Garfield
by the
pound

BY JIM DAVIS

Ballantine Books ● New York

2011 Ballantine Books Trade Paperback Edition

Copyright © 1992, 2011 by PAWS, Inc. All rights reserved.
"GARFIELD" and the GARFIELD characters are trademarks of PAWS, Inc.

Published in the United States by Ballantine Books, an imprint of The Random House Publishing Group,
a division of Random House, Inc., New York.

Ballantine and colophon are registered trademarks of Random House, Inc.

Originally published in slightly different form in the United States by Ballantine Books, an imprint of
The Random House Publishing Group, a division of Random House, Inc., in 1992.

ISBN 978-0-345-52558-1

Printed in the United States of America

www.ballantinebooks.com

9 8 7 6 5 4 3 2 1

First Colorized Edition

Sometime in the 21st century...

GARFIELD PREDICTS

Days will be made longer so cats can get more sleep

France will officially change its name to "The Francster"

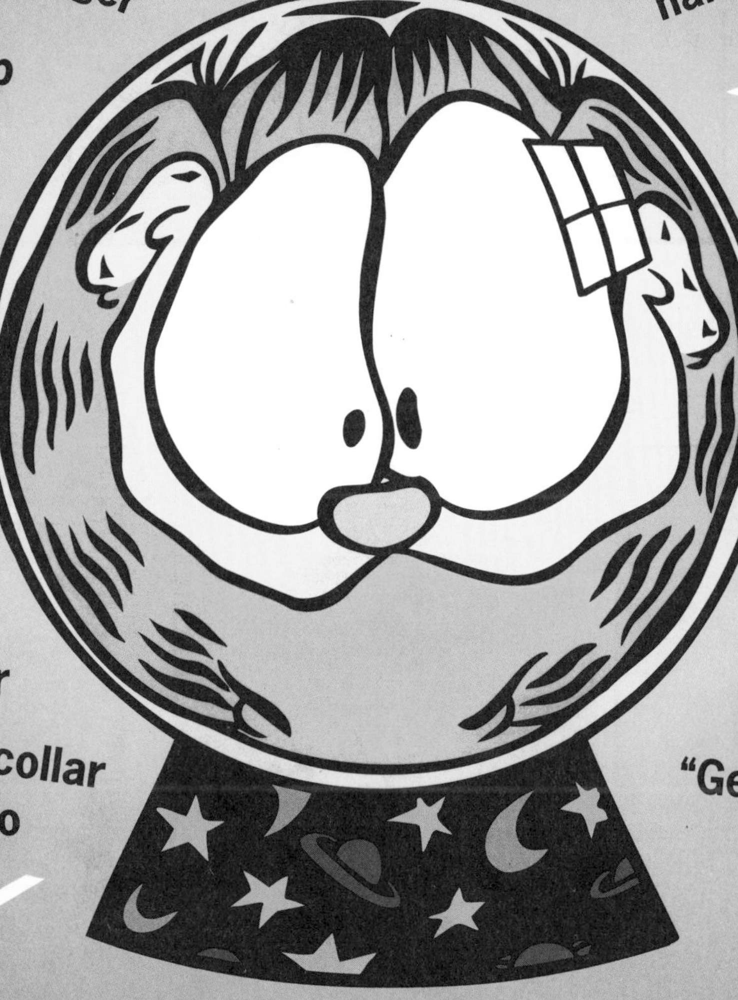

Scientists will develop a disposable dog

A large burp will devastate parts of Siberia

Astronomers will discover a huge flea collar encircling Pluto

Jon will be inducted into the "Geek Hall of Fame"

KNOW YOUR CAT MOODS

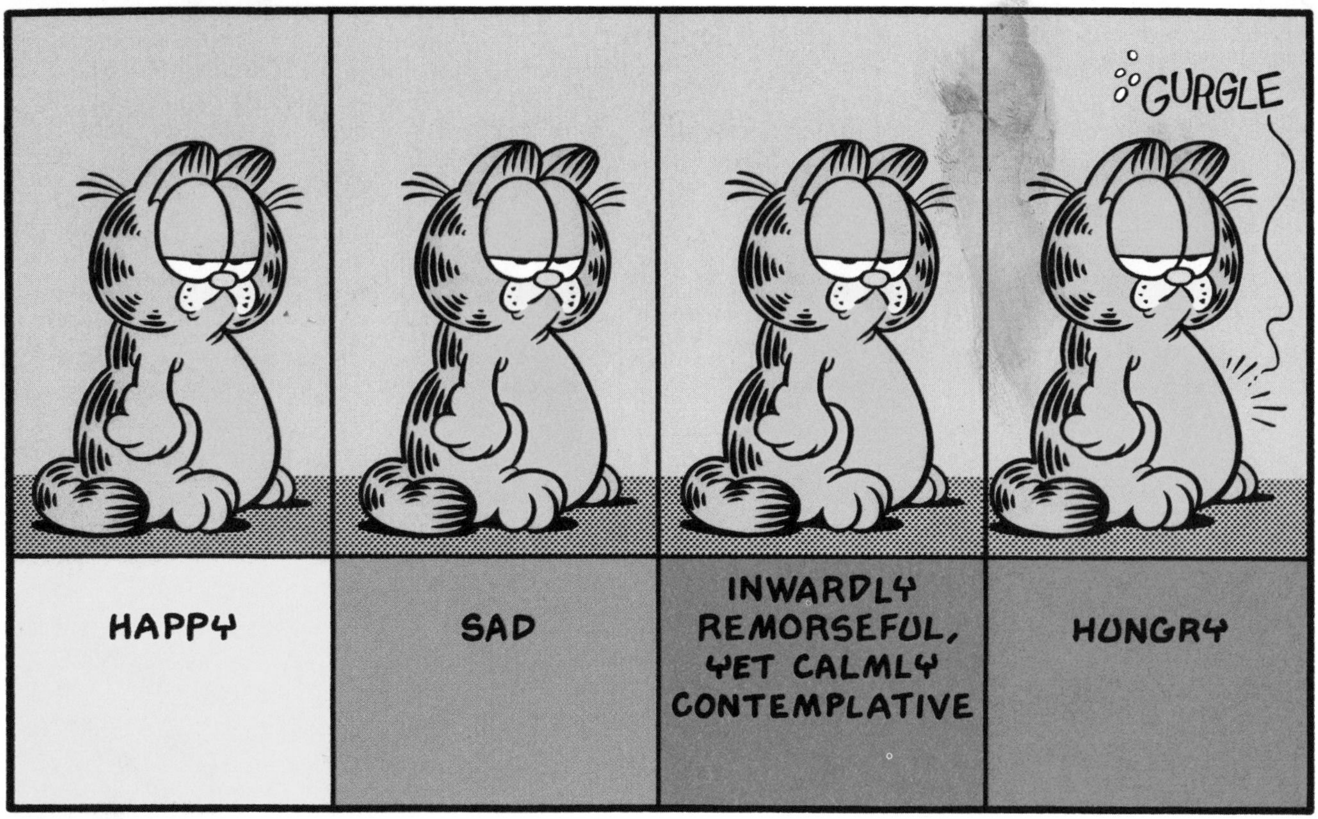
GURGLE
HAPPY
SAD
INWARDLY REMORSEFUL, YET CALMLY CONTEMPLATIVE
HUNGRY

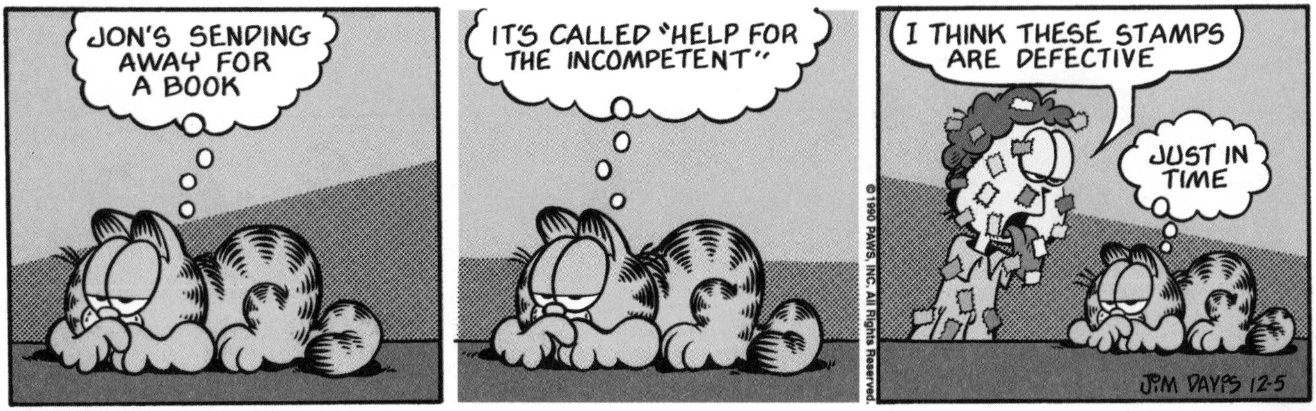
JON'S SENDING AWAY FOR A BOOK
IT'S CALLED "HELP FOR THE INCOMPETENT"
© 1990 PAWS, INC. All Rights Reserved.
I THINK THESE STAMPS ARE DEFECTIVE
JUST IN TIME
JIM DAVIS 12-5

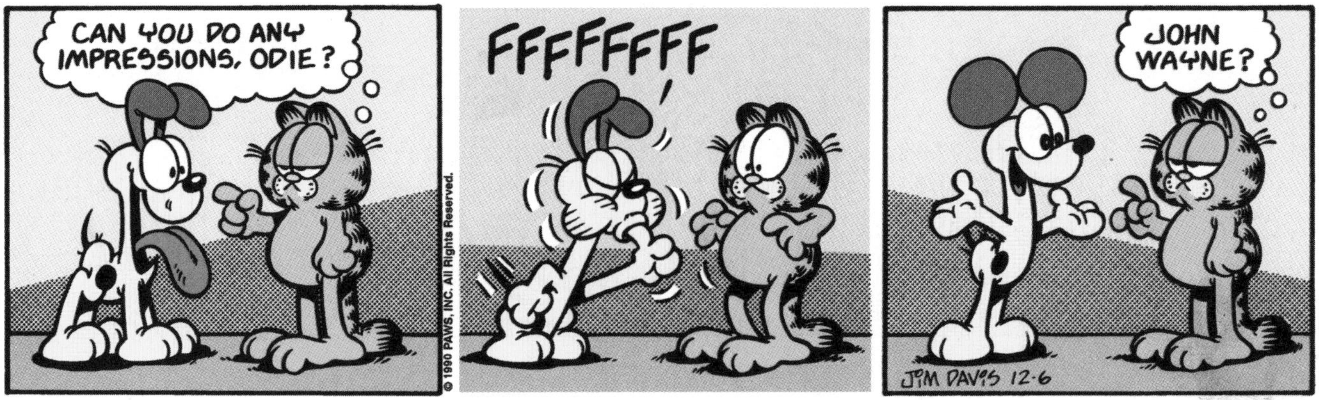
CAN YOU DO ANY IMPRESSIONS, ODIE?
FFFFFFFF
© 1990 PAWS, INC. All Rights Reserved.
JOHN WAYNE?
JIM DAVIS 12-6

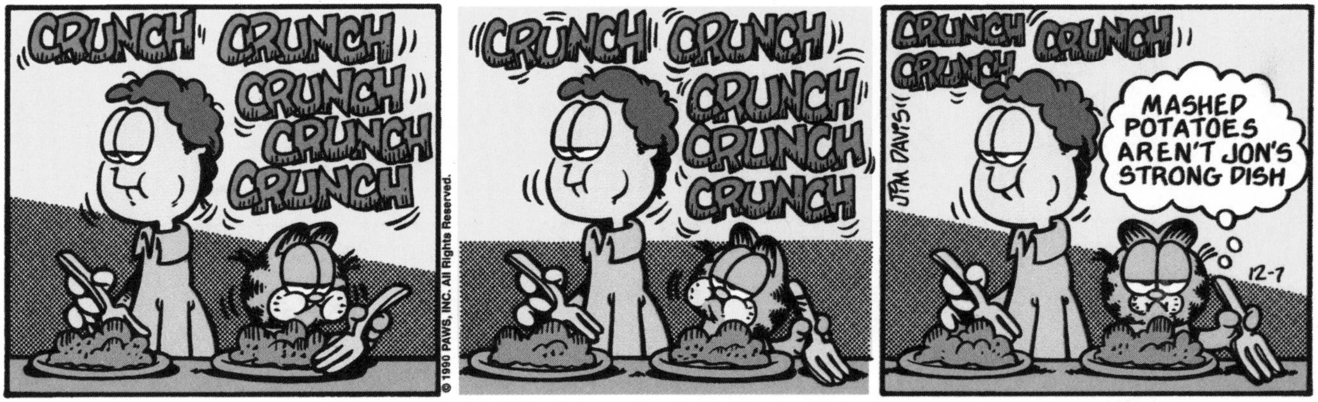
CRUNCH CRUNCH CRUNCH CRUNCH CRUNCH
© 1990 PAWS, INC. All Rights Reserved.
CRUNCH CRUNCH CRUNCH CRUNCH CRUNCH
CRUNCH CRUNCH CRUNCH
JIM DAVIS
MASHED POTATOES AREN'T JON'S STRONG DISH
12-7

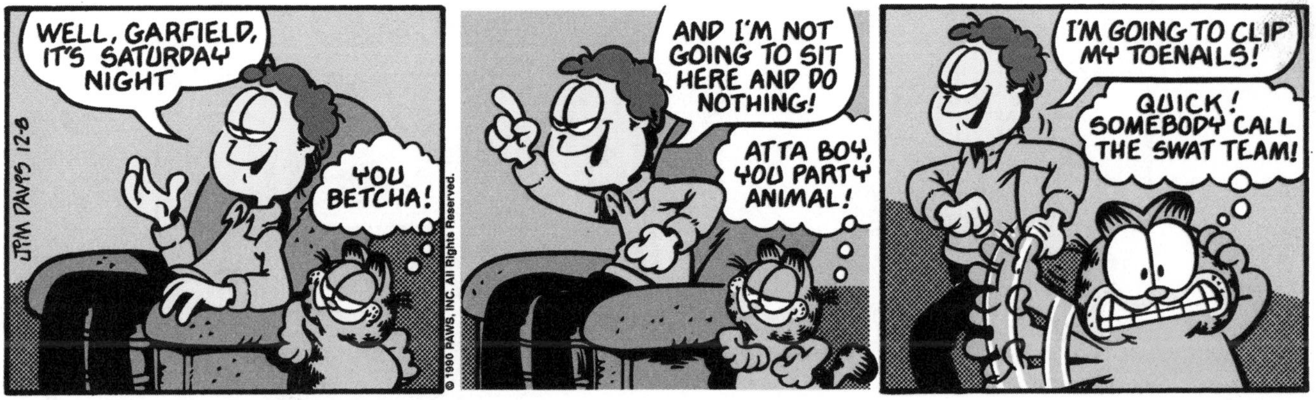
WELL, GARFIELD, IT'S SATURDAY NIGHT
YOU BETCHA!
JIM DAVIS 12-8
© 1990 PAWS, INC. All Rights Reserved.
AND I'M NOT GOING TO SIT HERE AND DO NOTHING!
ATTA BOY, YOU PARTY ANIMAL!
I'M GOING TO CLIP MY TOENAILS!
QUICK! SOMEBODY CALL THE SWAT TEAM!

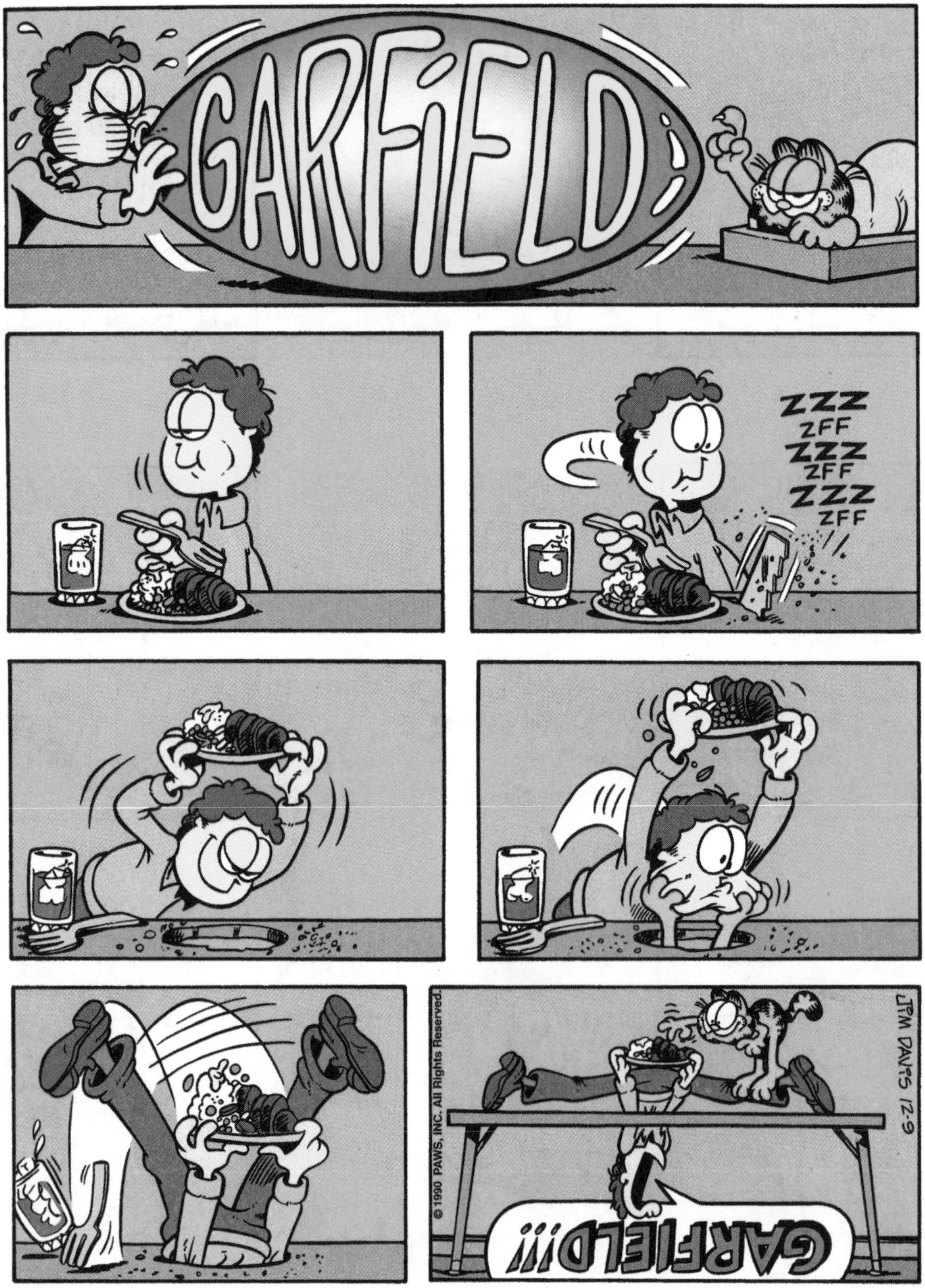
GARFIELD
ZZZ
ZFF
ZZZ
ZFF
ZZZ
ZFF
GARFIELD!!!
© 1990 PAWS, INC. All Rights Reserved.
JIM DAVIS 12-9

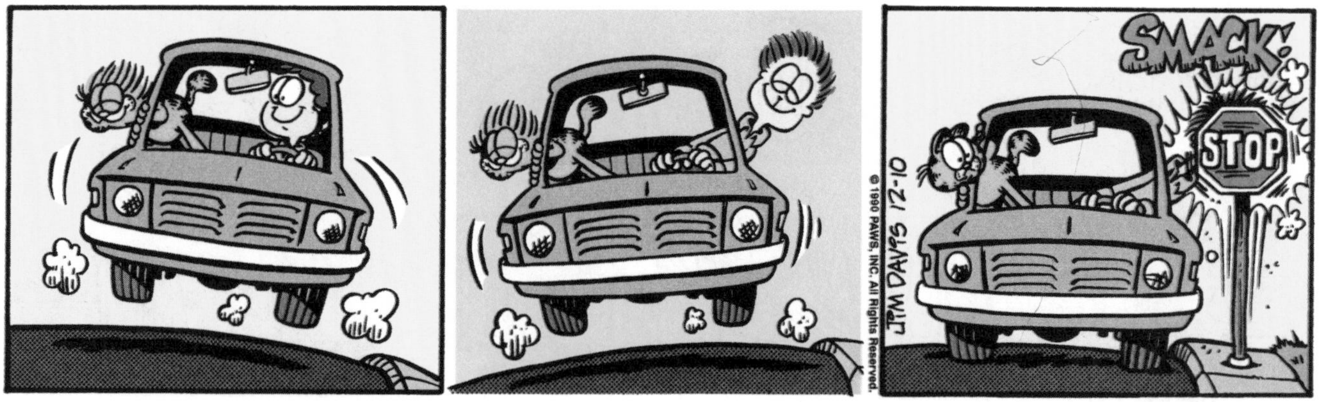
SMACK!
STOP
JIM DAVIS 12-10
© 1990 PAWS, INC. All Rights Reserved.

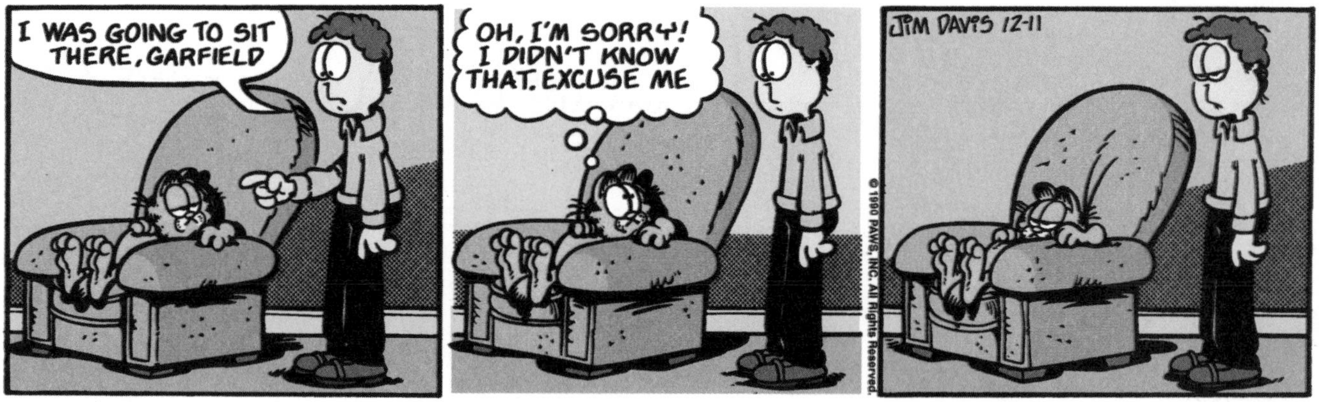
I WAS GOING TO SIT THERE, GARFIELD
OH, I'M SORRY! I DIDN'T KNOW THAT. EXCUSE ME
JIM DAVIS 12-11
© 1990 PAWS, INC. All Rights Reserved.

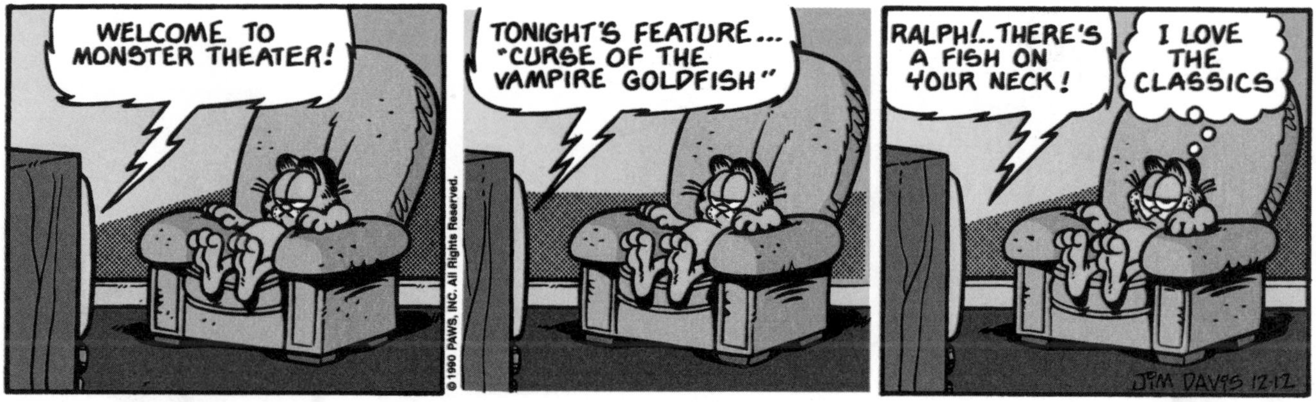
WELCOME TO MONSTER THEATER!
TONIGHT'S FEATURE... "CURSE OF THE VAMPIRE GOLDFISH"
RALPH!..THERE'S A FISH ON YOUR NECK!
I LOVE THE CLASSICS
JIM DAVIS 12-12
© 1990 PAWS, INC. All Rights Reserved.

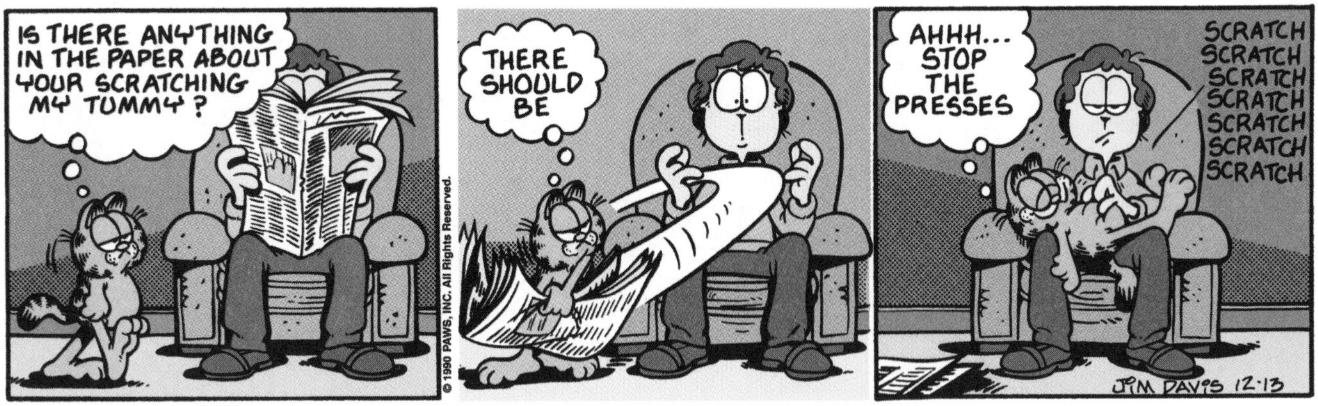
IS THERE ANYTHING IN THE PAPER ABOUT YOUR SCRATCHING MY TUMMY?
© 1990 PAWS, INC. All Rights Reserved.
THERE SHOULD BE
AHHH... STOP THE PRESSES
SCRATCH SCRATCH SCRATCH SCRATCH SCRATCH SCRATCH SCRATCH
JIM DAVIS 12-13

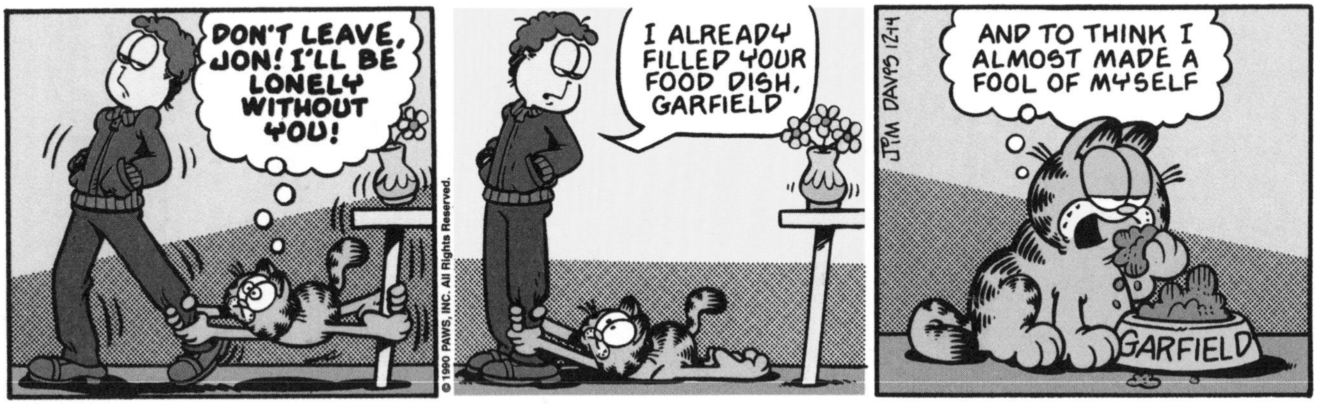
DON'T LEAVE, JON! I'LL BE LONELY WITHOUT YOU!
© 1990 PAWS, INC. All Rights Reserved.
I ALREADY FILLED YOUR FOOD DISH, GARFIELD
JIM DAVIS 12-14
AND TO THINK I ALMOST MADE A FOOL OF MYSELF
GARFIELD

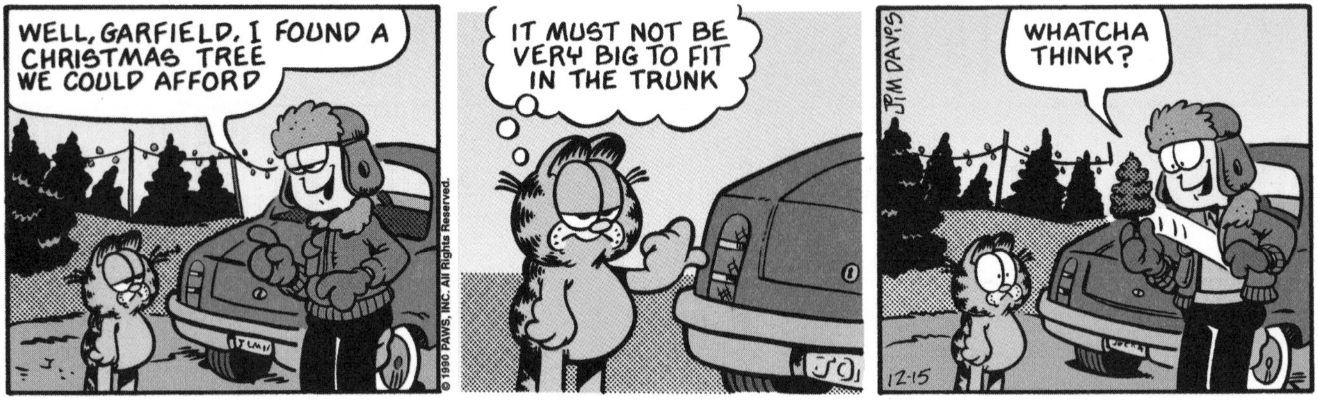
WELL, GARFIELD, I FOUND A CHRISTMAS TREE WE COULD AFFORD
© 1990 PAWS, INC. All Rights Reserved.
IT MUST NOT BE VERY BIG TO FIT IN THE TRUNK
JIM DAVIS
WHATCHA THINK?
12-15

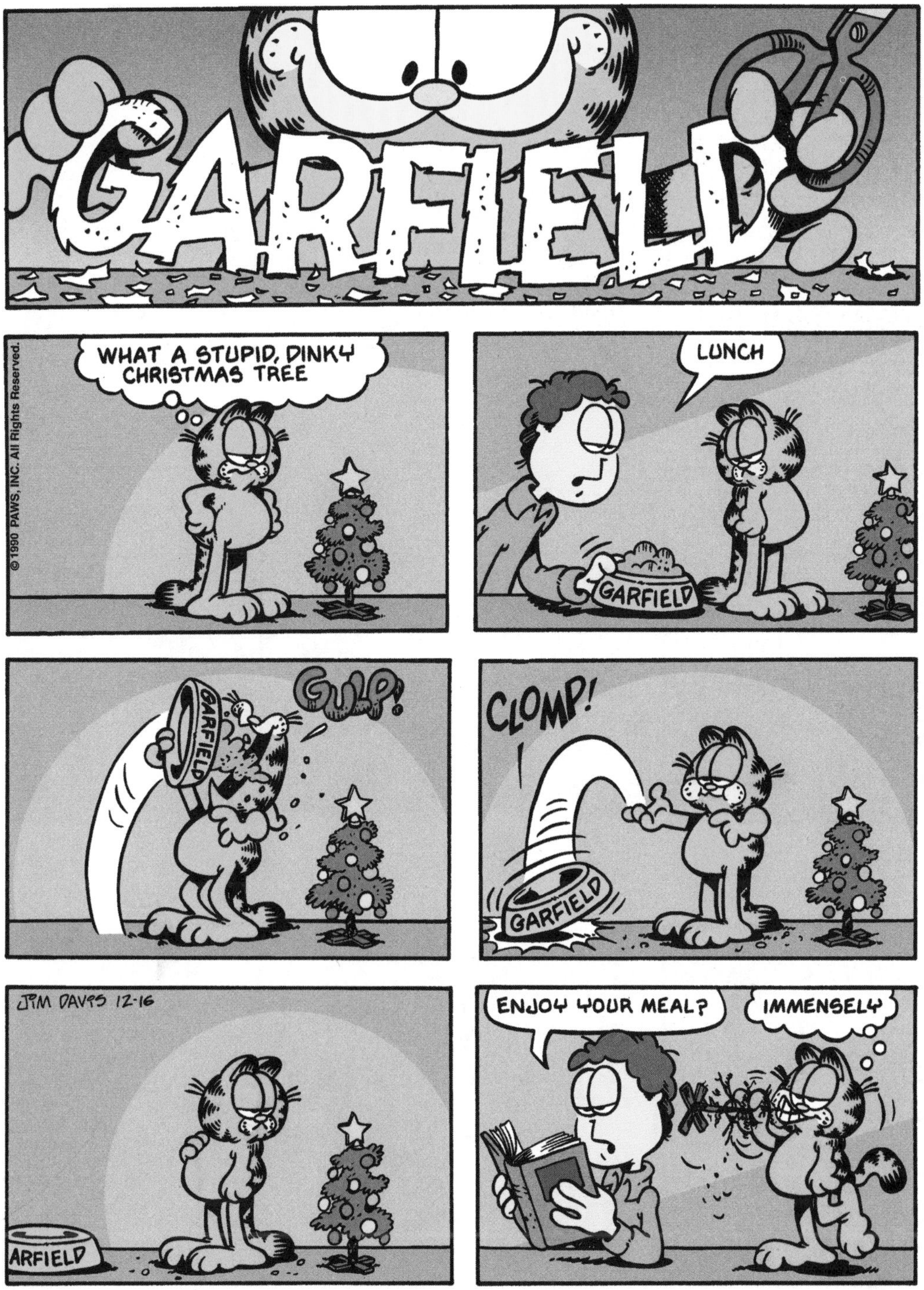
GARFIELD
WHAT A STUPID, DINKY CHRISTMAS TREE
LUNCH
GARFIELD
GARFIELD
GULP!
CLOMP!
GARFIELD
JIM DAVIS 12-16
ARFIELD
ENJOY YOUR MEAL?
IMMENSELY

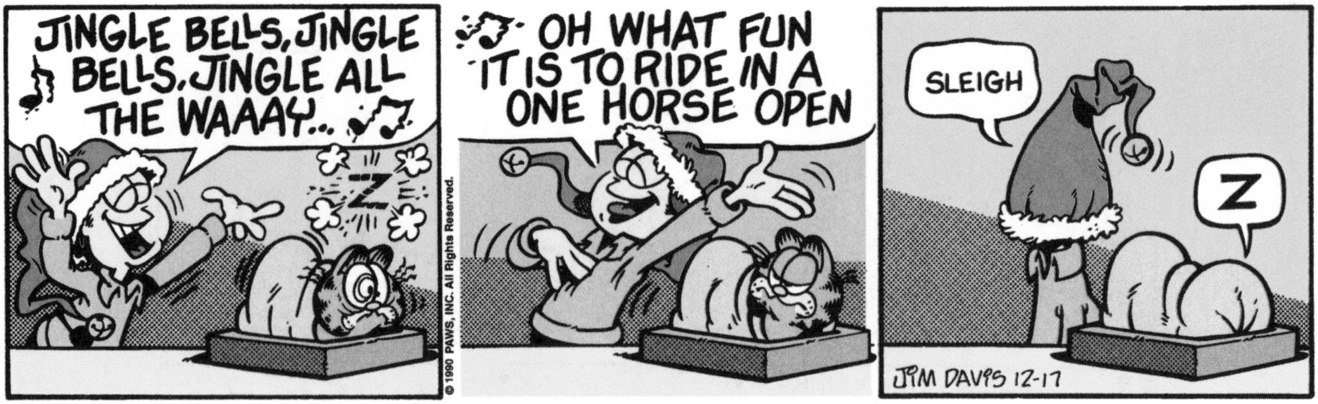
JINGLE BELLS, JINGLE BELLS, JINGLE ALL THE WAAAY...
Z
OH WHAT FUN IT IS TO RIDE IN A ONE HORSE OPEN
© 1990 PAWS, INC. All Rights Reserved.
SLEIGH
Z
JIM DAVIS 12-17

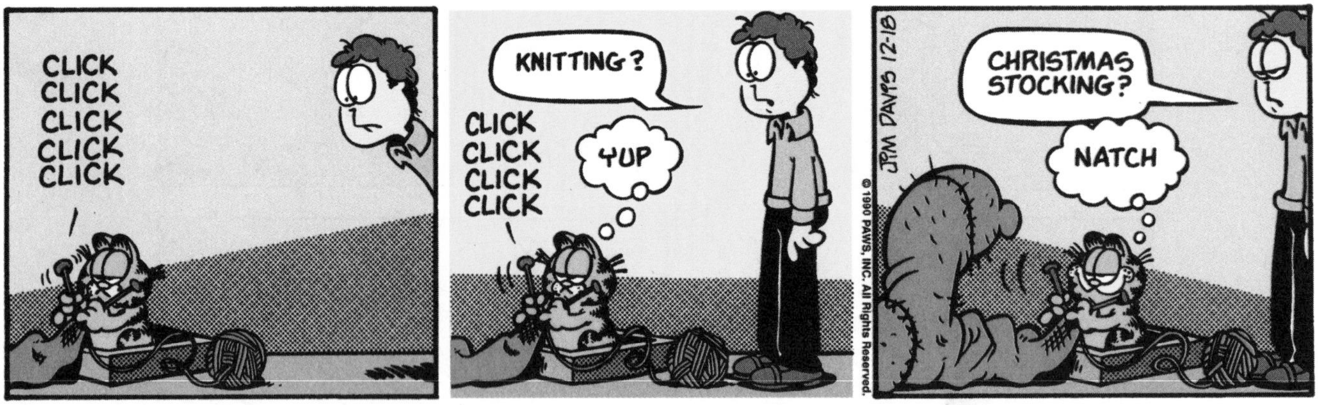
CLICK CLICK CLICK CLICK CLICK
KNITTING?
CLICK CLICK CLICK CLICK
YUP
© 1990 PAWS, INC. All Rights Reserved.
JIM DAVIS 12-18
CHRISTMAS STOCKING?
NATCH

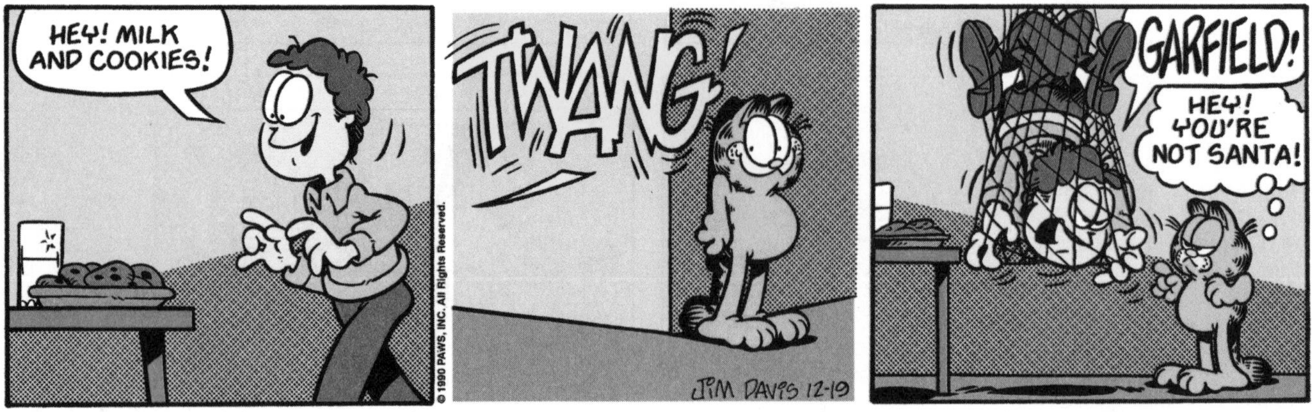
HEY! MILK AND COOKIES!
© 1990 PAWS, INC. All Rights Reserved.
TWANG!
JIM DAVIS 12-19
GARFIELD!
HEY! YOU'RE NOT SANTA!

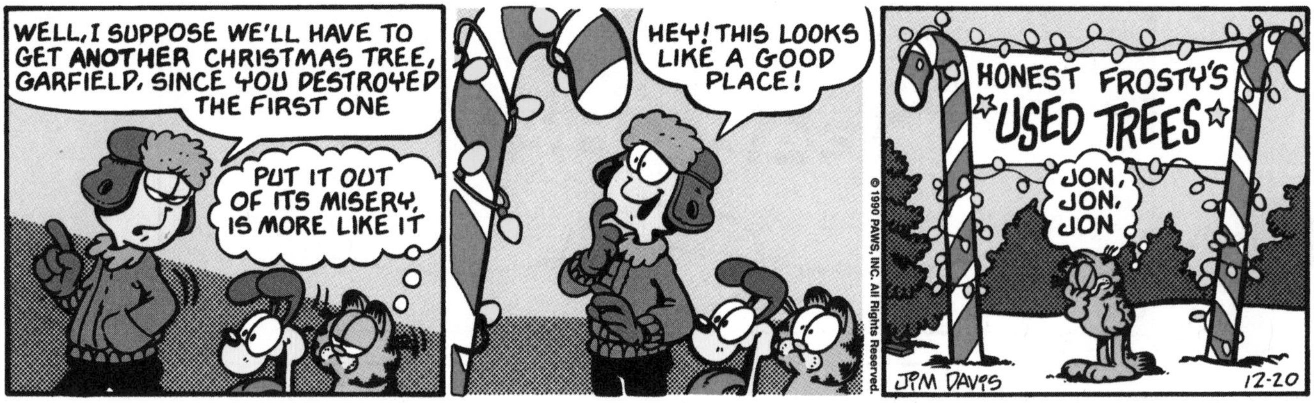
WELL, I SUPPOSE WE'LL HAVE TO GET ANOTHER CHRISTMAS TREE, GARFIELD, SINCE YOU DESTROYED THE FIRST ONE
PUT IT OUT OF ITS MISERY, IS MORE LIKE IT
HEY! THIS LOOKS LIKE A GOOD PLACE!
© 1990 PAWS, INC. All Rights Reserved.
HONEST FROSTY'S USED TREES
JON, JON, JON
JIM DAVIS 12-20

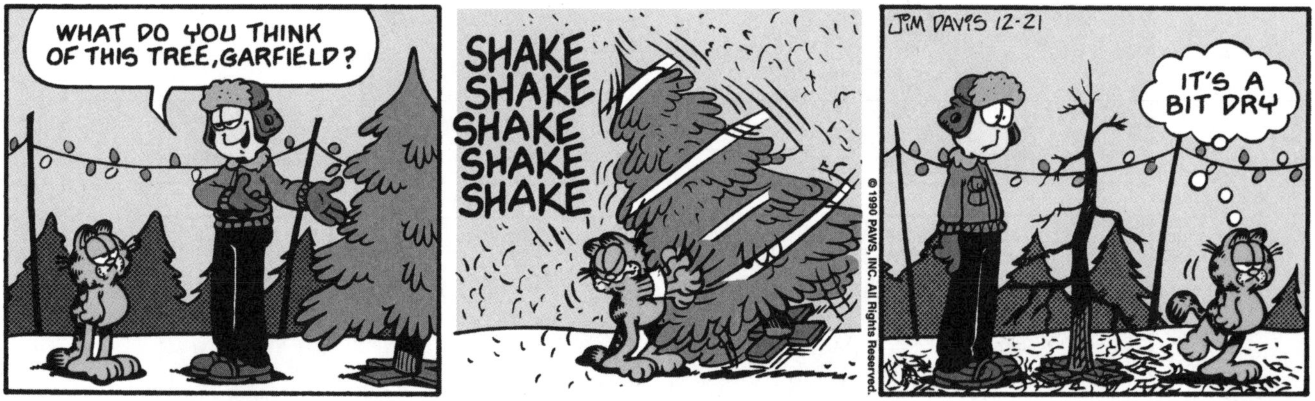
WHAT DO YOU THINK OF THIS TREE, GARFIELD?
SHAKE SHAKE SHAKE SHAKE SHAKE
© 1990 PAWS, INC. All Rights Reserved.
JIM DAVIS 12-21
IT'S A BIT DRY

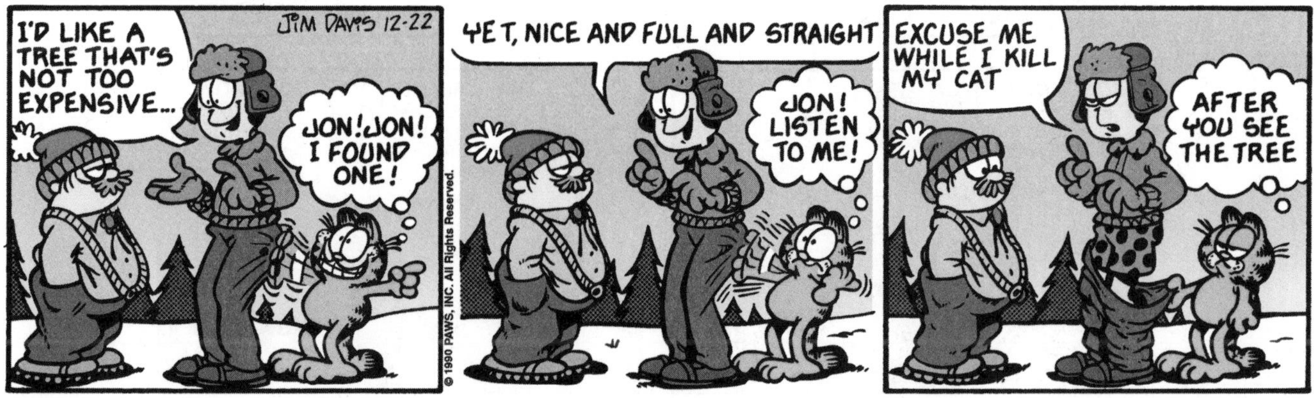
JIM DAVIS 12-22
I'D LIKE A TREE THAT'S NOT TOO EXPENSIVE...
JON! JON! I FOUND ONE!
© 1990 PAWS, INC. All Rights Reserved.
YET, NICE AND FULL AND STRAIGHT
JON! LISTEN TO ME!
EXCUSE ME WHILE I KILL MY CAT
AFTER YOU SEE THE TREE

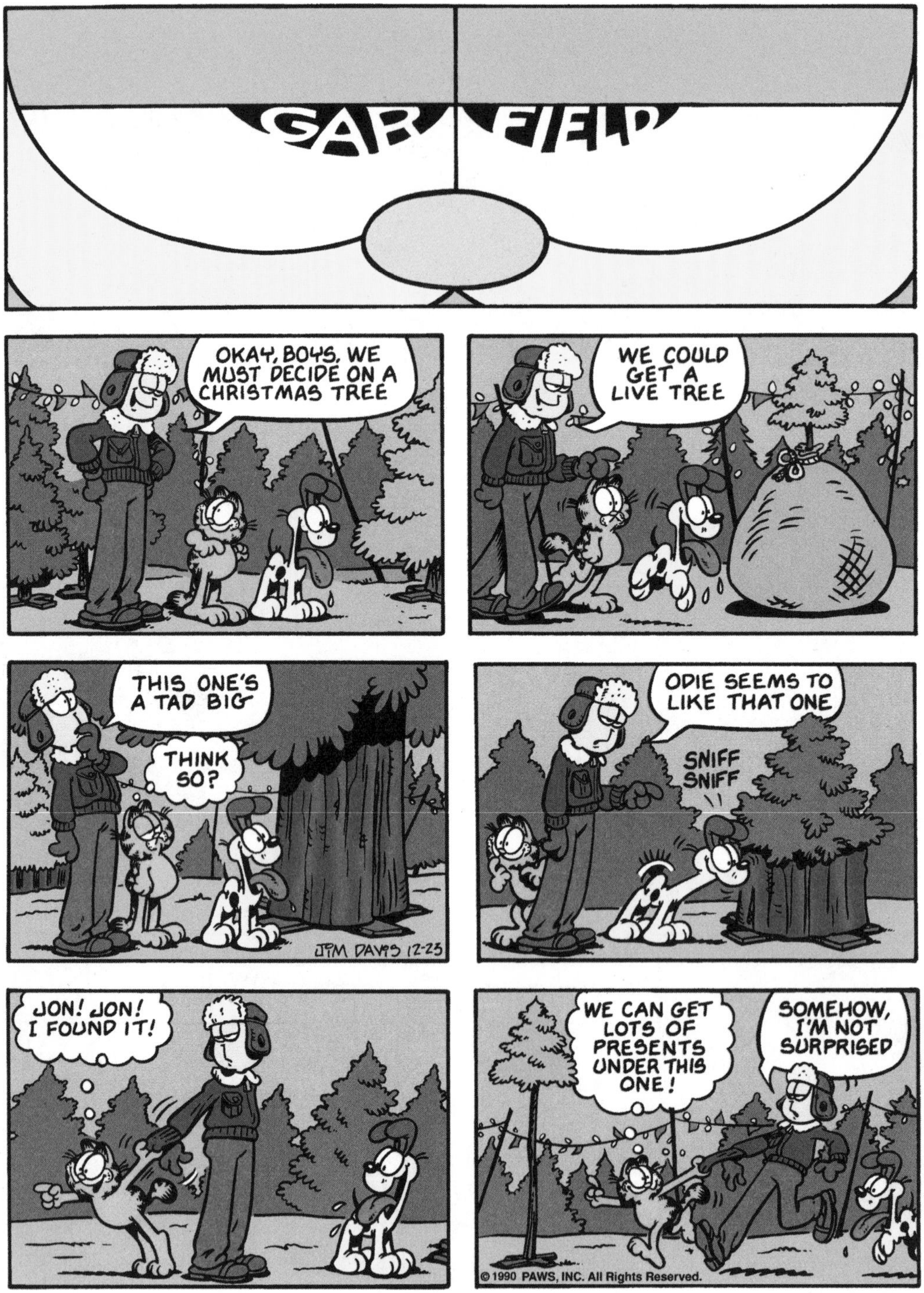
GARFIELD
OKAY, BOYS, WE MUST DECIDE ON A CHRISTMAS TREE
WE COULD GET A LIVE TREE
THIS ONE'S A TAD BIG
THINK SO?
JIM DAVIS 12-23
ODIE SEEMS TO LIKE THAT ONE
SNIFF SNIFF
JON! JON! I FOUND IT!
WE CAN GET LOTS OF PRESENTS UNDER THIS ONE!
SOMEHOW, I'M NOT SURPRISED

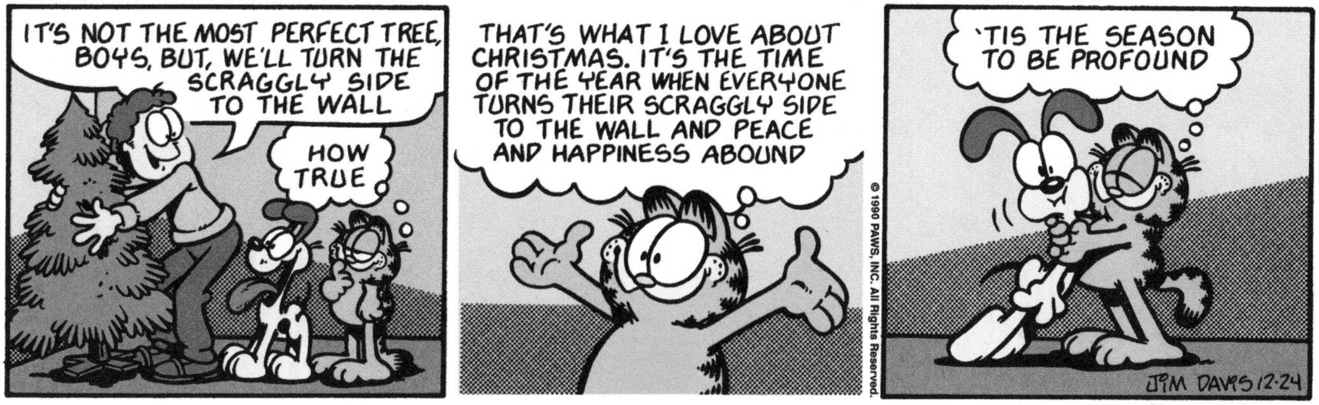
IT'S NOT THE MOST PERFECT TREE, BOYS, BUT, WE'LL TURN THE SCRAGGLY SIDE TO THE WALL
HOW TRUE
THAT'S WHAT I LOVE ABOUT CHRISTMAS. IT'S THE TIME OF THE YEAR WHEN EVERYONE TURNS THEIR SCRAGGLY SIDE TO THE WALL AND PEACE AND HAPPINESS ABOUND
'TIS THE SEASON TO BE PROFOUND
© 1990 PAWS, INC. All Rights Reserved.
JIM DAVIS 12-24

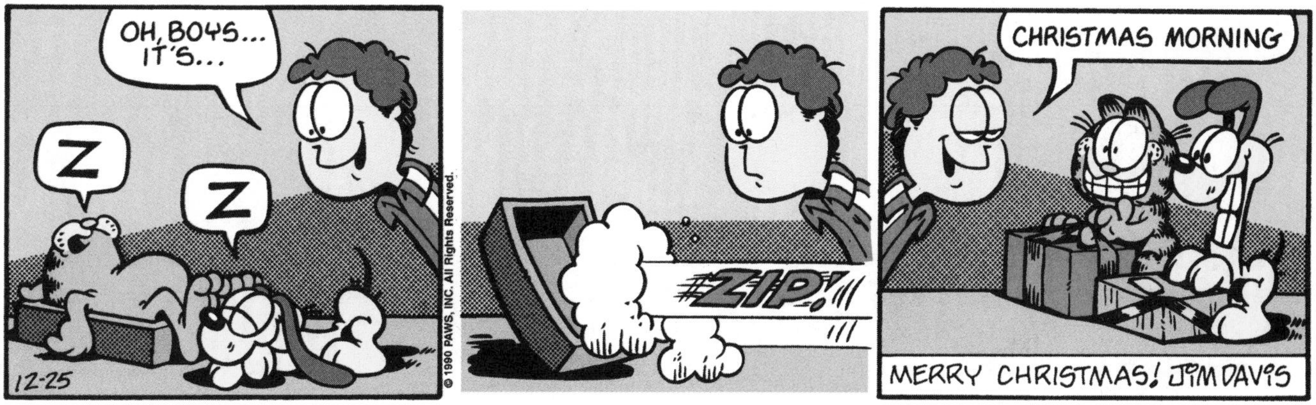
12-25
OH, BOYS... IT'S...
Z
Z
© 1990 PAWS, INC. All Rights Reserved.
ZIP!
CHRISTMAS MORNING
MERRY CHRISTMAS! JIM DAVIS

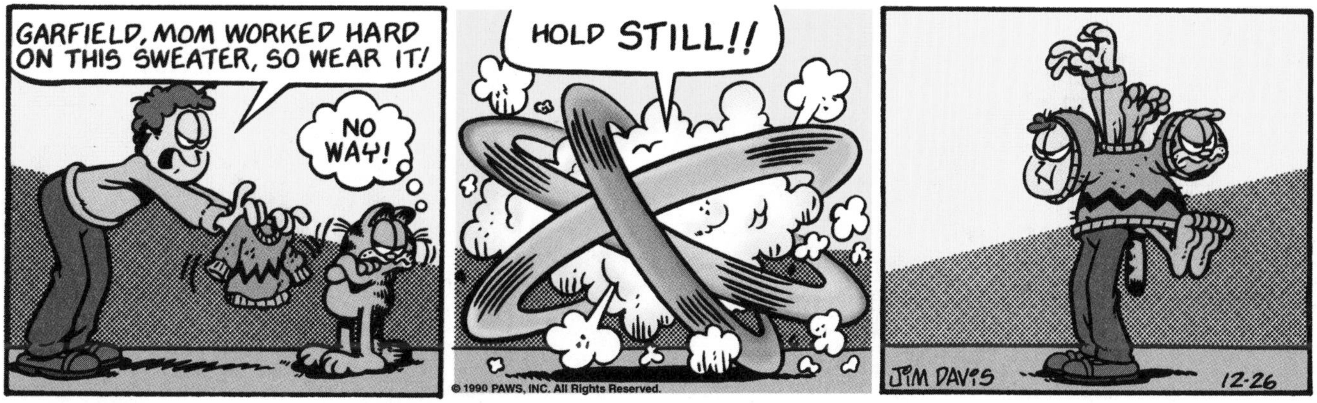
GARFIELD, MOM WORKED HARD ON THIS SWEATER, SO WEAR IT!
NO WAY!
HOLD STILL!!
© 1990 PAWS, INC. All Rights Reserved.
JIM DAVIS
12-26

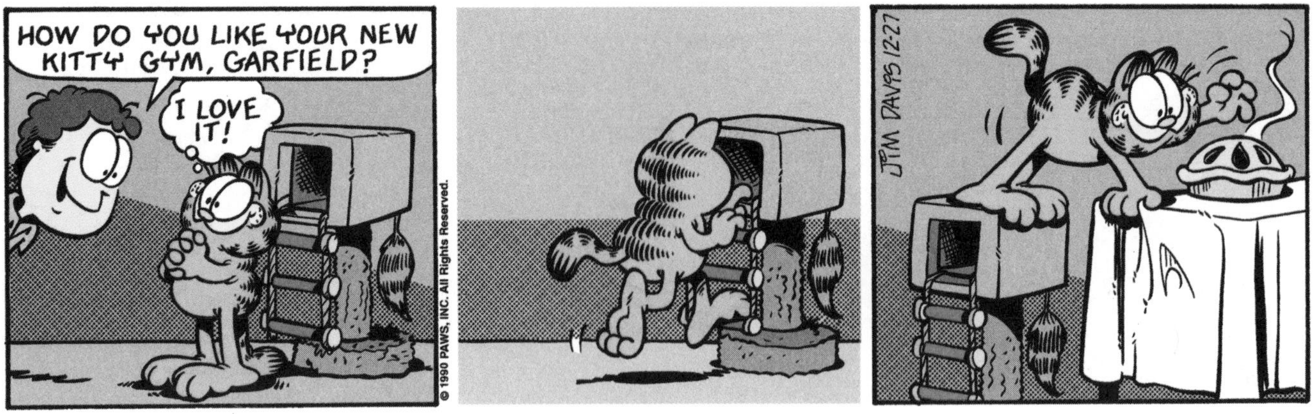
HOW DO YOU LIKE YOUR NEW KITTY GYM, GARFIELD?
I LOVE IT!
© 1990 PAWS, INC. All Rights Reserved.
JIM DAVIS 12-27

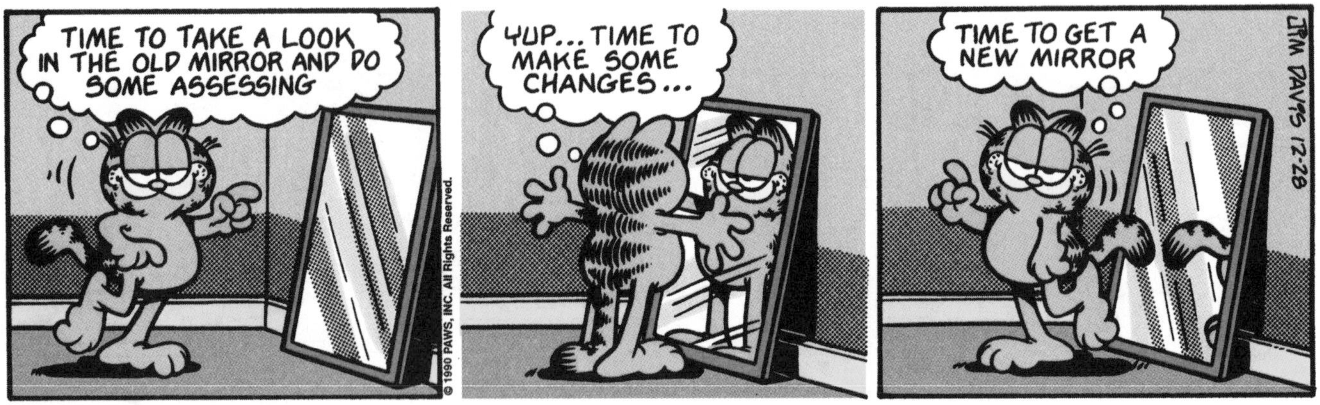
TIME TO TAKE A LOOK IN THE OLD MIRROR AND DO SOME ASSESSING
© 1990 PAWS, INC. All Rights Reserved.
YUP... TIME TO MAKE SOME CHANGES...
TIME TO GET A NEW MIRROR
JIM DAVIS 12-28

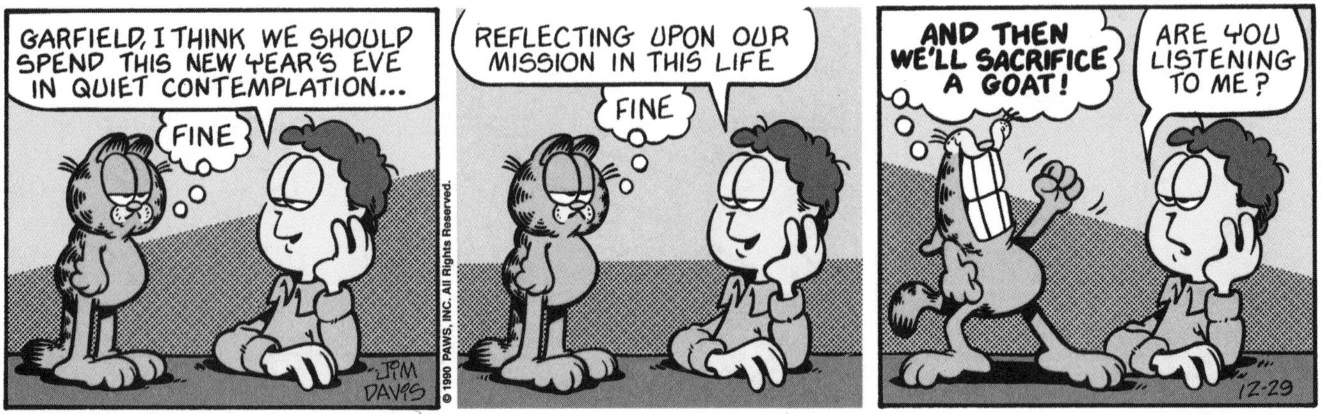
GARFIELD, I THINK WE SHOULD SPEND THIS NEW YEAR'S EVE IN QUIET CONTEMPLATION...
FINE
JIM DAVIS
© 1990 PAWS, INC. All Rights Reserved.
REFLECTING UPON OUR MISSION IN THIS LIFE
FINE
AND THEN WE'LL SACRIFICE A GOAT!
ARE YOU LISTENING TO ME?
12-29

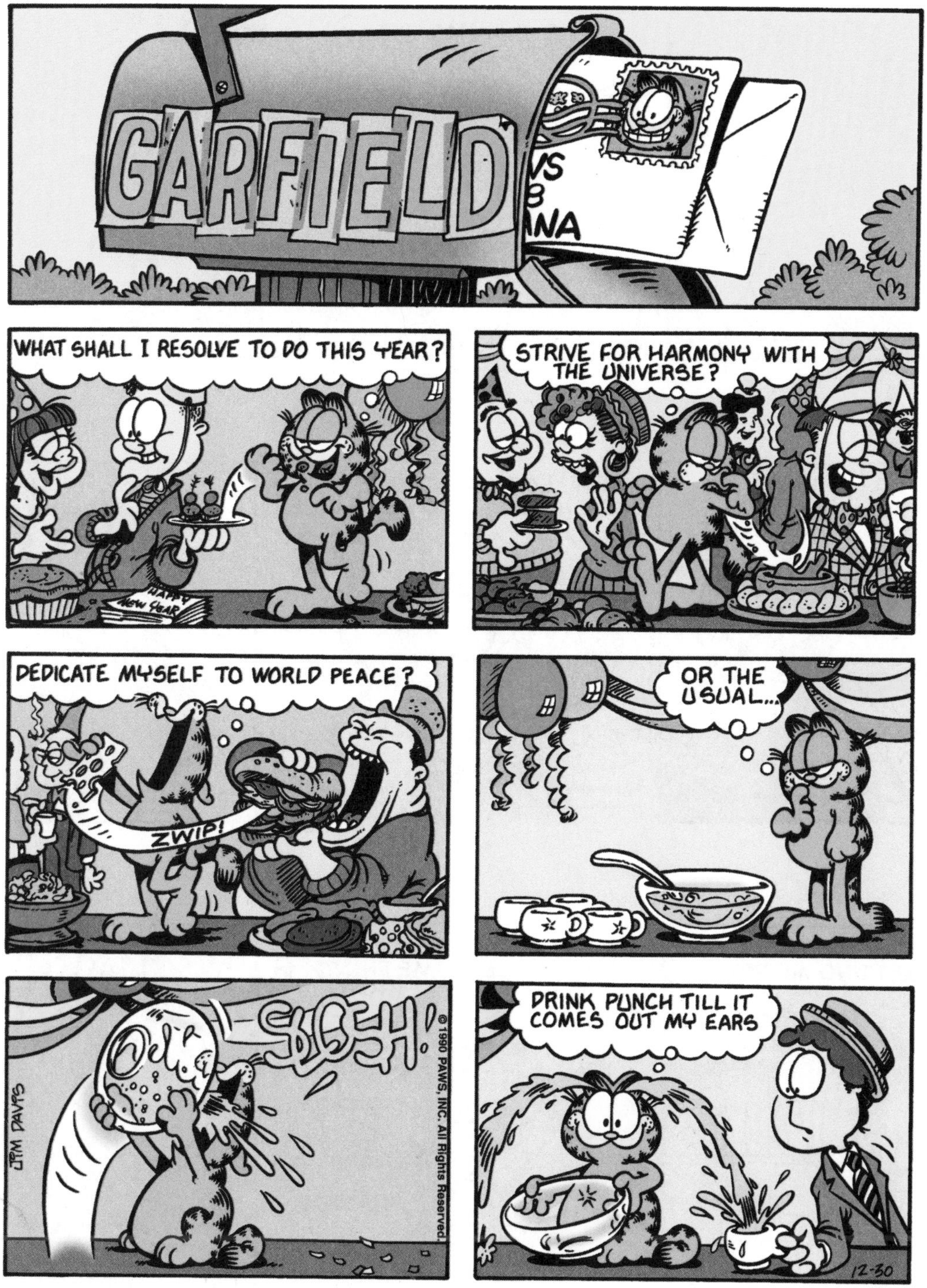
GARFIELD
WHAT SHALL I RESOLVE TO DO THIS YEAR?
HAPPY NEW YEAR
STRIVE FOR HARMONY WITH THE UNIVERSE?
DEDICATE MYSELF TO WORLD PEACE?
ZWIP!
OR THE USUAL...
SLOOSH!
JPM DAVPS
© 1990 PAWS, INC. All Rights Reserved.
DRINK PUNCH TILL IT COMES OUT MY EARS
12-30

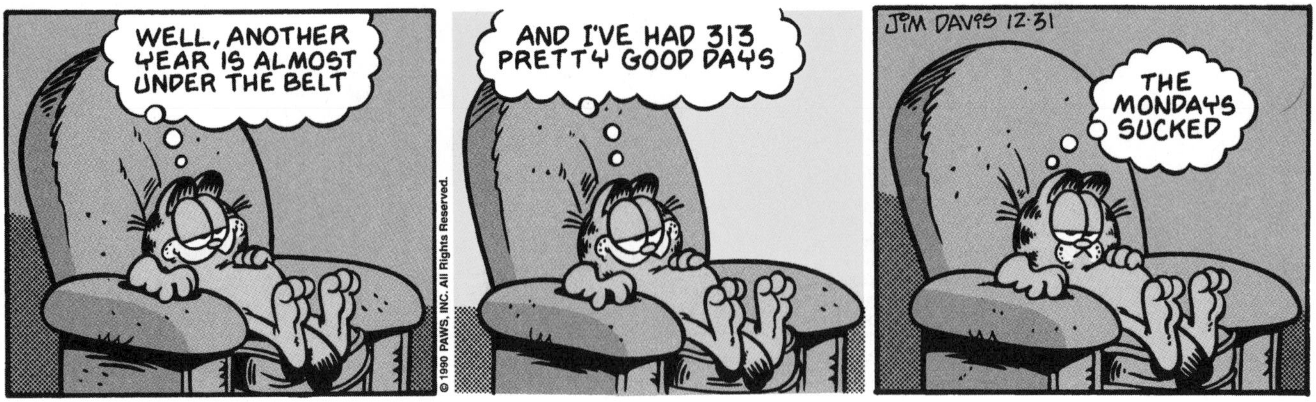
WELL, ANOTHER YEAR IS ALMOST UNDER THE BELT
AND I'VE HAD 313 PRETTY GOOD DAYS
JIM DAVIS 12-31
THE MONDAYS SUCKED
© 1990 PAWS, INC. All Rights Reserved.

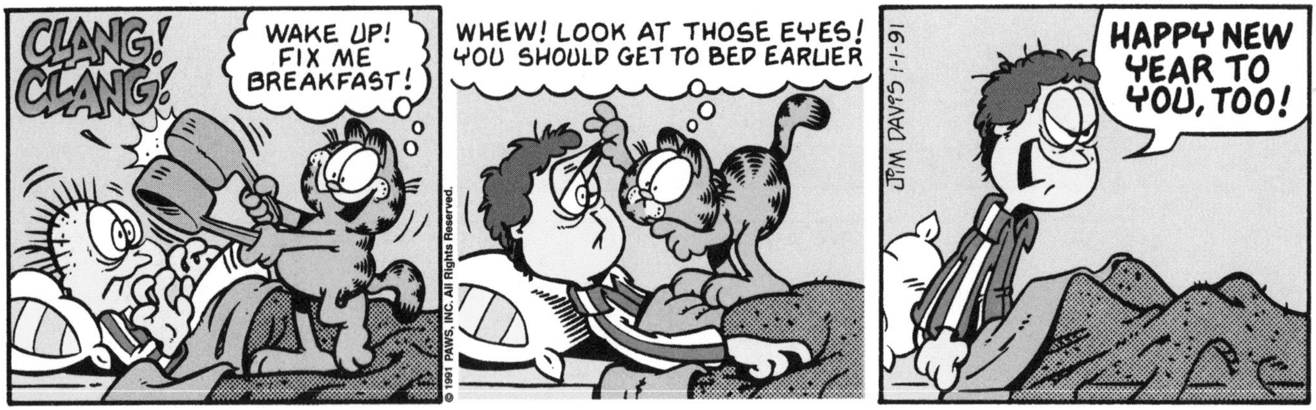
CLANG! CLANG!
WAKE UP! FIX ME BREAKFAST!
WHEW! LOOK AT THOSE EYES! YOU SHOULD GET TO BED EARLIER
JIM DAVIS 1-1-91
HAPPY NEW YEAR TO YOU, TOO!
© 1991 PAWS, INC. All Rights Reserved.

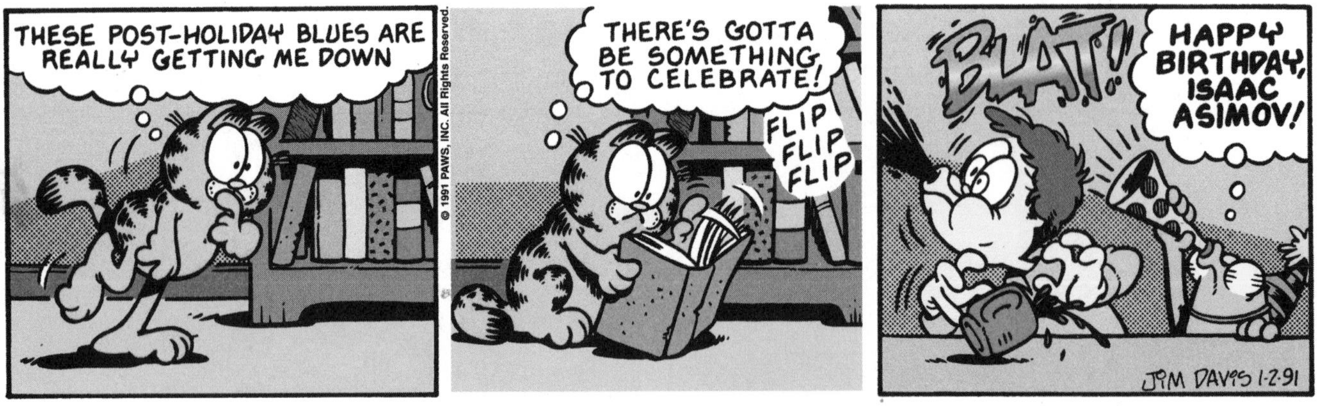
THESE POST-HOLIDAY BLUES ARE REALLY GETTING ME DOWN
THERE'S GOTTA BE SOMETHING TO CELEBRATE!
FLIP FLIP FLIP
BLAT!
HAPPY BIRTHDAY, ISAAC ASIMOV!
JIM DAVIS 1-2-91
© 1991 PAWS, INC. All Rights Reserved.

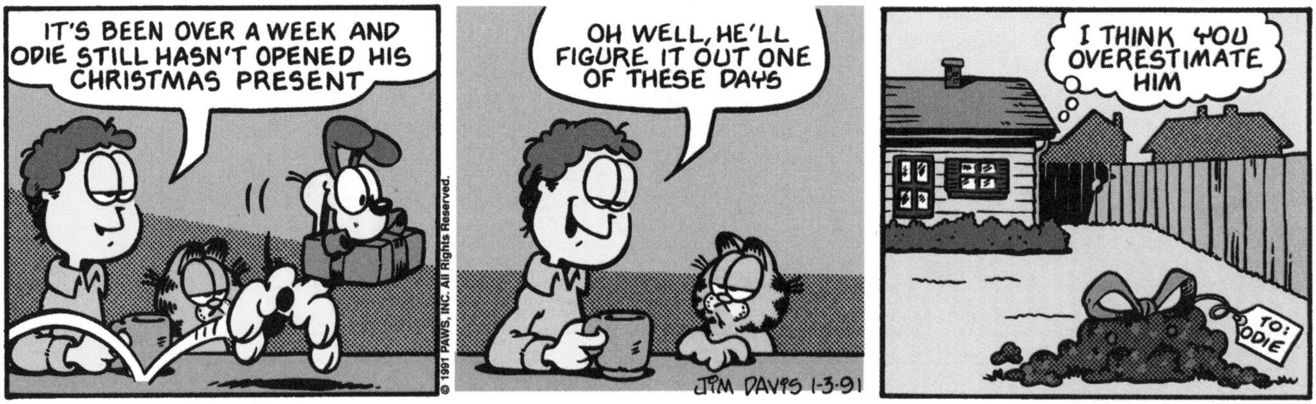
IT'S BEEN OVER A WEEK AND ODIE STILL HASN'T OPENED HIS CHRISTMAS PRESENT
© 1991 PAWS, INC. All Rights Reserved.
OH WELL, HE'LL FIGURE IT OUT ONE OF THESE DAYS
JIM DAVIS 1-3-91
I THINK YOU OVERESTIMATE HIM
TO: ODIE

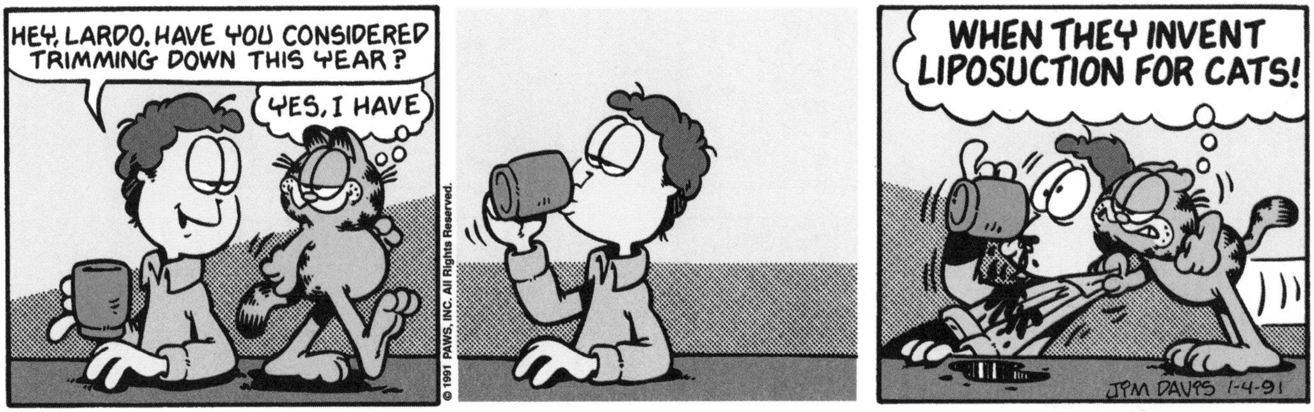
HEY, LARDO. HAVE YOU CONSIDERED TRIMMING DOWN THIS YEAR?
YES, I HAVE
© 1991 PAWS, INC. All Rights Reserved.
WHEN THEY INVENT LIPOSUCTION FOR CATS!
JIM DAVIS 1-4-91

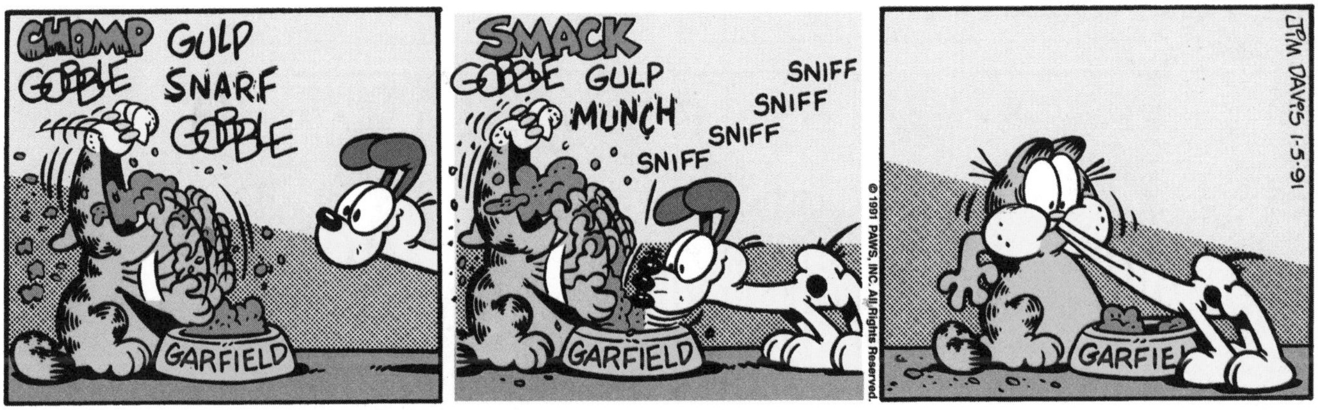
CHOMP GULP
GOBBLE SNARF
GOBBLE
GARFIELD
SMACK
GOBBLE GULP
MUNCH
SNIFF
SNIFF
SNIFF
SNIFF
GARFIELD
© 1991 PAWS, INC. All Rights Reserved.
JIM DAVIS 1-5-91
GARFIE

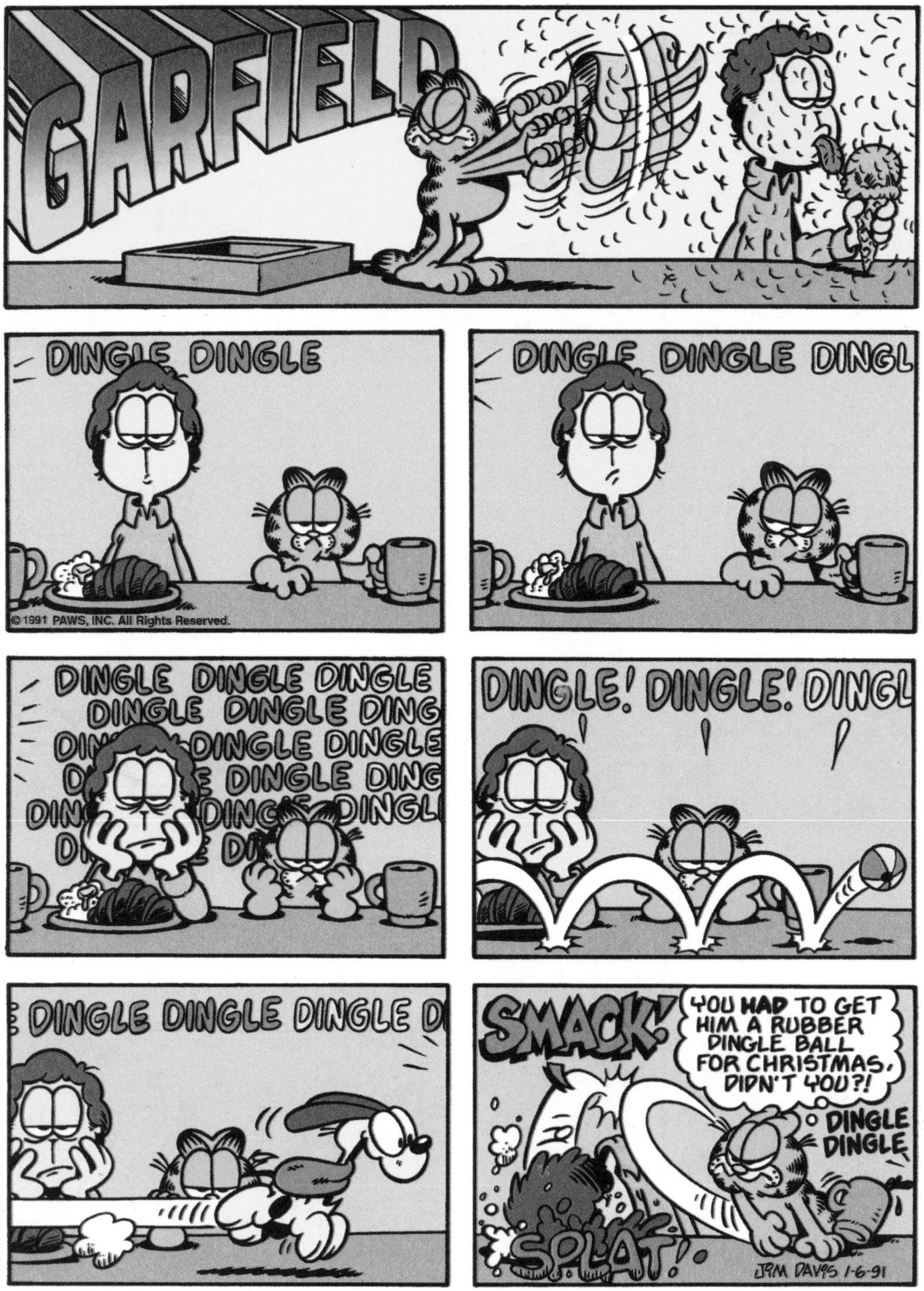
GARFIELD
DINGLE DINGLE
© 1991 PAWS, INC. All Rights Reserved.
DINGLE DINGLE DINGL
DINGLE DINGLE DINGLE
DINGLE DINGLE DING
DINGLE DINGLE
DINGLE DING
DINGLE! DINGLE! DINGL
DINGLE DINGLE DINGLE
SMACK!
YOU HAD TO GET HIM A RUBBER DINGLE BALL FOR CHRISTMAS, DIDN'T YOU?!
DINGLE DINGLE
SPLAT!
JIM DAVIS 1-6-91

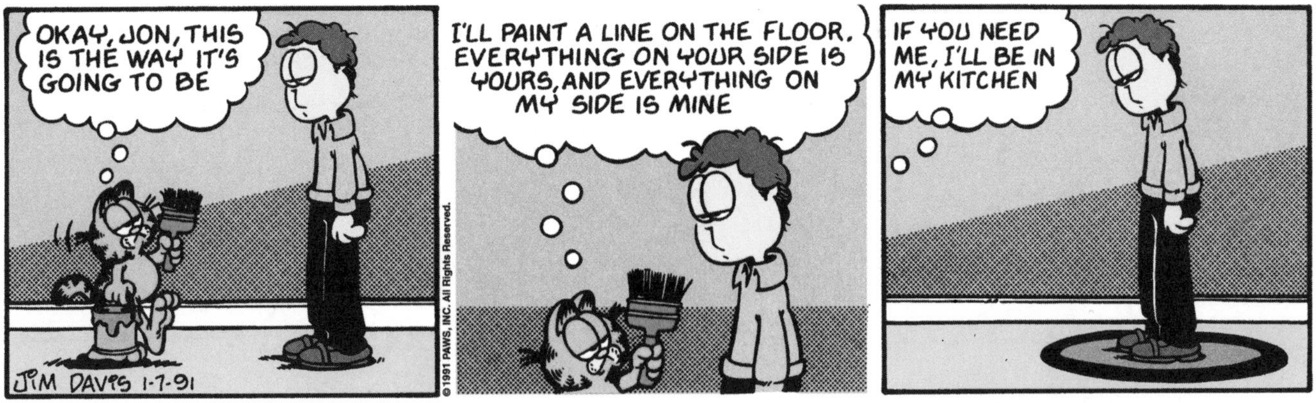
OKAY, JON, THIS IS THE WAY IT'S GOING TO BE
JIM DAVIS 1-7-91
© 1991 PAWS, INC. All Rights Reserved.
I'LL PAINT A LINE ON THE FLOOR. EVERYTHING ON YOUR SIDE IS YOURS, AND EVERYTHING ON MY SIDE IS MINE
IF YOU NEED ME, I'LL BE IN MY KITCHEN

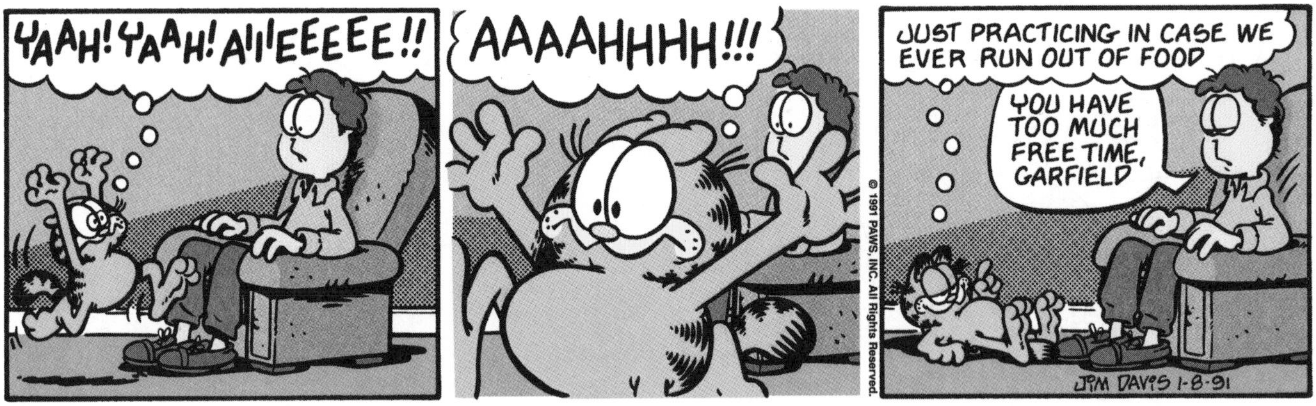
YAAH! YAAH! AIIEEEEEE!!
AAAAHHHH!!!
© 1991 PAWS, INC. All Rights Reserved.
JUST PRACTICING IN CASE WE EVER RUN OUT OF FOOD
YOU HAVE TOO MUCH FREE TIME, GARFIELD
JIM DAVIS 1-8-91

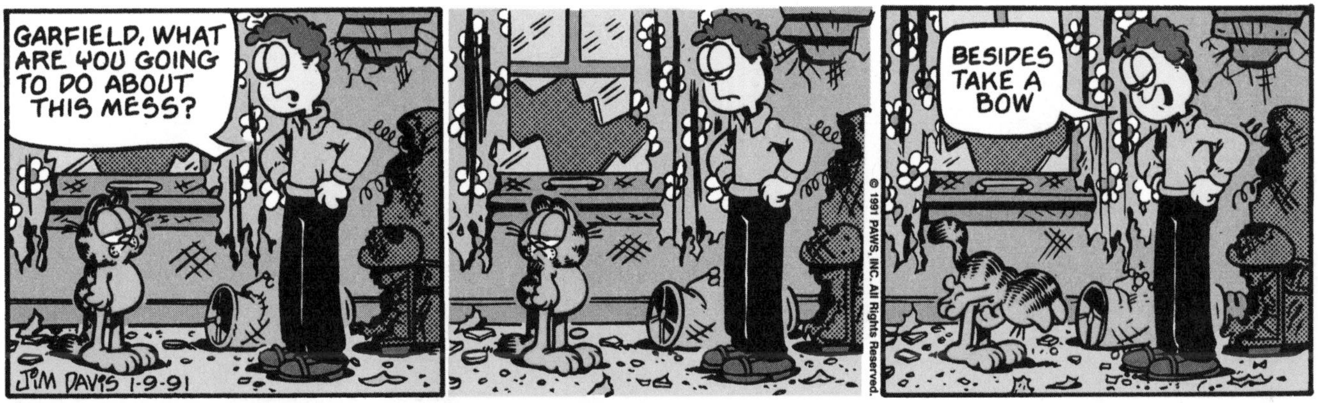
GARFIELD, WHAT ARE YOU GOING TO DO ABOUT THIS MESS?
JIM DAVIS 1-9-91
© 1991 PAWS, INC. All Rights Reserved.
BESIDES TAKE A BOW

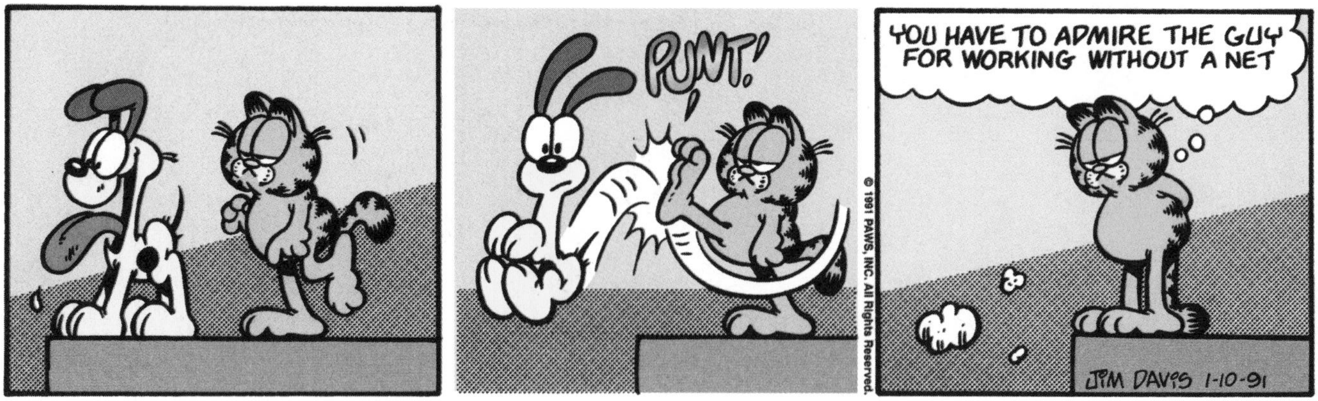
PUNT!
YOU HAVE TO ADMIRE THE GUY FOR WORKING WITHOUT A NET
© 1991 PAWS, INC. All Rights Reserved.
JIM DAVIS 1-10-91

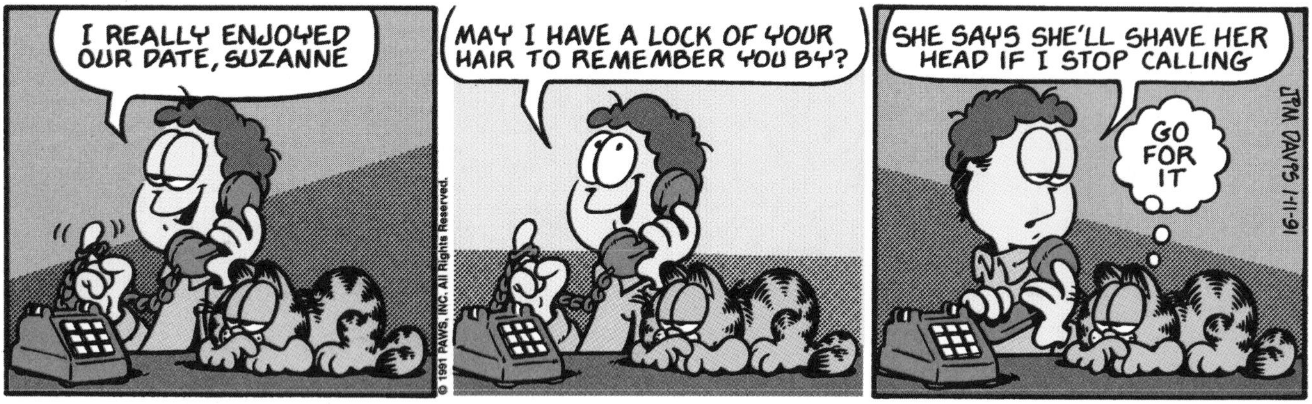
I REALLY ENJOYED OUR DATE, SUZANNE
MAY I HAVE A LOCK OF YOUR HAIR TO REMEMBER YOU BY?
SHE SAYS SHE'LL SHAVE HER HEAD IF I STOP CALLING
GO FOR IT
© 1991 PAWS, INC. All Rights Reserved.
JIM DAVIS 1-11-91

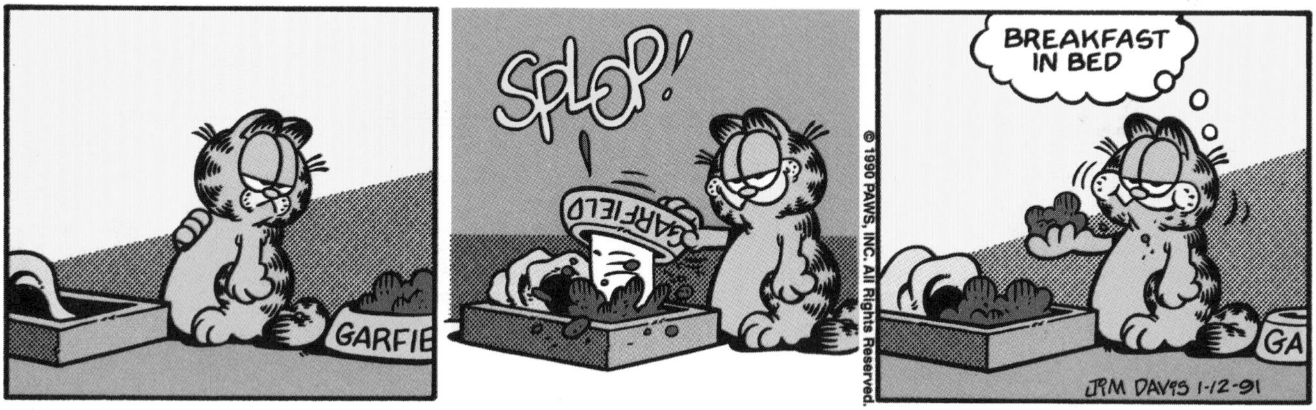
GARFIE
SPLOP!
GARFIELD
BREAKFAST IN BED
GA
© 1990 PAWS, INC. All Rights Reserved.
JIM DAVIS 1-12-91

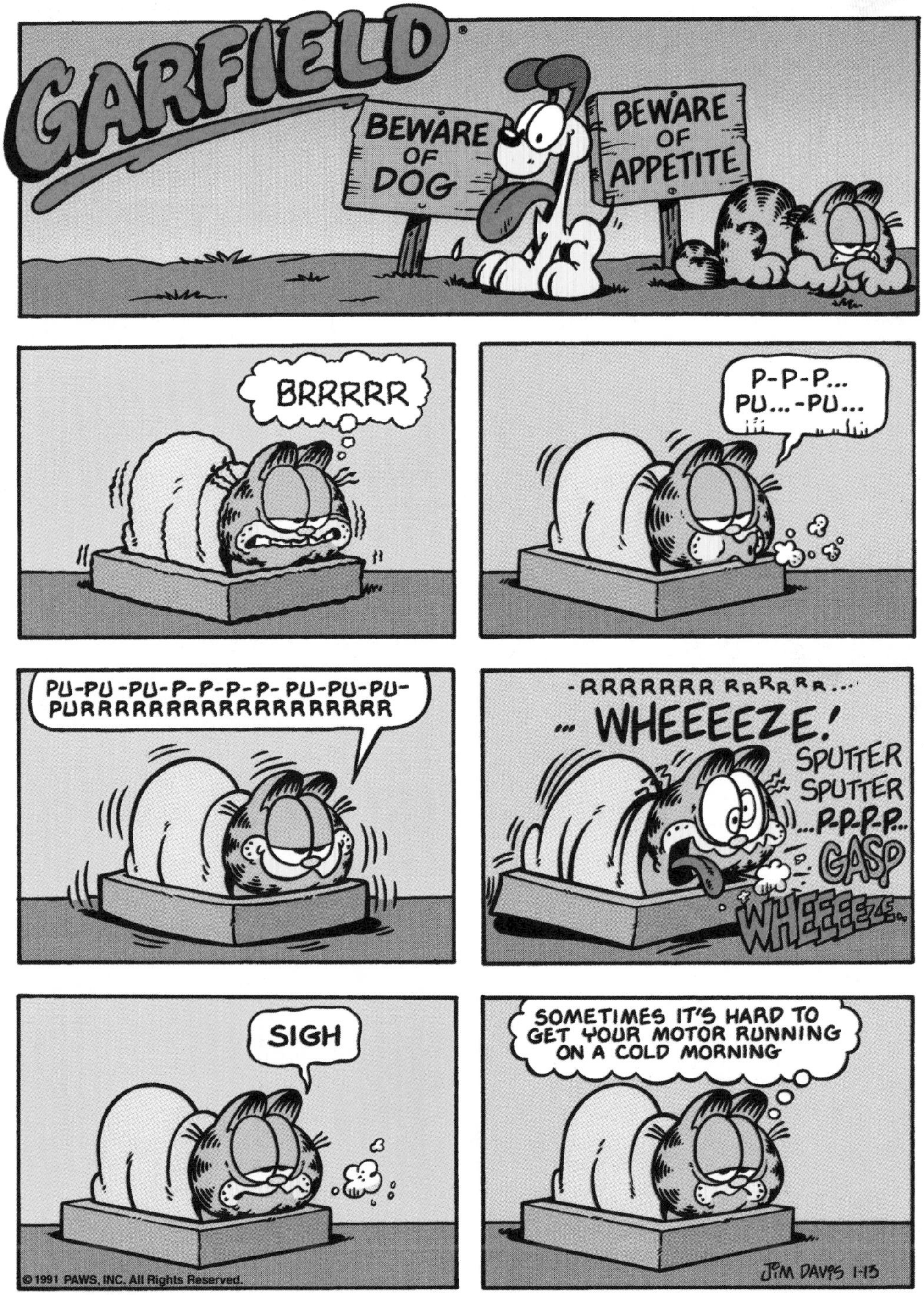
GARFIELD®
BEWARE OF DOG
BEWARE OF APPETITE
BRRRRR
P-P-P...
PU...-PU...
PU-PU-PU-P-P-P-P-PU-PU-PU-PURRRRRRRRRRRRRRRRRRR
-RRRRRRR RRRRRR....
... WHEEEEZE!
SPUTTER
SPUTTER
...P-P-P-P...
GASP
WHEEEEZE..
SIGH
SOMETIMES IT'S HARD TO GET YOUR MOTOR RUNNING ON A COLD MORNING
JIM DAVIS 1-13

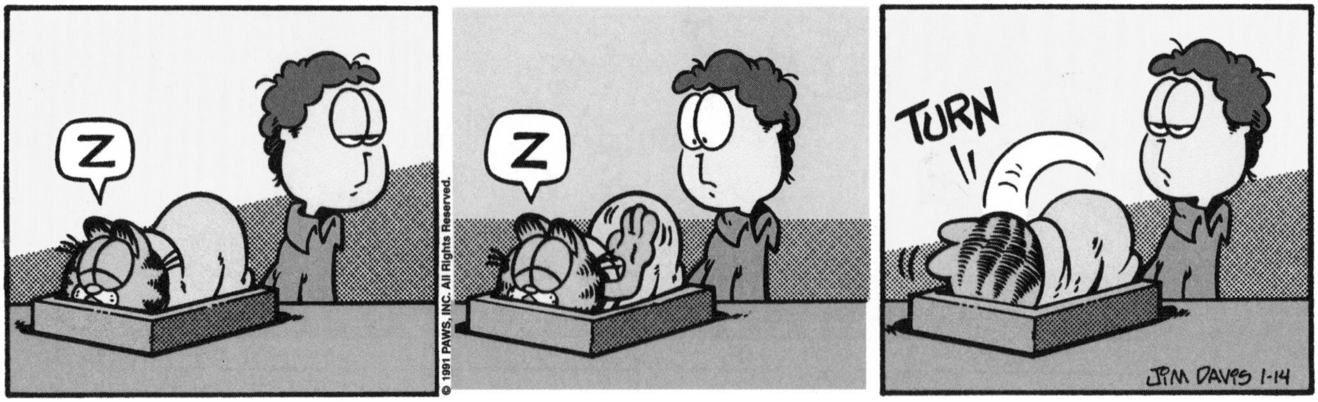
Z
Z
TURN
© 1991 PAWS, INC. All Rights Reserved.
JIM DAVIS 1-14

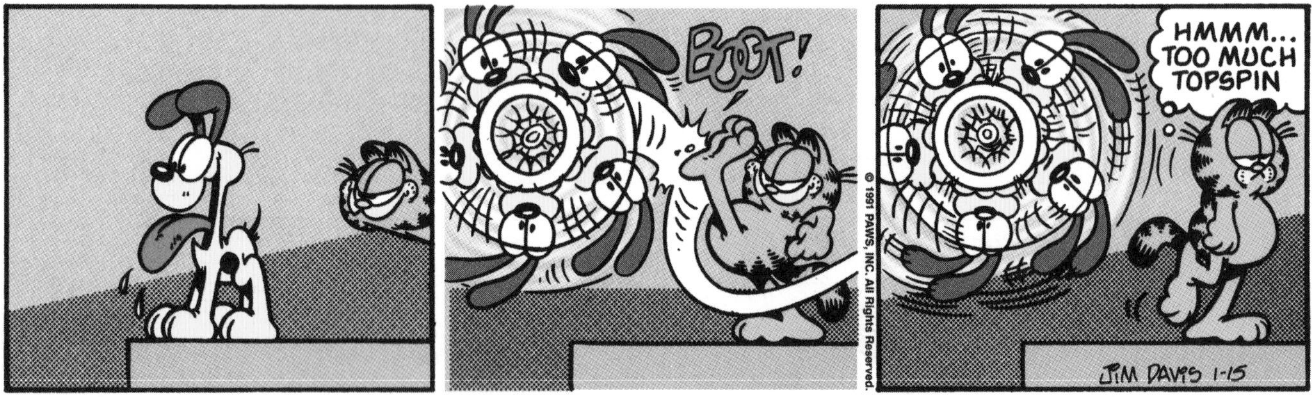
BOOT!
HMMM... TOO MUCH TOPSPIN
© 1991 PAWS, INC. All Rights Reserved.
JIM DAVIS 1-15

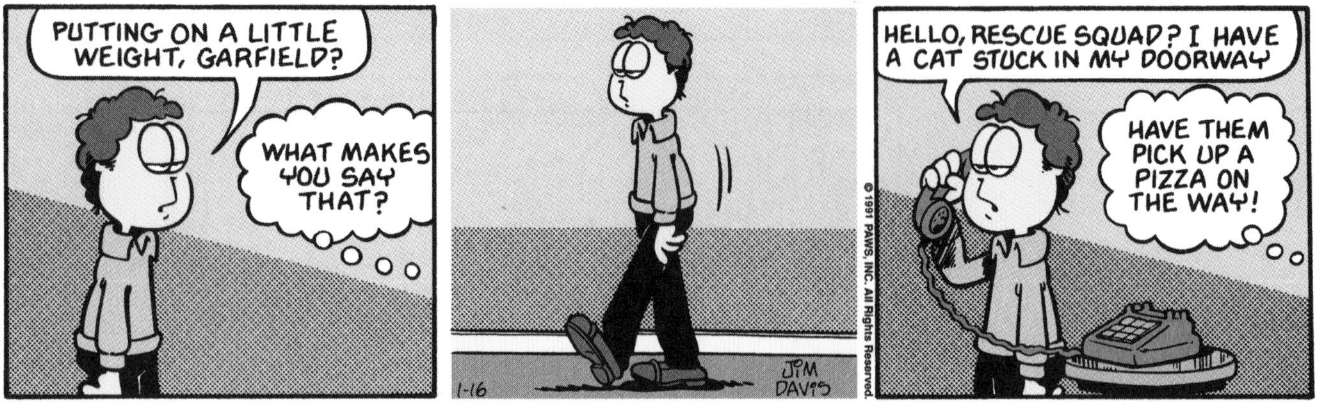
PUTTING ON A LITTLE WEIGHT, GARFIELD?
WHAT MAKES YOU SAY THAT?
1-16
JIM DAVIS
HELLO, RESCUE SQUAD? I HAVE A CAT STUCK IN MY DOORWAY
HAVE THEM PICK UP A PIZZA ON THE WAY!
© 1991 PAWS, INC. All Rights Reserved.

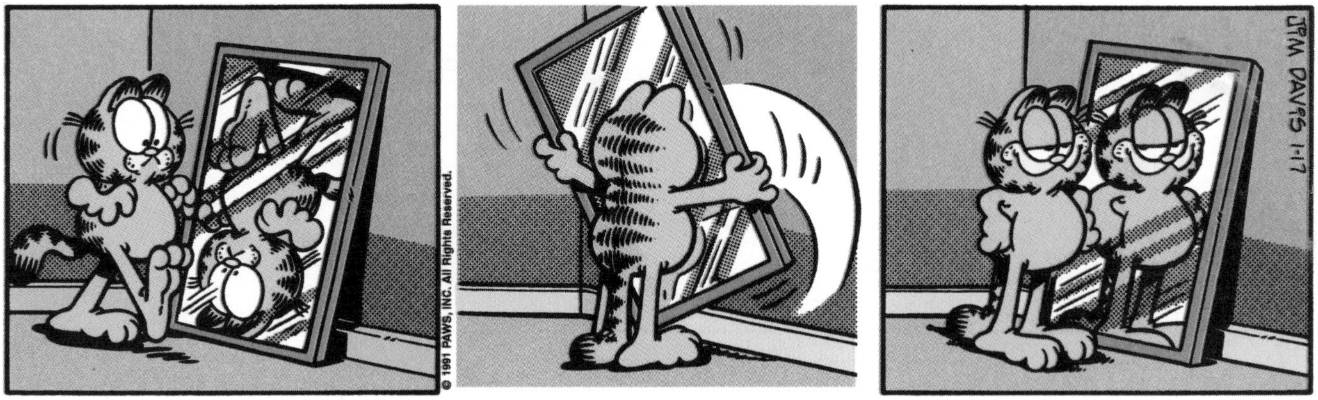
© 1991 PAWS, INC. All Rights Reserved.
JIM DAVIS 1-17

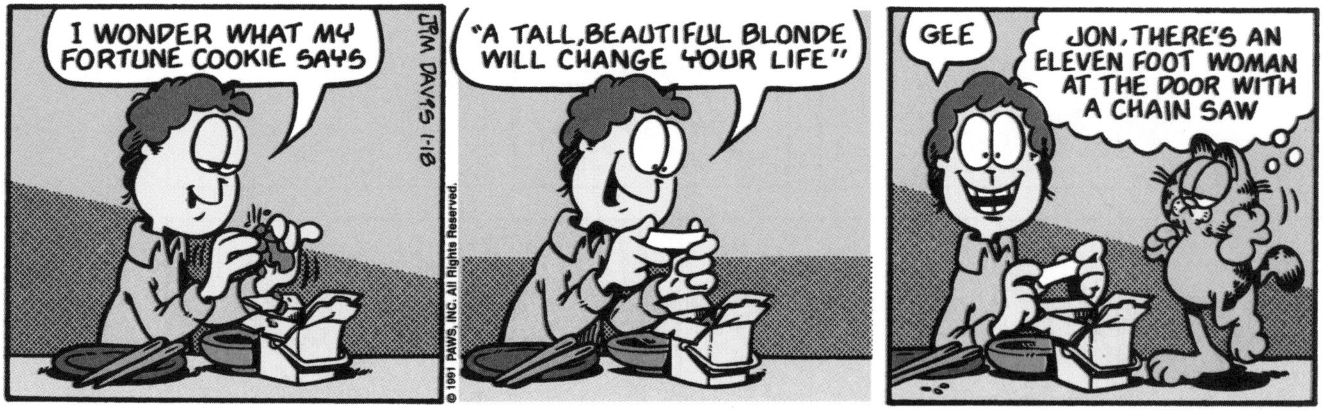
I WONDER WHAT MY FORTUNE COOKIE SAYS
JIM DAVIS 1-18
© 1991 PAWS, INC. All Rights Reserved.
"A TALL, BEAUTIFUL BLONDE WILL CHANGE YOUR LIFE"
GEE
JON, THERE'S AN ELEVEN FOOT WOMAN AT THE DOOR WITH A CHAIN SAW

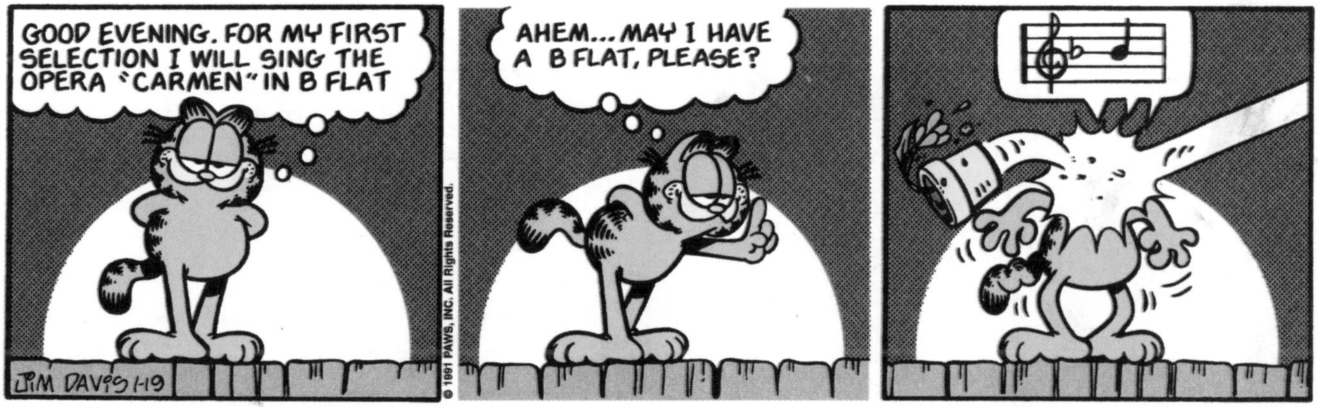
GOOD EVENING. FOR MY FIRST SELECTION I WILL SING THE OPERA "CARMEN" IN B FLAT
JIM DAVIS 1-19
© 1991 PAWS, INC. All Rights Reserved.
AHEM... MAY I HAVE A B FLAT, PLEASE?

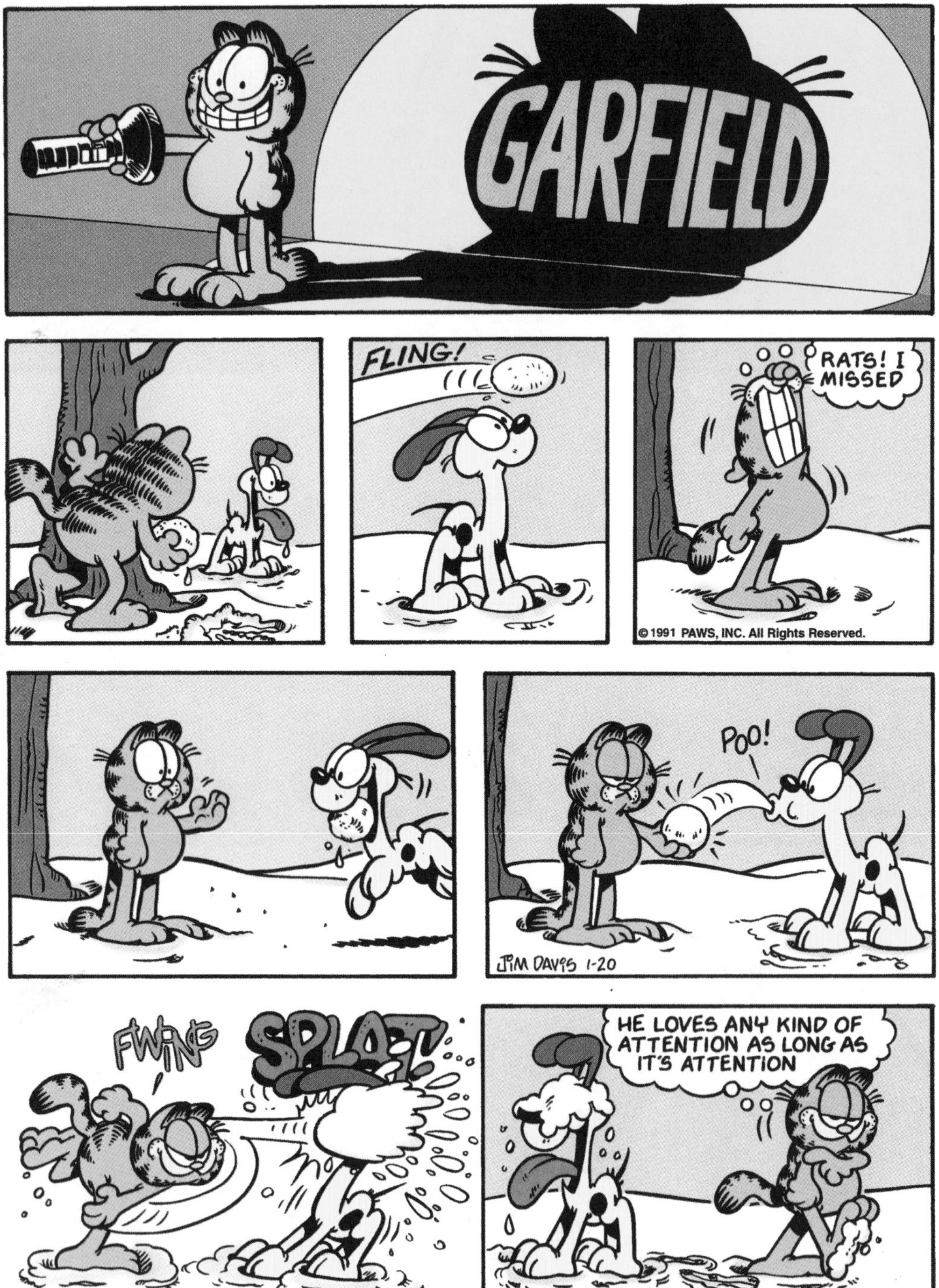
GARFIELD
FLING!
RATS! I MISSED
© 1991 PAWS, INC. All Rights Reserved.
POO!
JIM DAVIS 1-20
FWING
SPLAT
HE LOVES ANY KIND OF ATTENTION AS LONG AS IT'S ATTENTION

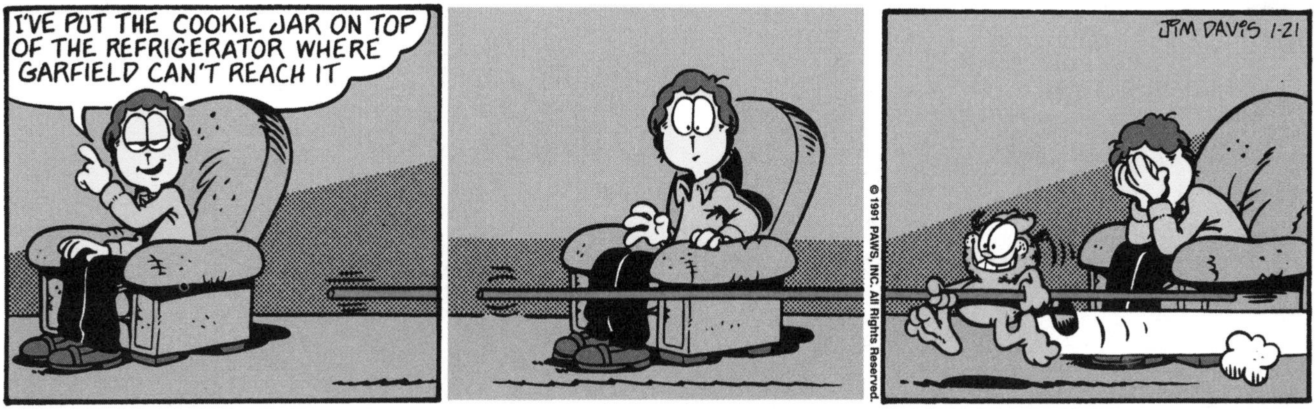
I'VE PUT THE COOKIE JAR ON TOP OF THE REFRIGERATOR WHERE GARFIELD CAN'T REACH IT
© 1991 PAWS, INC. All Rights Reserved.
JIM DAVIS 1-21

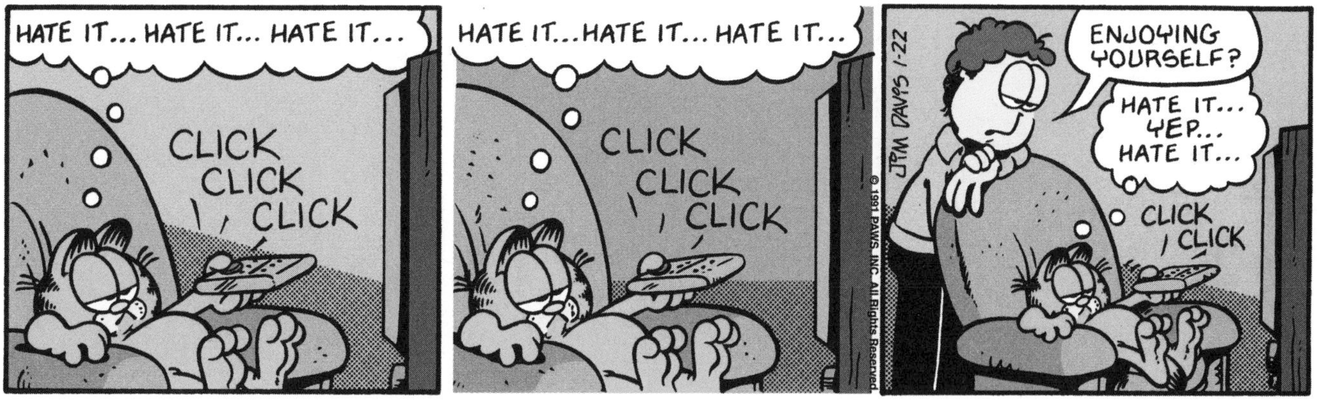
HATE IT... HATE IT... HATE IT...
CLICK CLICK CLICK
HATE IT... HATE IT... HATE IT...
CLICK CLICK CLICK
© 1991 PAWS, INC. All Rights Reserved.
JIM DAVIS 1-22
ENJOYING YOURSELF?
HATE IT... YEP... HATE IT...
CLICK CLICK

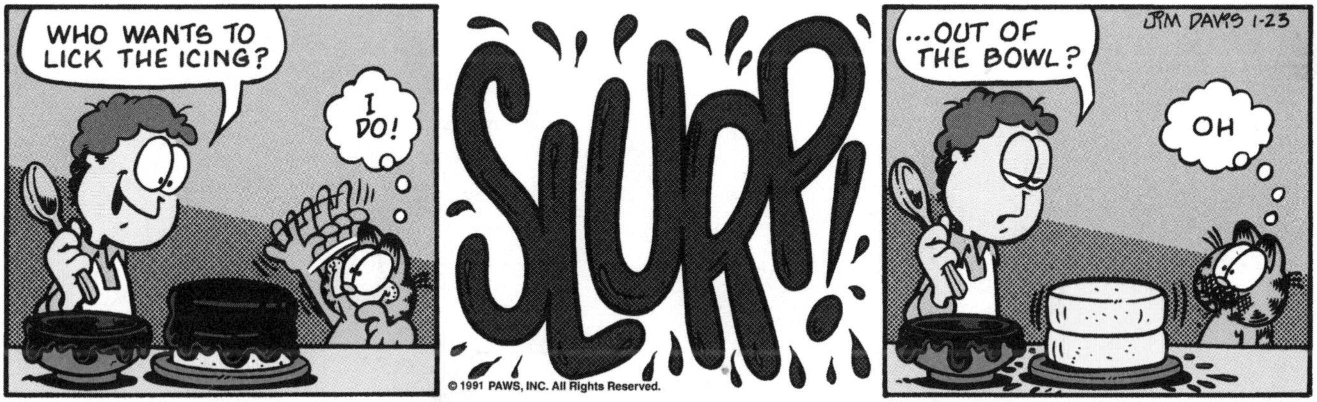
WHO WANTS TO LICK THE ICING?
I DO!
SLURP!
© 1991 PAWS, INC. All Rights Reserved.
JIM DAVIS 1-23
...OUT OF THE BOWL?
OH

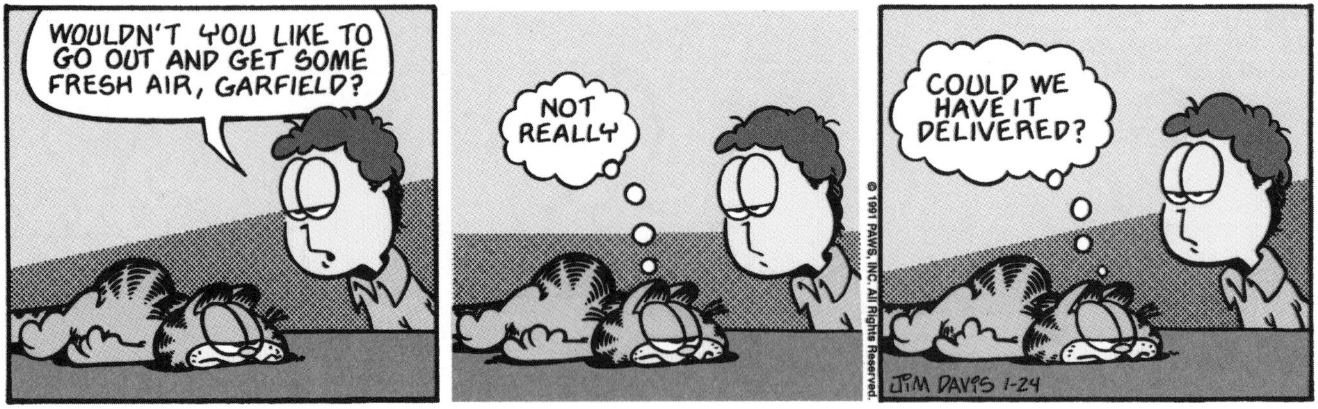
WOULDN'T YOU LIKE TO GO OUT AND GET SOME FRESH AIR, GARFIELD?
NOT REALLY
© 1991 PAWS, INC. All Rights Reserved.
COULD WE HAVE IT DELIVERED?
JIM DAVIS 1-24

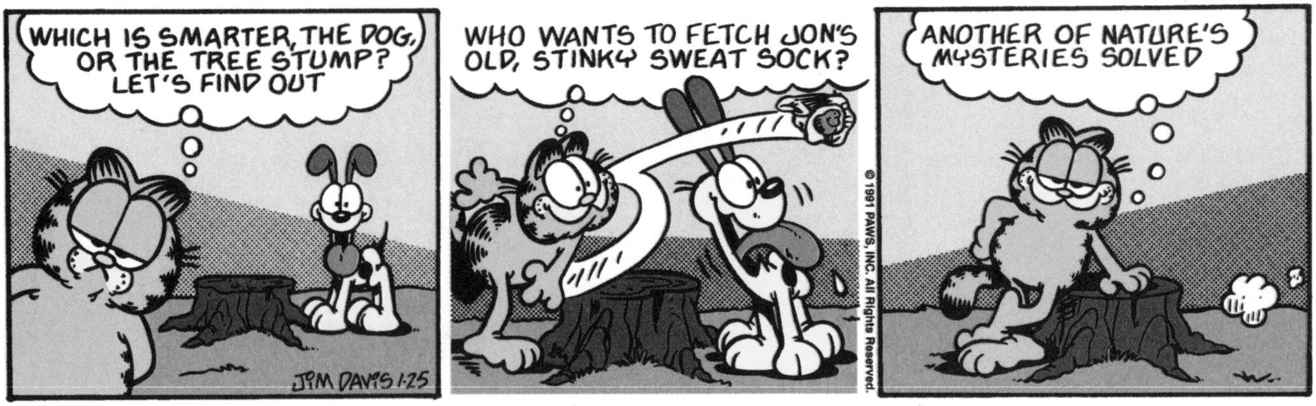
WHICH IS SMARTER, THE DOG, OR THE TREE STUMP? LET'S FIND OUT
JIM DAVIS 1-25
WHO WANTS TO FETCH JON'S OLD, STINKY SWEAT SOCK?
© 1991 PAWS, INC. All Rights Reserved.
ANOTHER OF NATURE'S MYSTERIES SOLVED

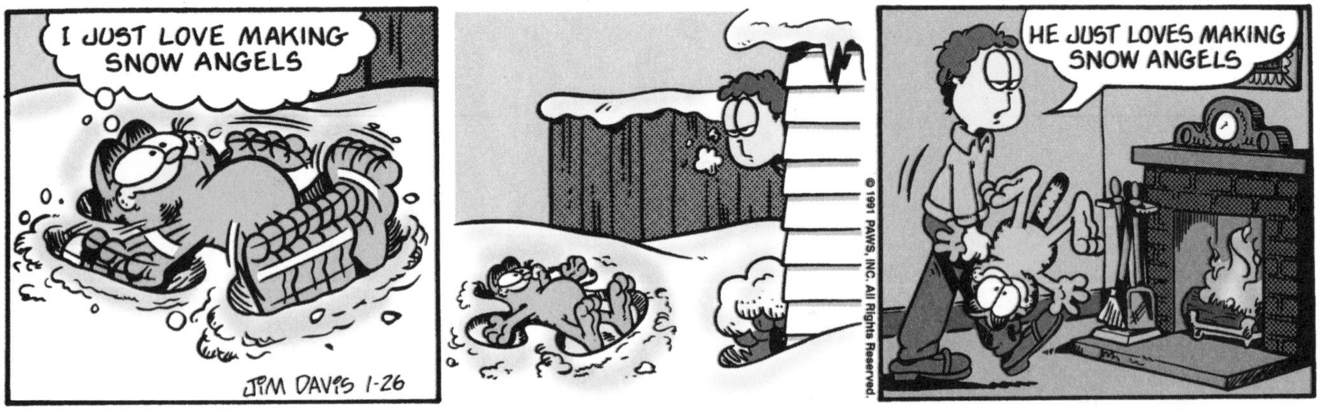
I JUST LOVE MAKING SNOW ANGELS
JIM DAVIS 1-26
© 1991 PAWS, INC. All Rights Reserved.
HE JUST LOVES MAKING SNOW ANGELS

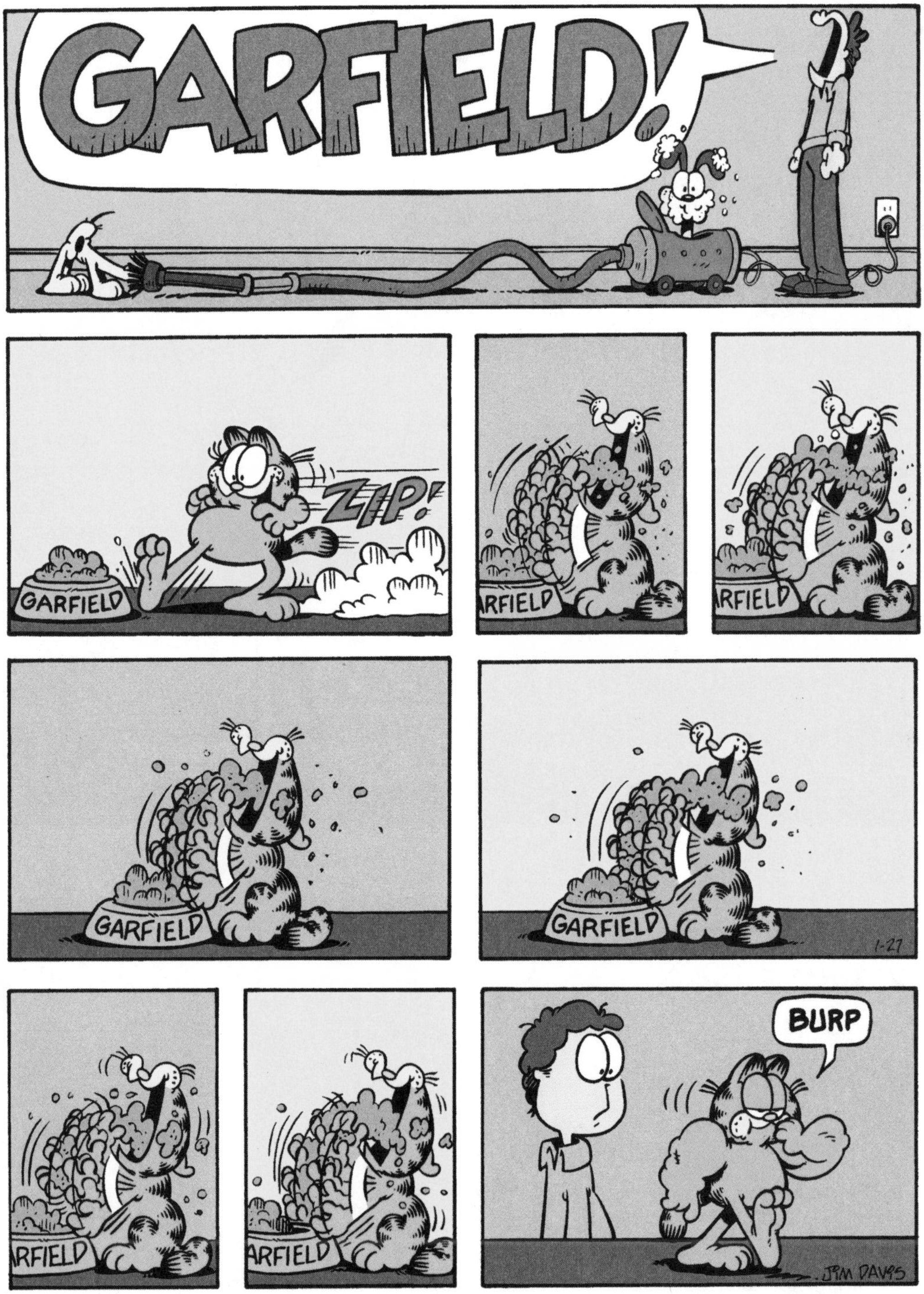
GARFIELD!
ZIP!
GARFIELD
1-27
BURP
JIM DAVIS

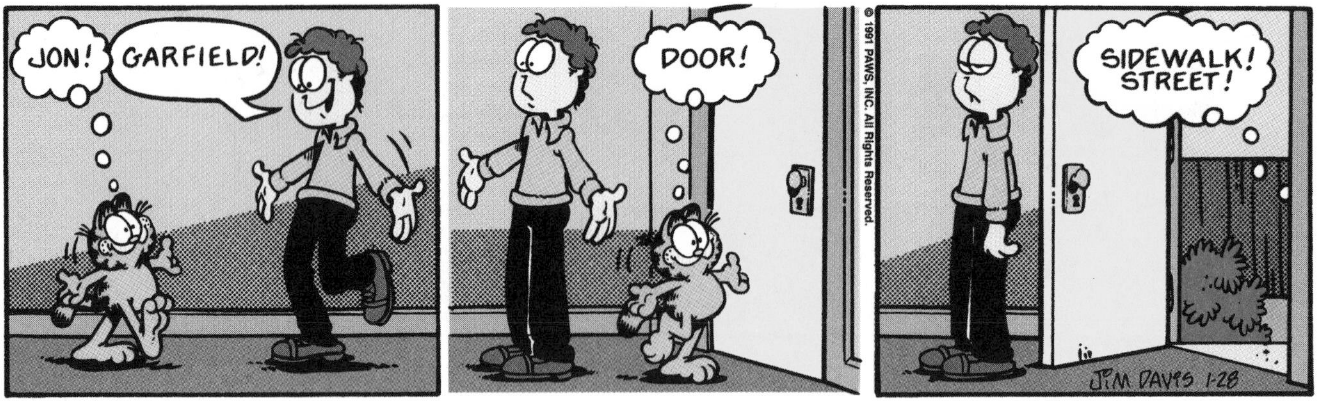
JON!
GARFIELD!
DOOR!
SIDEWALK! STREET!
© 1991 PAWS, INC. All Rights Reserved.
JIM DAVIS 1-28

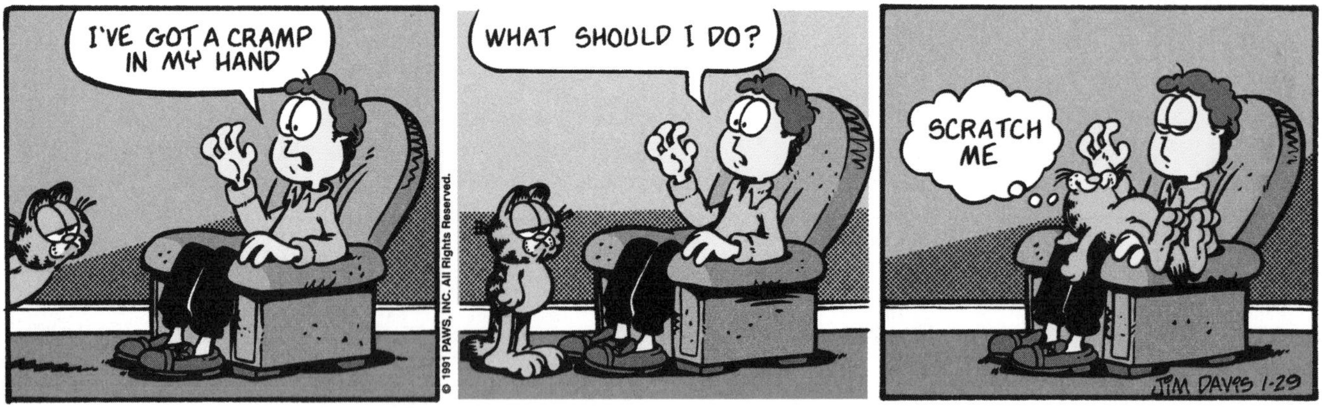
I'VE GOT A CRAMP IN MY HAND
WHAT SHOULD I DO?
SCRATCH ME
© 1991 PAWS, INC. All Rights Reserved.
JIM DAVIS 1-29

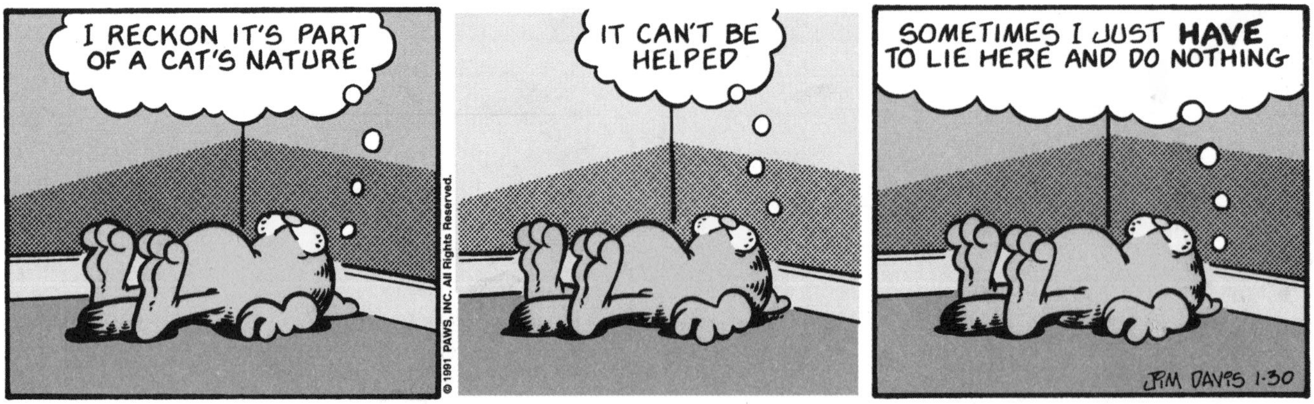
I RECKON IT'S PART OF A CAT'S NATURE
IT CAN'T BE HELPED
SOMETIMES I JUST **HAVE** TO LIE HERE AND DO NOTHING
© 1991 PAWS, INC. All Rights Reserved.
JIM DAVIS 1-30

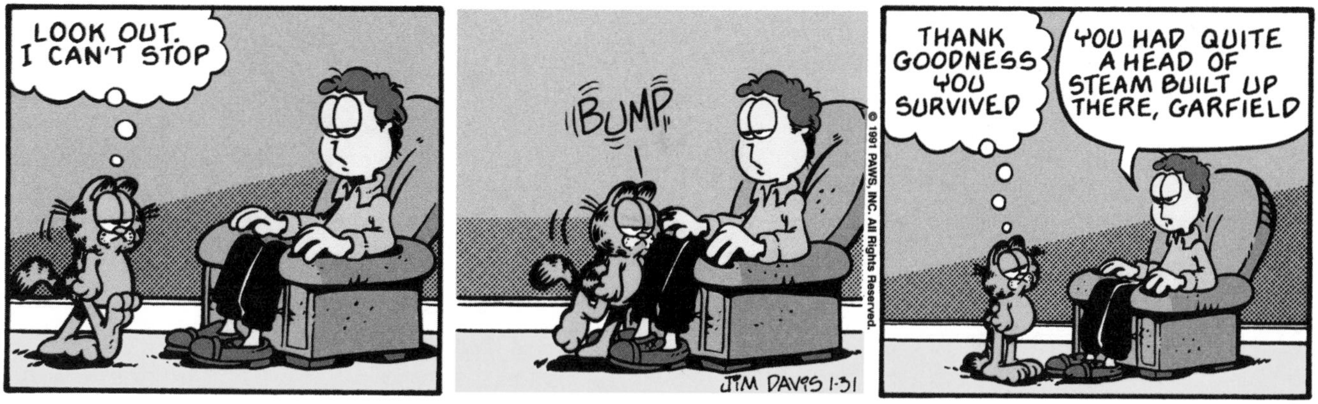
LOOK OUT. I CAN'T STOP
BUMP
© 1991 PAWS, INC. All Rights Reserved.
JIM DAVIS 1-31
THANK GOODNESS YOU SURVIVED
YOU HAD QUITE A HEAD OF STEAM BUILT UP THERE, GARFIELD

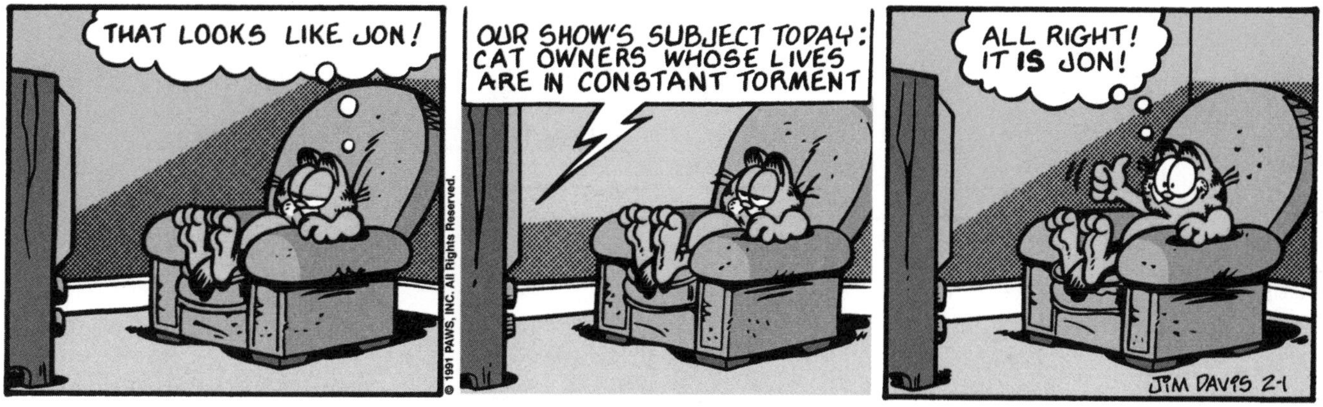
THAT LOOKS LIKE JON!
© 1991 PAWS, INC. All Rights Reserved.
OUR SHOW'S SUBJECT TODAY: CAT OWNERS WHOSE LIVES ARE IN CONSTANT TORMENT
ALL RIGHT! IT **IS** JON!
JIM DAVIS 2-1

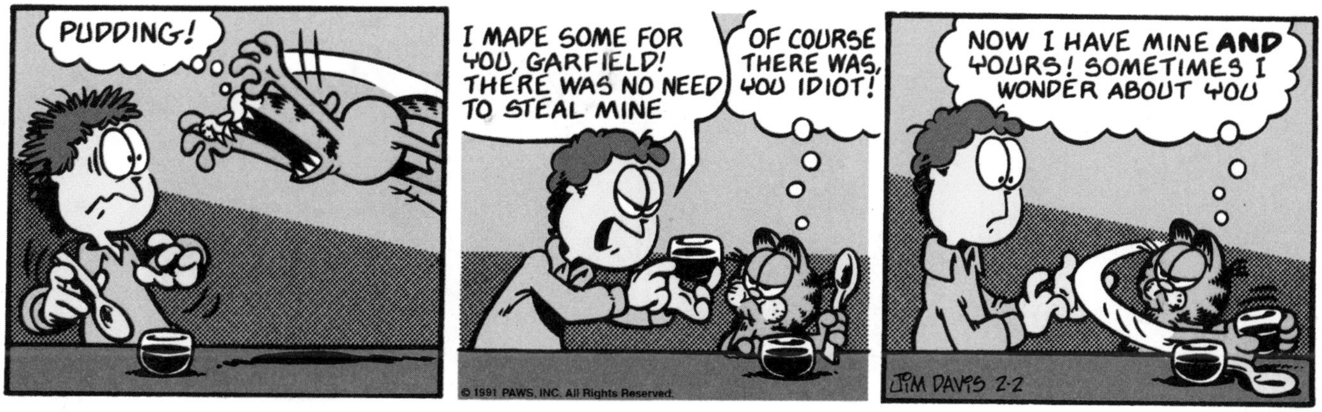
PUDDING!
I MADE SOME FOR YOU, GARFIELD! THERE WAS NO NEED TO STEAL MINE
OF COURSE THERE WAS, YOU IDIOT!
© 1991 PAWS, INC. All Rights Reserved.
NOW I HAVE MINE **AND** YOURS! SOMETIMES I WONDER ABOUT YOU
JIM DAVIS 2-2

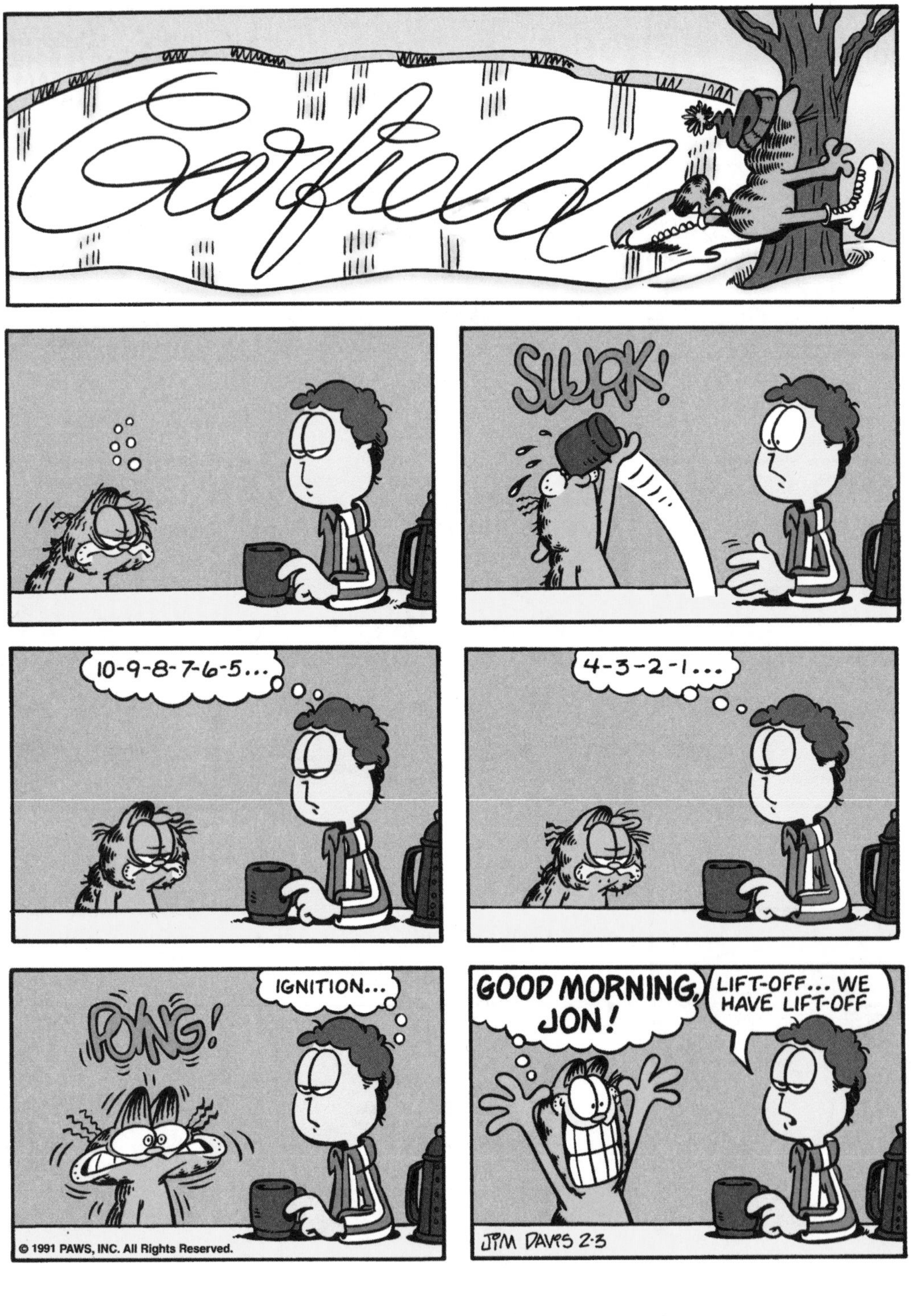
Garfield
SLURK!
10-9-8-7-6-5...
4-3-2-1...
PONG!
IGNITION...
GOOD MORNING, JON!
LIFT-OFF... WE HAVE LIFT-OFF
JIM DAVIS 2-3

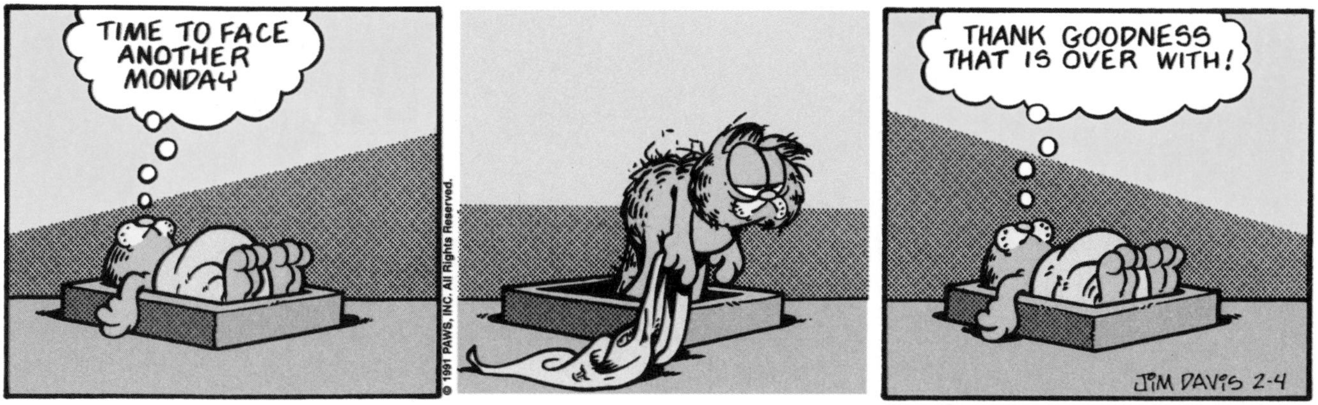
TIME TO FACE ANOTHER MONDAY
THANK GOODNESS THAT IS OVER WITH!
JIM DAVIS 2-4
© 1991 PAWS, INC. All Rights Reserved.

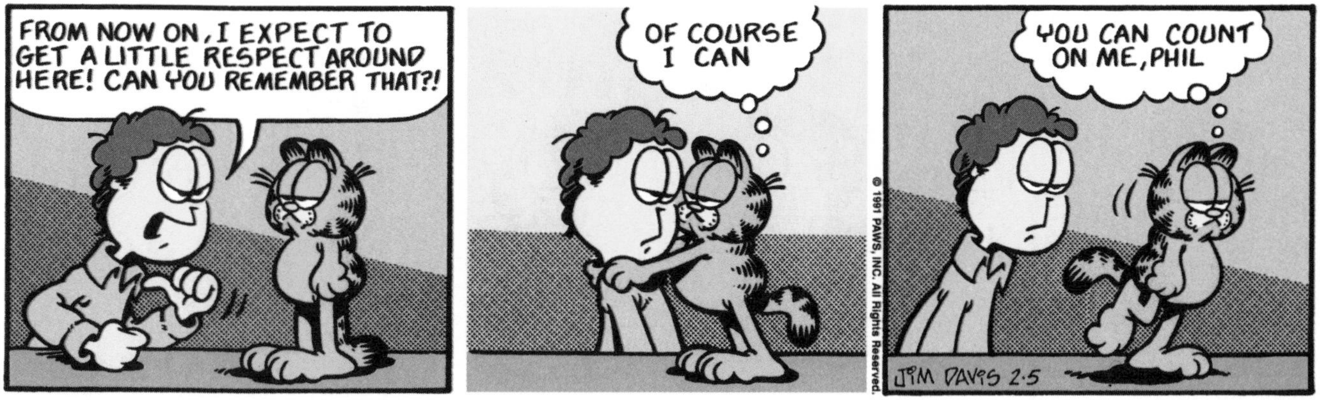
FROM NOW ON, I EXPECT TO GET A LITTLE RESPECT AROUND HERE! CAN YOU REMEMBER THAT?!
OF COURSE I CAN
YOU CAN COUNT ON ME, PHIL
JIM DAVIS 2-5
© 1991 PAWS, INC. All Rights Reserved.

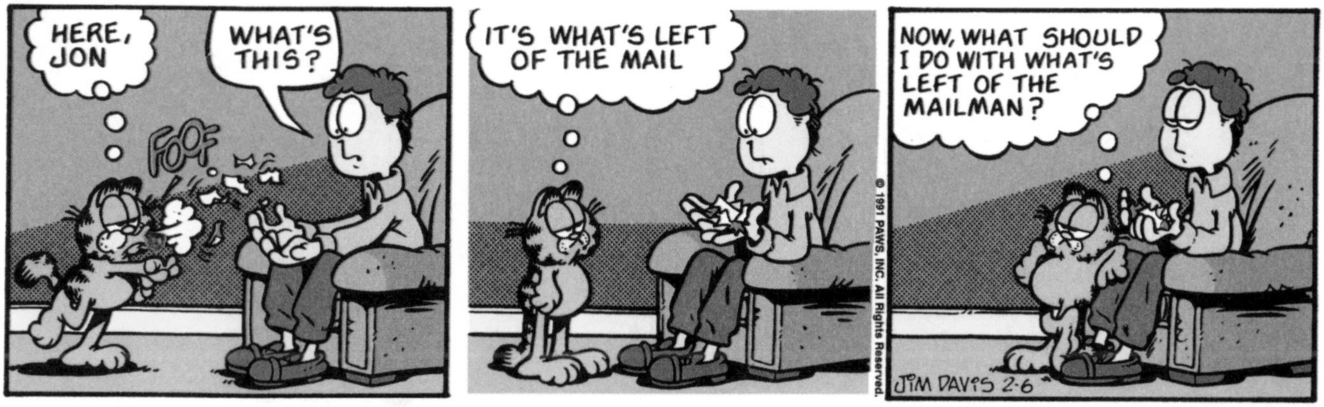
HERE, JON
FOOF
WHAT'S THIS?
IT'S WHAT'S LEFT OF THE MAIL
NOW, WHAT SHOULD I DO WITH WHAT'S LEFT OF THE MAILMAN?
JIM DAVIS 2-6
© 1991 PAWS, INC. All Rights Reserved.

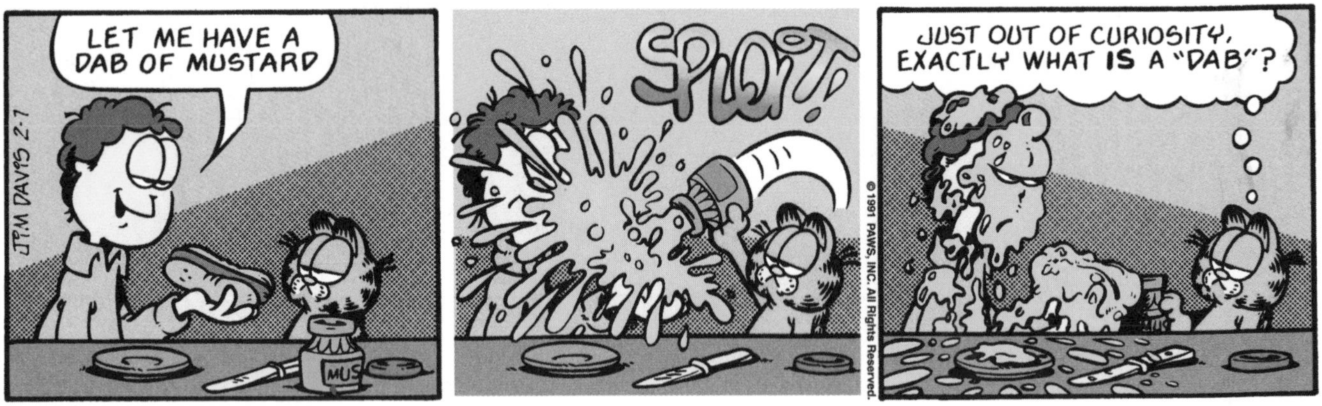
JIM DAVIS 2-7
LET ME HAVE A DAB OF MUSTARD
MUS
SPLOOT!
JUST OUT OF CURIOSITY, EXACTLY WHAT IS A "DAB"?

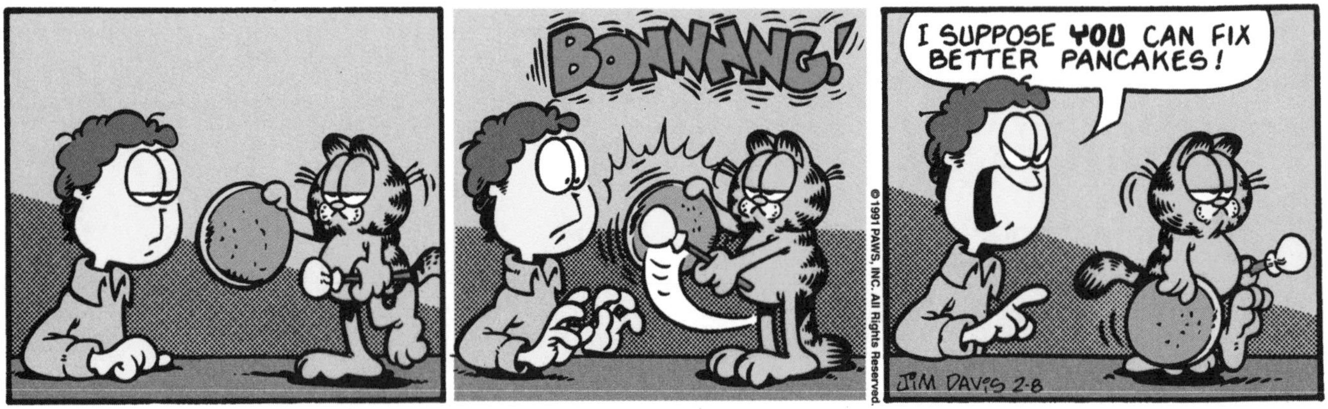
BONNNG!
I SUPPOSE YOU CAN FIX BETTER PANCAKES!
JIM DAVIS 2-8

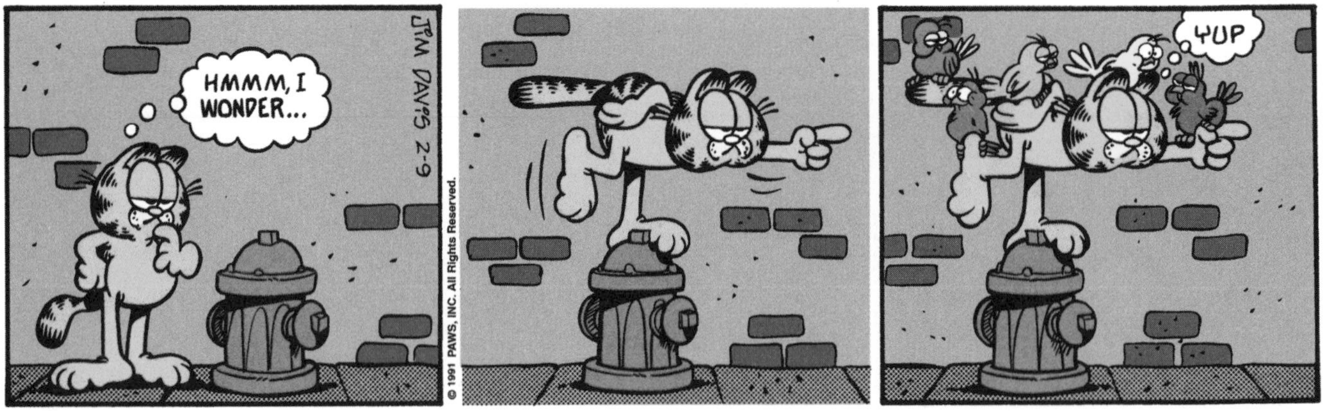
JIM DAVIS 2-9
HMMM, I WONDER...
YUP

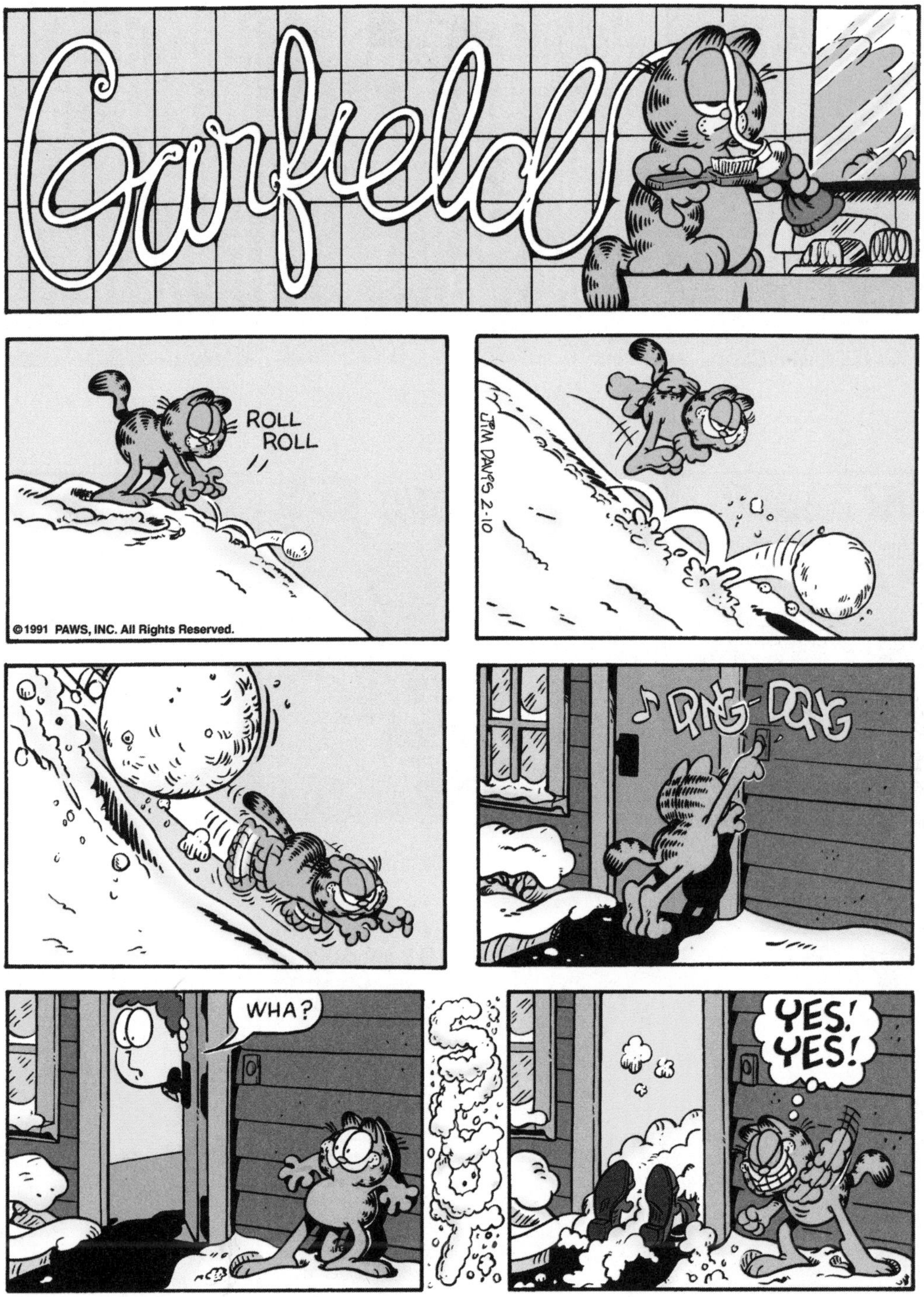
Garfield
ROLL
ROLL
©1991 PAWS, INC. All Rights Reserved.
JPM DAVPS 2-10
DING-DONG
WHA?
YES! YES!

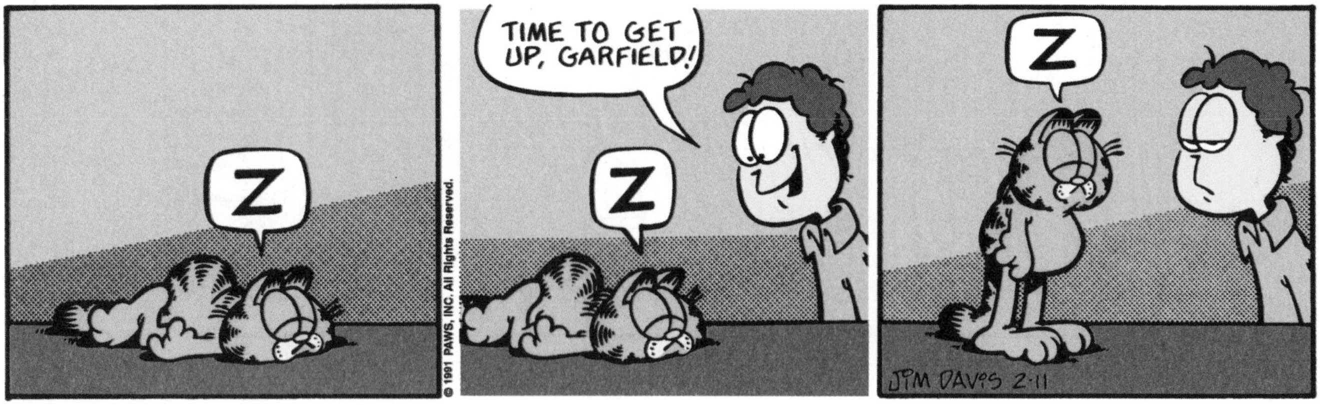
Z
TIME TO GET UP, GARFIELD!
Z
Z
© 1991 PAWS, INC. All Rights Reserved.
JIM DAVIS 2-11

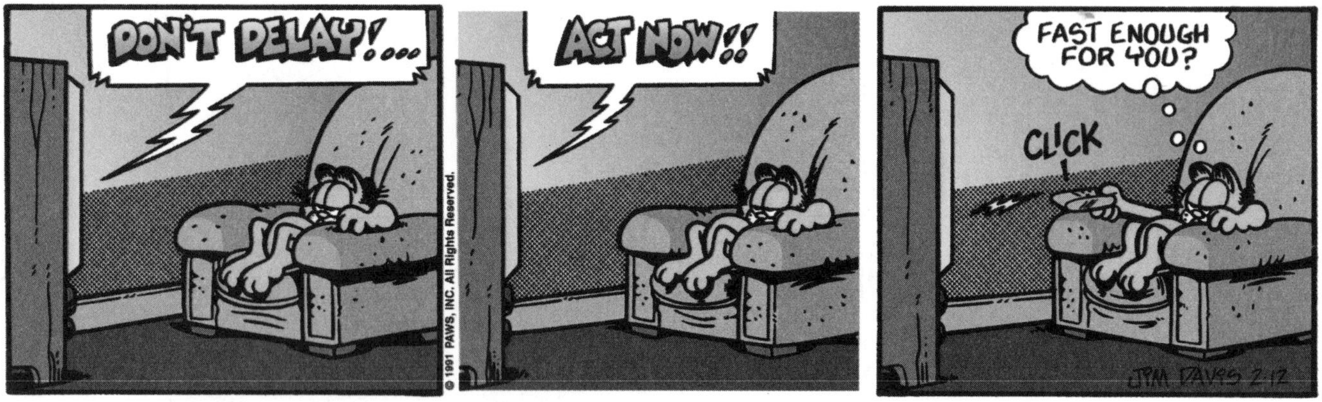
DON'T DELAY!....
ACT NOW!!
FAST ENOUGH FOR YOU?
CLICK
© 1991 PAWS, INC. All Rights Reserved.
JIM DAVIS 2-12

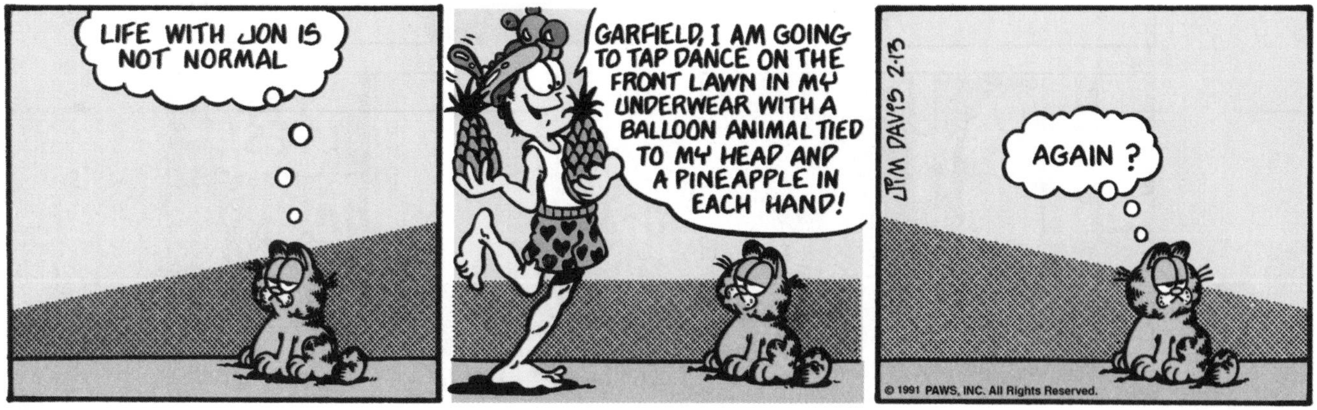
LIFE WITH JON IS NOT NORMAL
GARFIELD, I AM GOING TO TAP DANCE ON THE FRONT LAWN IN MY UNDERWEAR WITH A BALLOON ANIMAL TIED TO MY HEAD AND A PINEAPPLE IN EACH HAND!
JIM DAVIS 2-13
AGAIN ?
© 1991 PAWS, INC. All Rights Reserved.

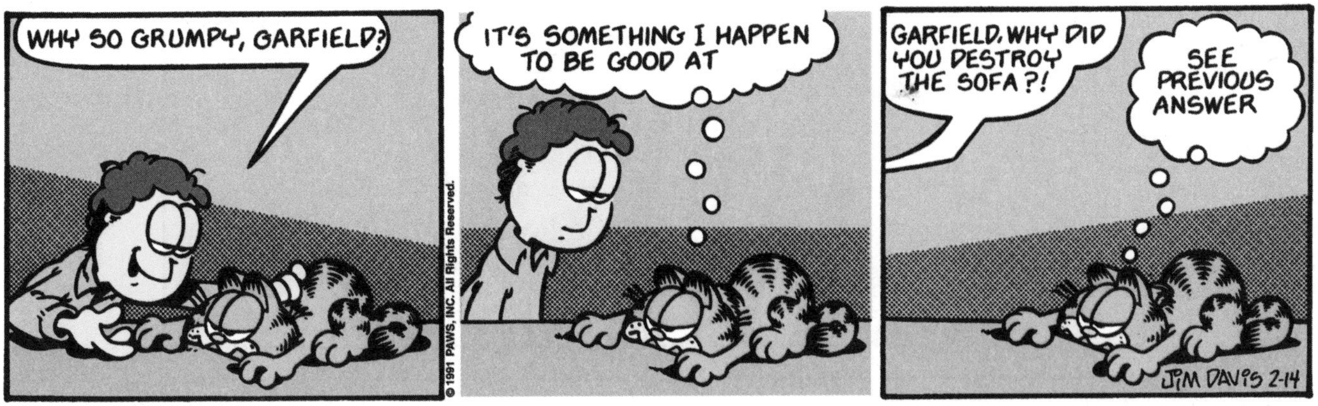
WHY SO GRUMPY, GARFIELD?
© 1991 PAWS, INC. All Rights Reserved.
IT'S SOMETHING I HAPPEN TO BE GOOD AT
GARFIELD, WHY DID YOU DESTROY THE SOFA?!
SEE PREVIOUS ANSWER
JIM DAVIS 2-14

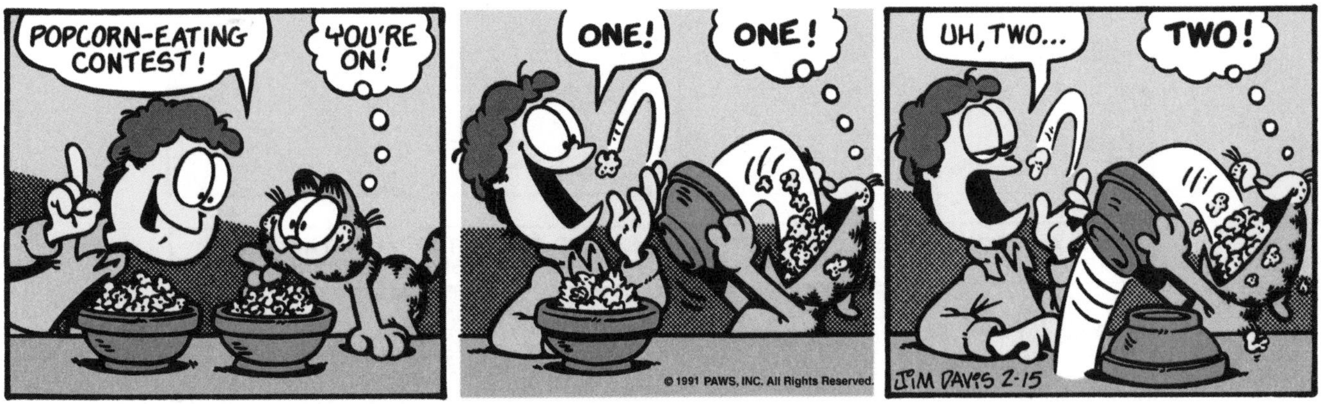
POPCORN-EATING CONTEST!
YOU'RE ON!
ONE!
ONE!
© 1991 PAWS, INC. All Rights Reserved.
UH, TWO...
TWO!
JIM DAVIS 2-15

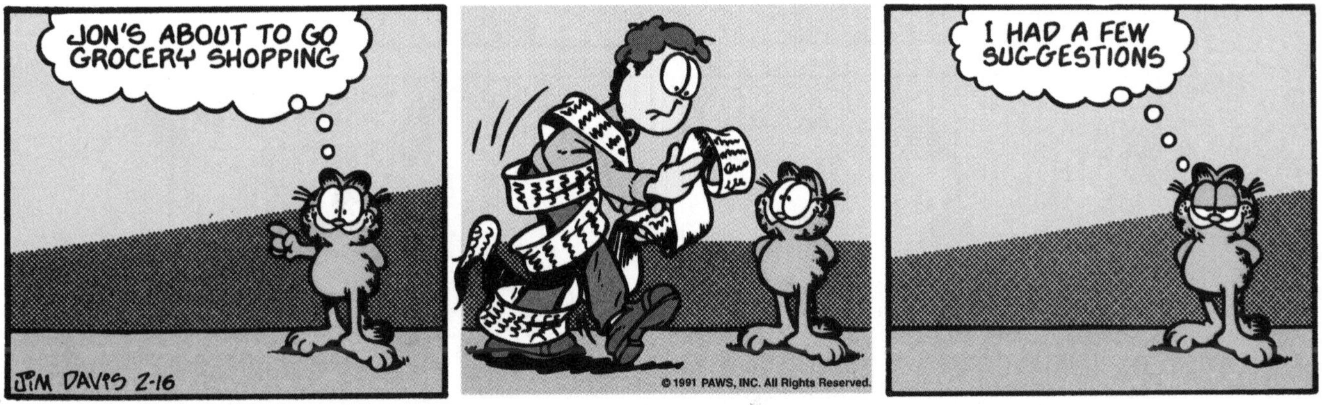
JON'S ABOUT TO GO GROCERY SHOPPING
JIM DAVIS 2-16
© 1991 PAWS, INC. All Rights Reserved.
I HAD A FEW SUGGESTIONS

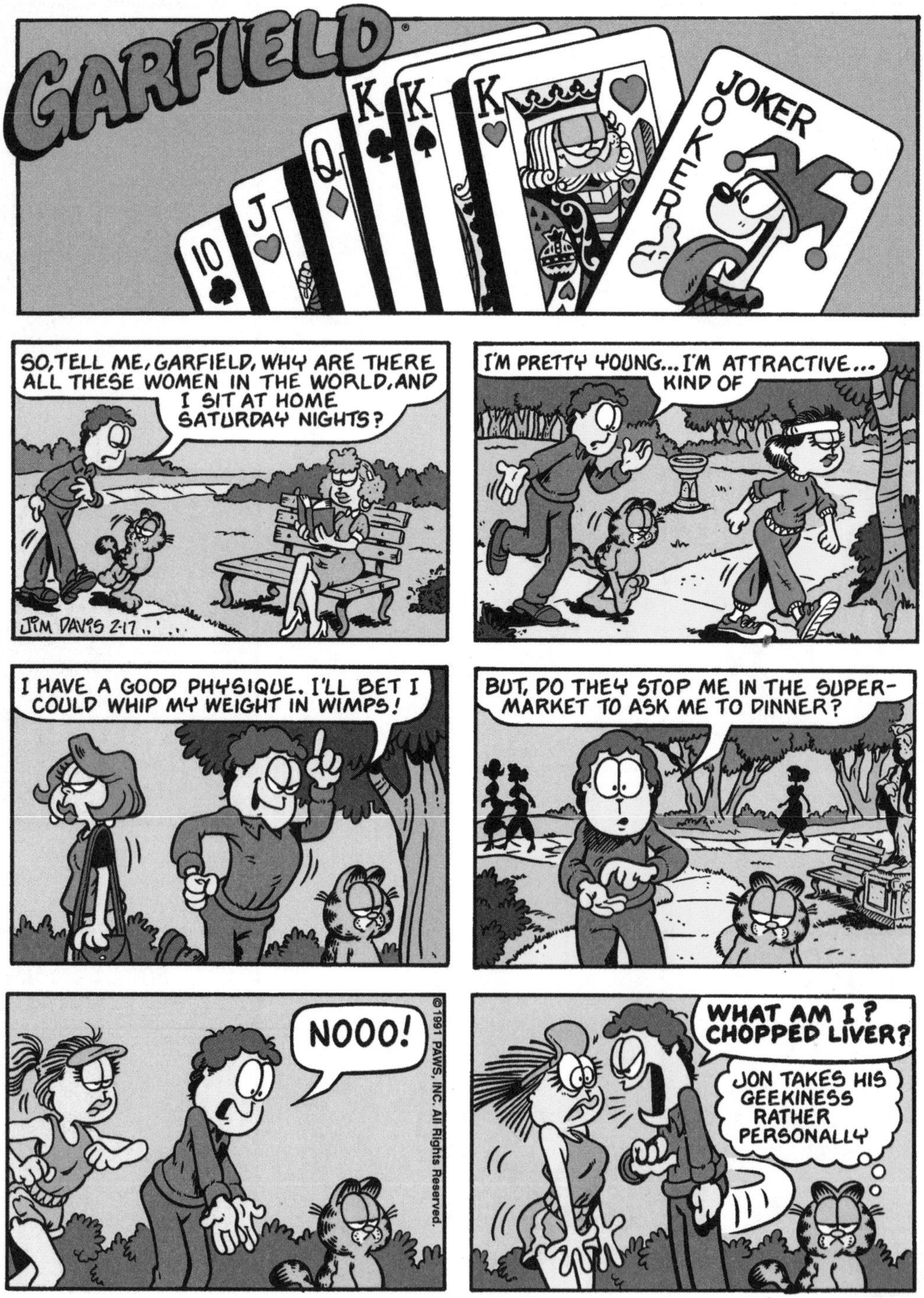
GARFIELD®
JOKER
SO, TELL ME, GARFIELD, WHY ARE THERE ALL THESE WOMEN IN THE WORLD, AND I SIT AT HOME SATURDAY NIGHTS?
JIM DAVIS 2-17
I'M PRETTY YOUNG... I'M ATTRACTIVE... KIND OF
I HAVE A GOOD PHYSIQUE. I'LL BET I COULD WHIP MY WEIGHT IN WIMPS!
BUT, DO THEY STOP ME IN THE SUPER-MARKET TO ASK ME TO DINNER?
NOOO!
WHAT AM I? CHOPPED LIVER?
JON TAKES HIS GEEKINESS RATHER PERSONALLY

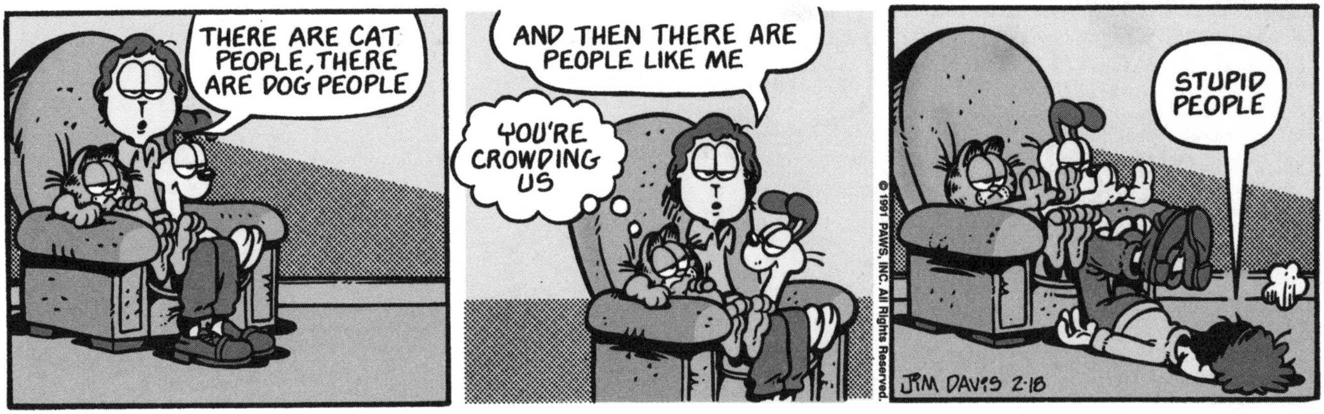
THERE ARE CAT PEOPLE, THERE ARE DOG PEOPLE
AND THEN THERE ARE PEOPLE LIKE ME
YOU'RE CROWDING US
STUPID PEOPLE
© 1991 PAWS, INC. All Rights Reserved.
JIM DAVIS 2-18

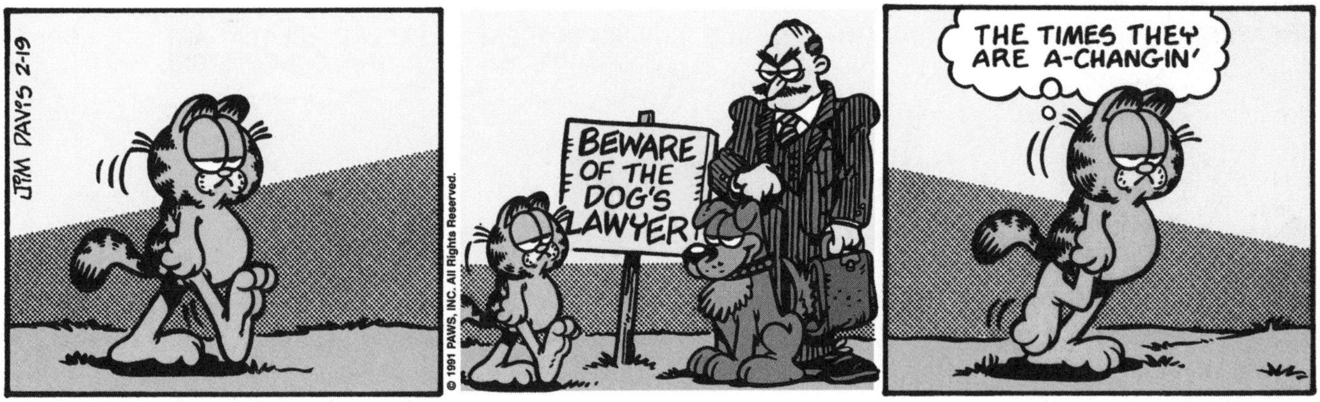
JIM DAVIS 2-19
© 1991 PAWS, INC. All Rights Reserved.
BEWARE OF THE DOG'S LAWYER
THE TIMES THEY ARE A-CHANGIN'

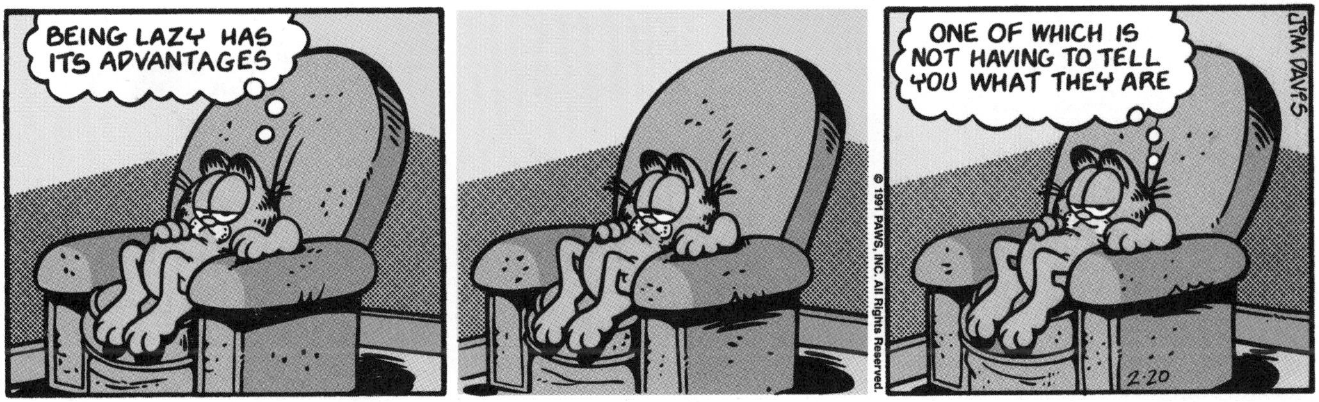
BEING LAZY HAS ITS ADVANTAGES
© 1991 PAWS, INC. All Rights Reserved.
ONE OF WHICH IS NOT HAVING TO TELL YOU WHAT THEY ARE
JIM DAVIS
2-20

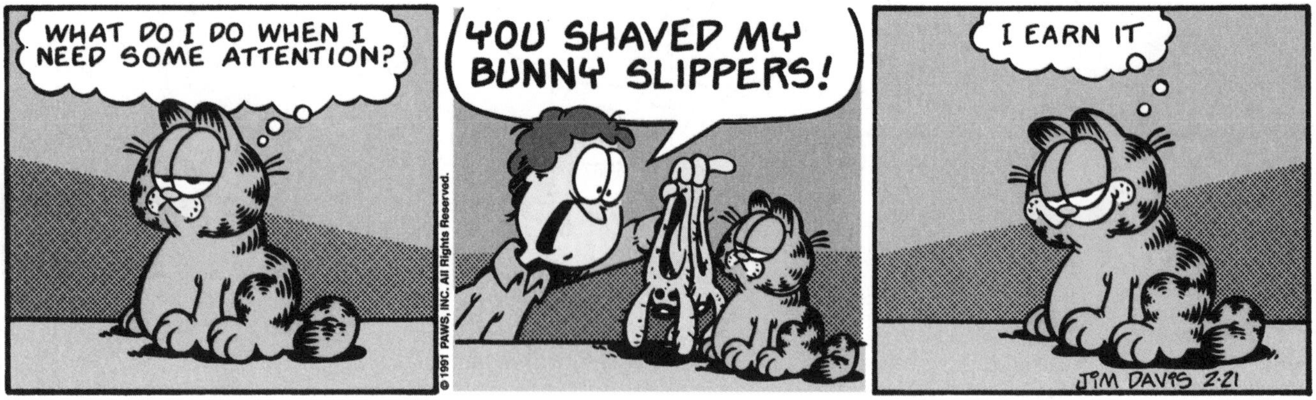
WHAT DO I DO WHEN I NEED SOME ATTENTION?
YOU SHAVED MY BUNNY SLIPPERS!
© 1991 PAWS, INC. All Rights Reserved.
I EARN IT
JIM DAVIS 2-21

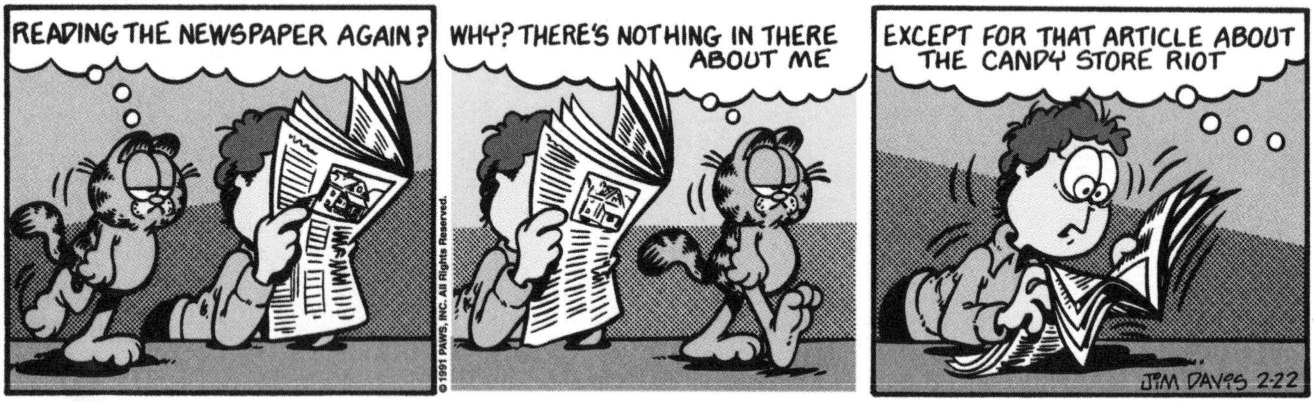
READING THE NEWSPAPER AGAIN?
WHY? THERE'S NOTHING IN THERE ABOUT ME
© 1991 PAWS, INC. All Rights Reserved.
EXCEPT FOR THAT ARTICLE ABOUT THE CANDY STORE RIOT
JIM DAVIS 2-22

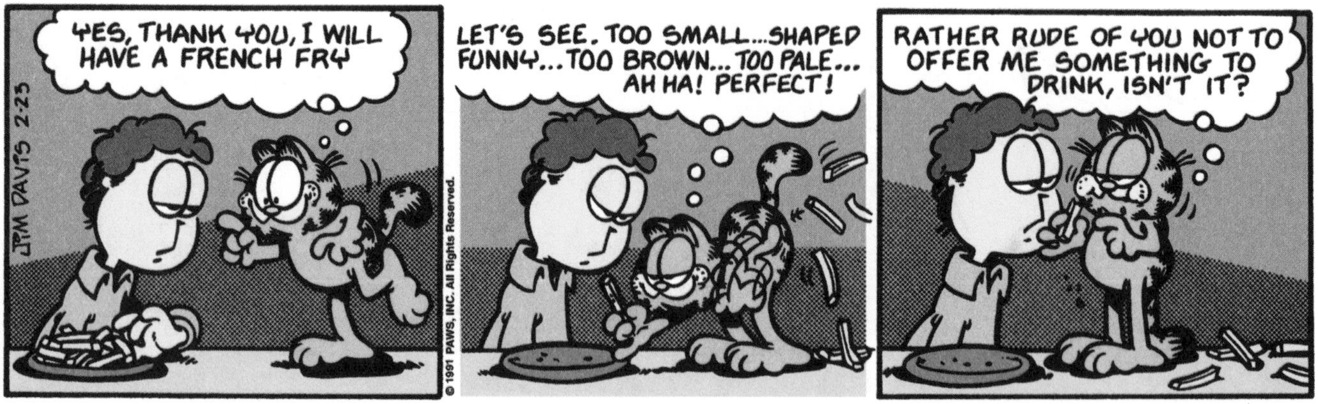
YES, THANK YOU, I WILL HAVE A FRENCH FRY
JIM DAVIS 2-23
LET'S SEE. TOO SMALL...SHAPED FUNNY...TOO BROWN...TOO PALE... AH HA! PERFECT!
© 1991 PAWS, INC. All Rights Reserved.
RATHER RUDE OF YOU NOT TO OFFER ME SOMETHING TO DRINK, ISN'T IT?

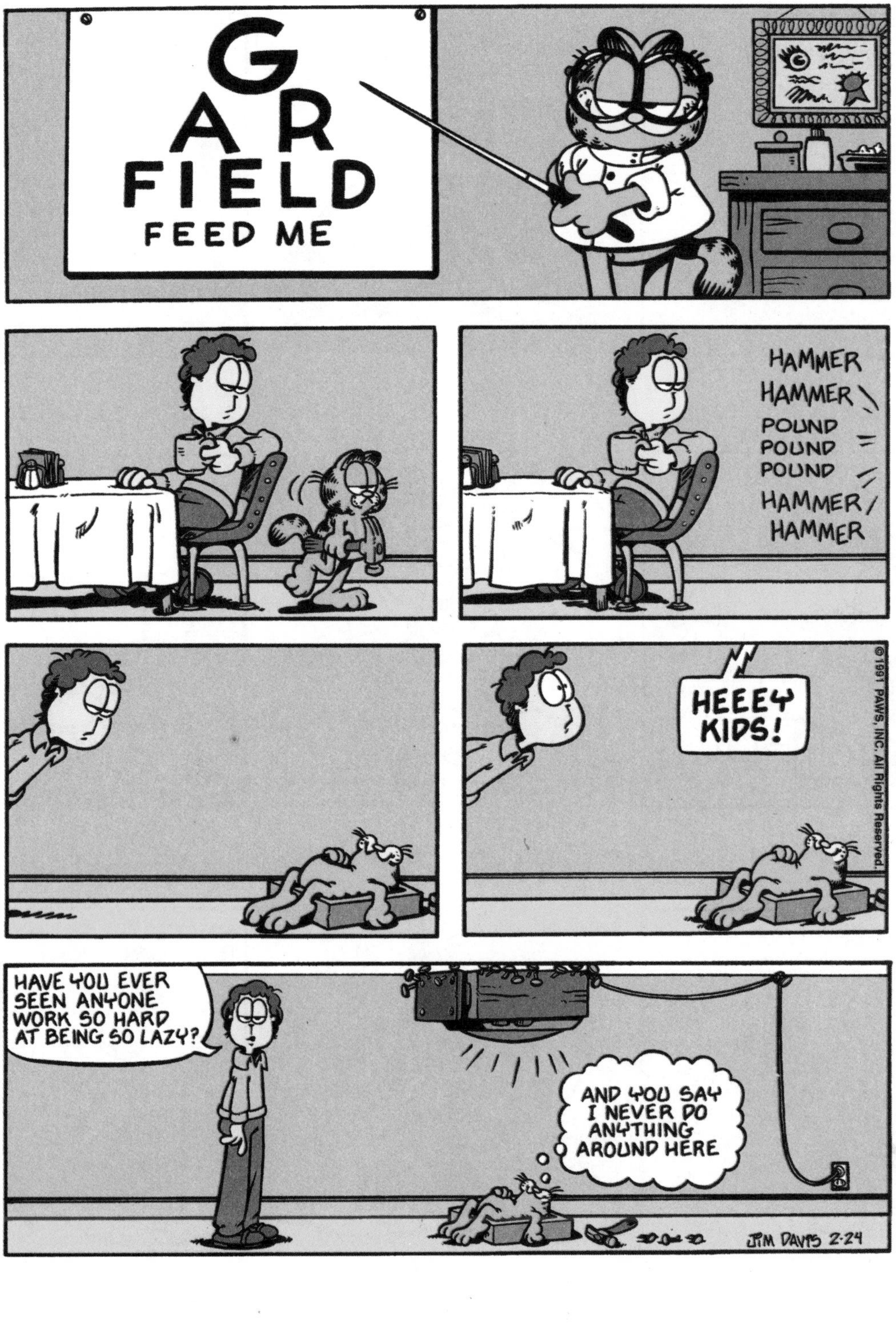

G
A R
FIELD
FEED ME
HAMMER
HAMMER
POUND
POUND
POUND
HAMMER
HAMMER
HEEEY KIDS!
© 1991 PAWS, INC. All Rights Reserved.
HAVE YOU EVER SEEN ANYONE WORK SO HARD AT BEING SO LAZY?
AND YOU SAY I NEVER DO ANYTHING AROUND HERE
JIM DAVIS 2-24

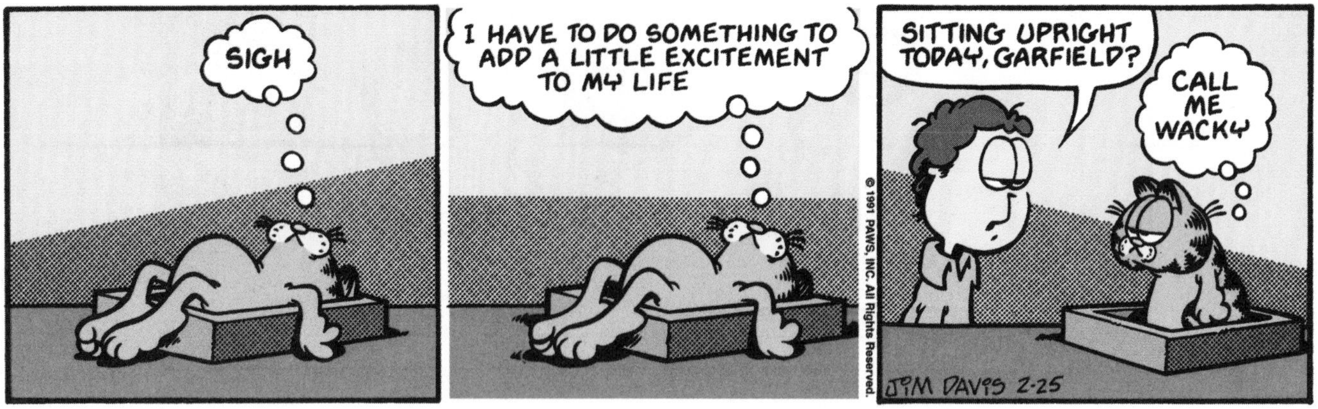
SIGH
I HAVE TO DO SOMETHING TO ADD A LITTLE EXCITEMENT TO MY LIFE
SITTING UPRIGHT TODAY, GARFIELD?
CALL ME WACKY
JIM DAVIS 2-25
© 1991 PAWS, INC. All Rights Reserved.

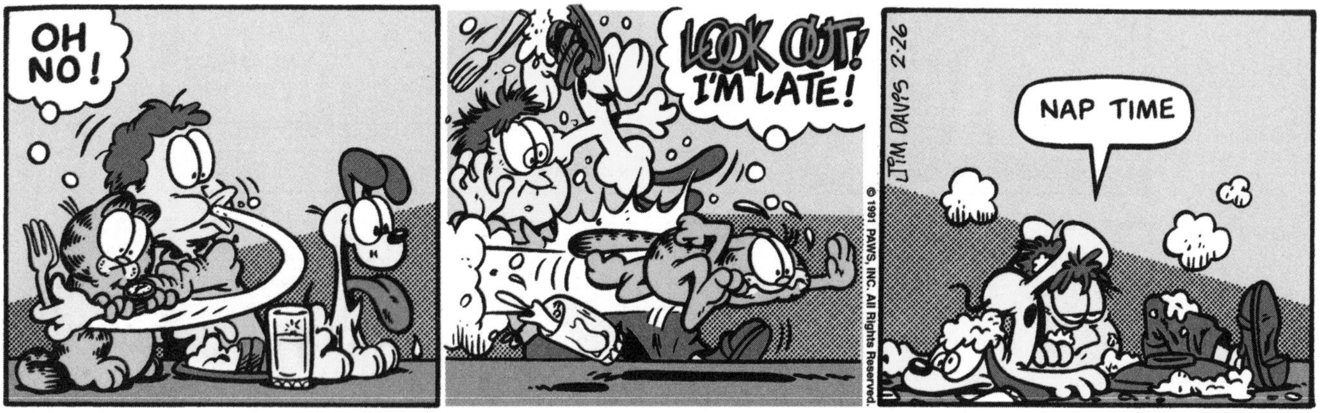
OH NO!
LOOK OUT! I'M LATE!
NAP TIME
JIM DAVIS 2-26
© 1991 PAWS, INC. All Rights Reserved.

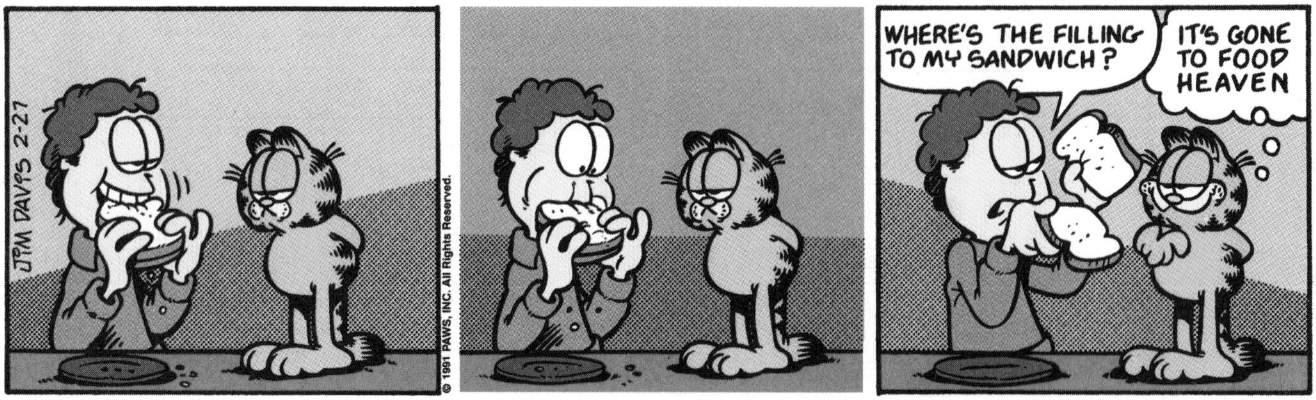
JIM DAVIS 2-27
© 1991 PAWS, INC. All Rights Reserved.
WHERE'S THE FILLING TO MY SANDWICH?
IT'S GONE TO FOOD HEAVEN

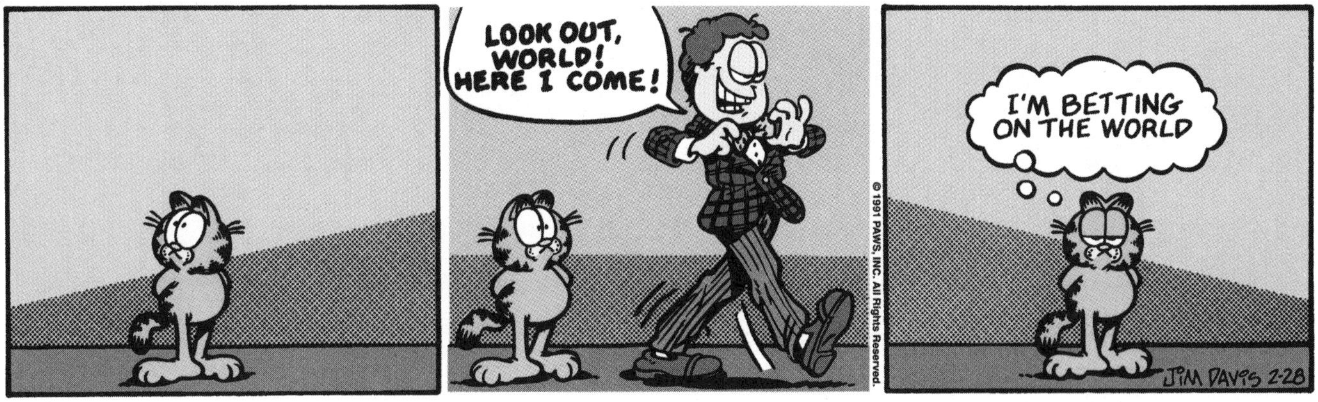
LOOK OUT, WORLD! HERE I COME!
© 1991 PAWS, INC. All Rights Reserved.
I'M BETTING ON THE WORLD
JIM DAVIS 2-28

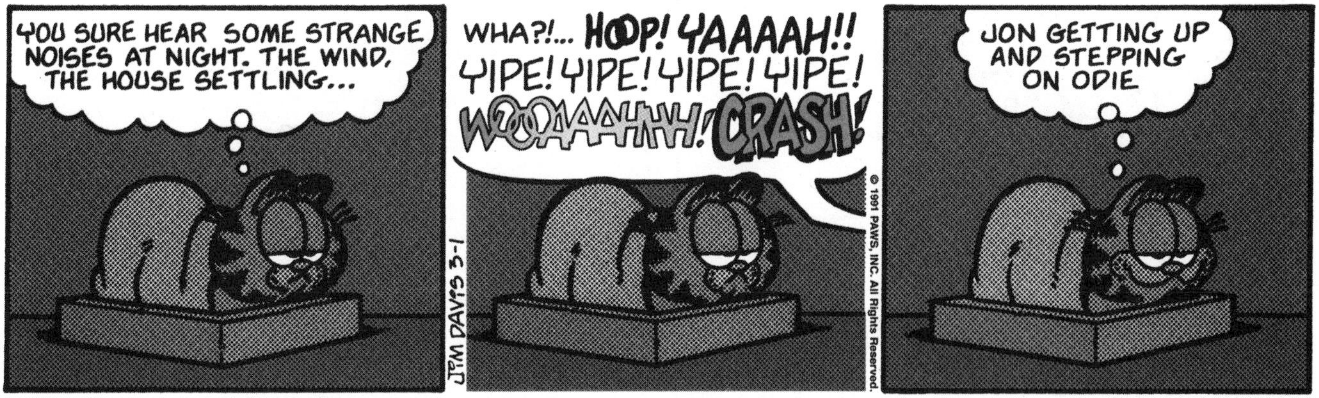
YOU SURE HEAR SOME STRANGE NOISES AT NIGHT. THE WIND, THE HOUSE SETTLING...
JIM DAVIS 3-1
WHA?!... HOOP! YAAAAH!! YIPE! YIPE! YIPE! YIPE! WOOAAAHHH! CRASH!
© 1991 PAWS, INC. All Rights Reserved.
JON GETTING UP AND STEPPING ON ODIE

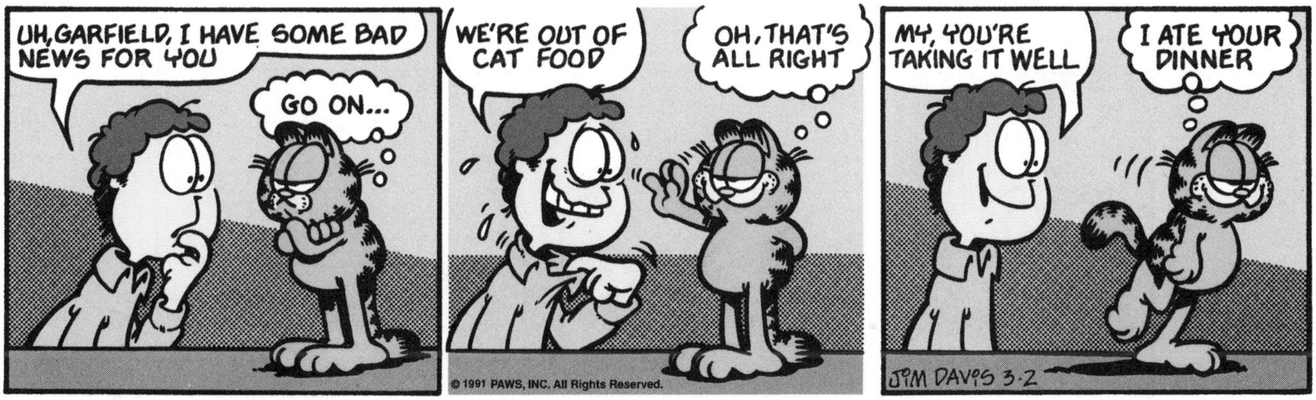
UH, GARFIELD, I HAVE SOME BAD NEWS FOR YOU
GO ON...
WE'RE OUT OF CAT FOOD
OH, THAT'S ALL RIGHT
© 1991 PAWS, INC. All Rights Reserved.
MY, YOU'RE TAKING IT WELL
I ATE YOUR DINNER
JIM DAVIS 3-2

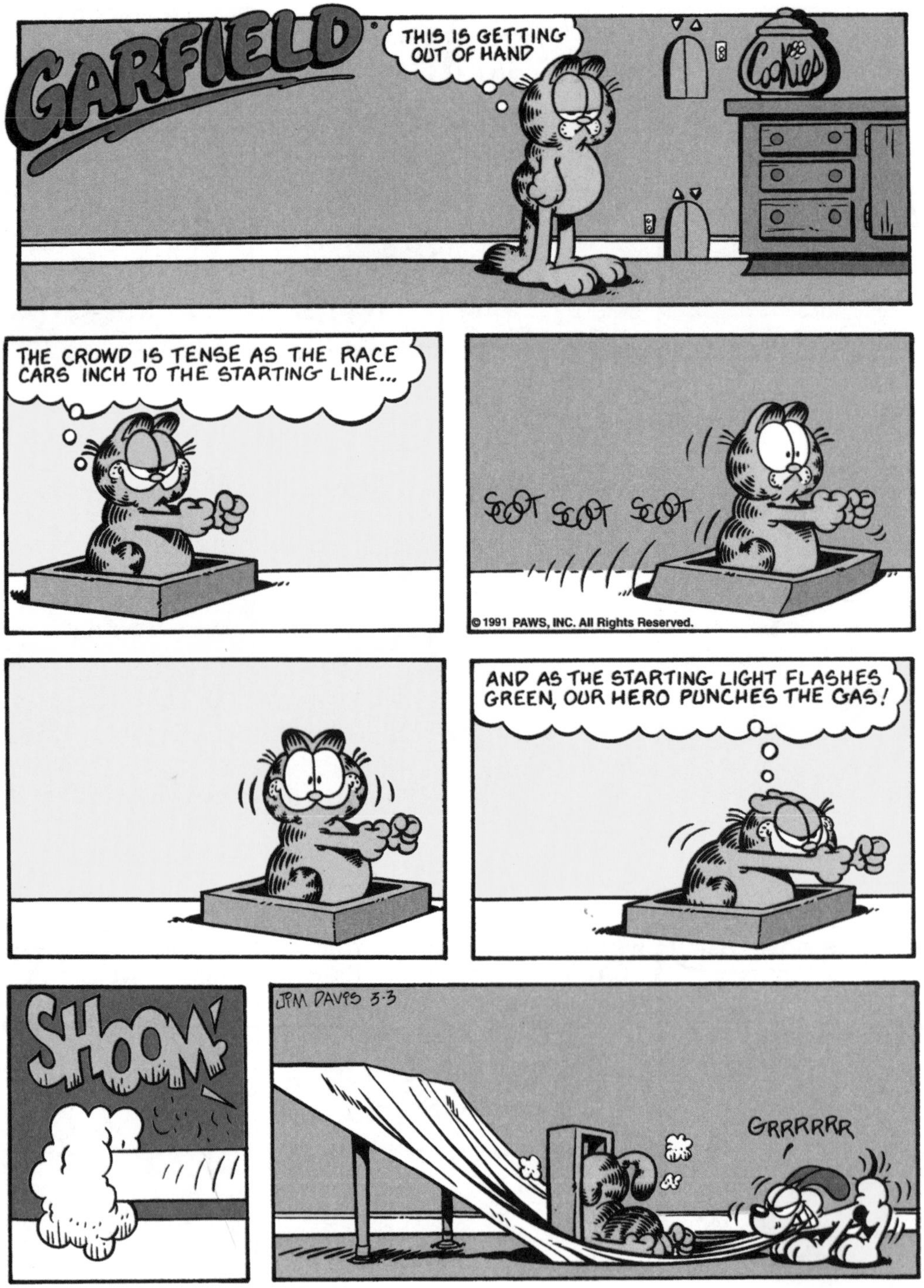
GARFIELD
THIS IS GETTING OUT OF HAND
Cookies
THE CROWD IS TENSE AS THE RACE CARS INCH TO THE STARTING LINE...
SCOOT SCOOT SCOOT
© 1991 PAWS, INC. All Rights Reserved.
AND AS THE STARTING LIGHT FLASHES GREEN, OUR HERO PUNCHES THE GAS!
SHOOM!
JIM DAVIS 3-3
GRRRRRR

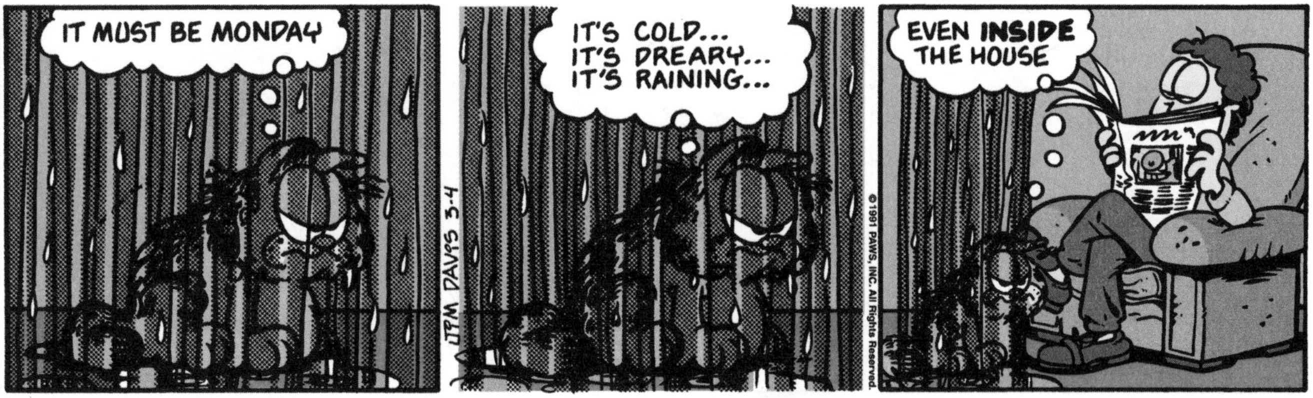
IT MUST BE MONDAY
JIM DAVIS 3-4
IT'S COLD...
IT'S DREARY...
IT'S RAINING...
© 1991 PAWS, INC. All Rights Reserved.
EVEN **INSIDE** THE HOUSE

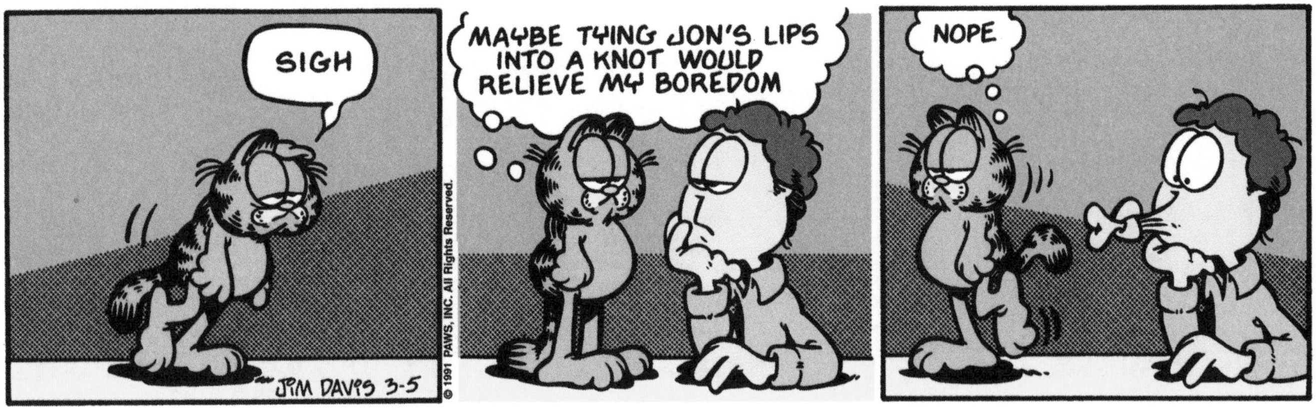
SIGH
JIM DAVIS 3-5
© 1991 PAWS, INC. All Rights Reserved.
MAYBE TYING JON'S LIPS INTO A KNOT WOULD RELIEVE MY BOREDOM
NOPE

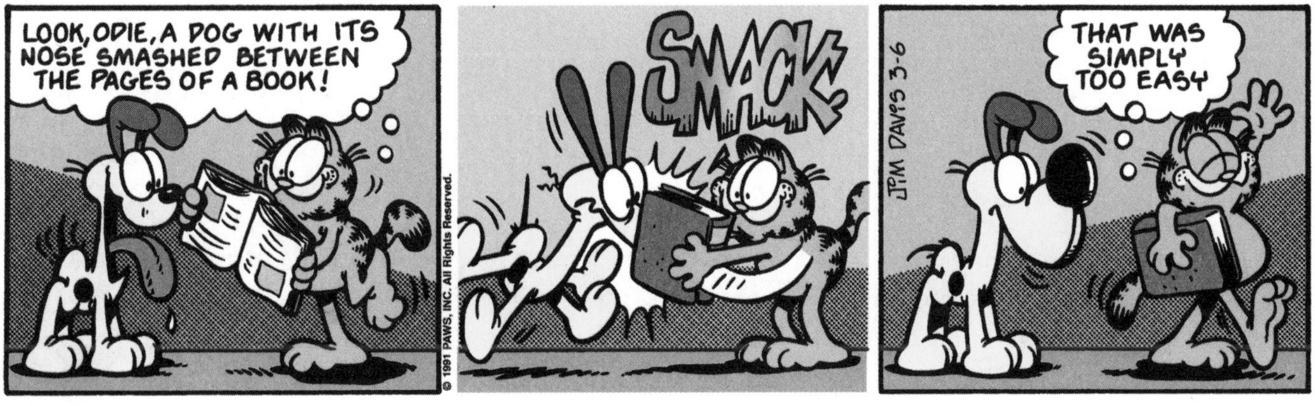
LOOK, ODIE, A DOG WITH ITS NOSE SMASHED BETWEEN THE PAGES OF A BOOK!
© 1991 PAWS, INC. All Rights Reserved.
SMACK
JIM DAVIS 3-6
THAT WAS SIMPLY TOO EASY

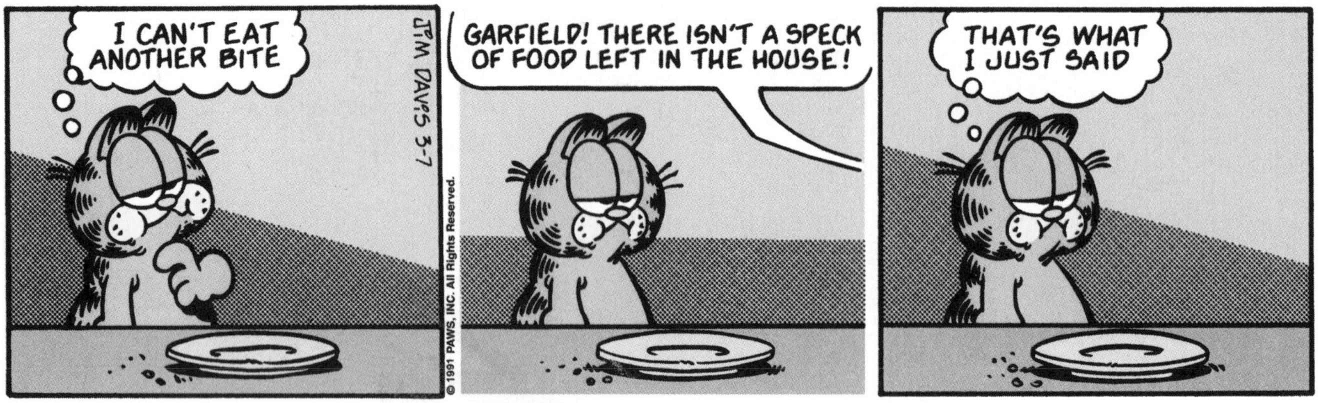
I CAN'T EAT ANOTHER BITE
JIM DAVIS 3-7
© 1991 PAWS, INC. All Rights Reserved.
GARFIELD! THERE ISN'T A SPECK OF FOOD LEFT IN THE HOUSE!
THAT'S WHAT I JUST SAID

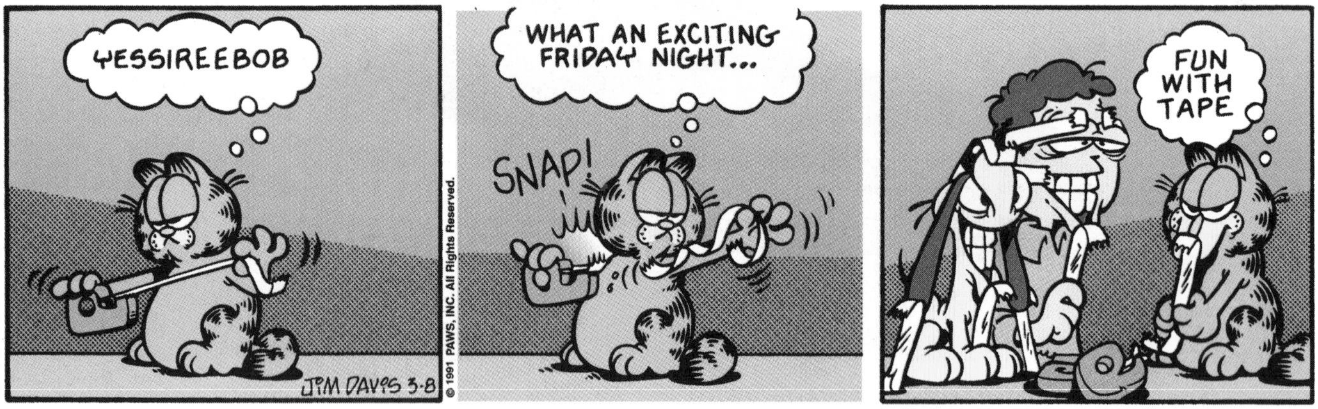
YESSIREEBOB
JIM DAVIS 3-8
© 1991 PAWS, INC. All Rights Reserved.
WHAT AN EXCITING FRIDAY NIGHT...
SNAP!
FUN WITH TAPE

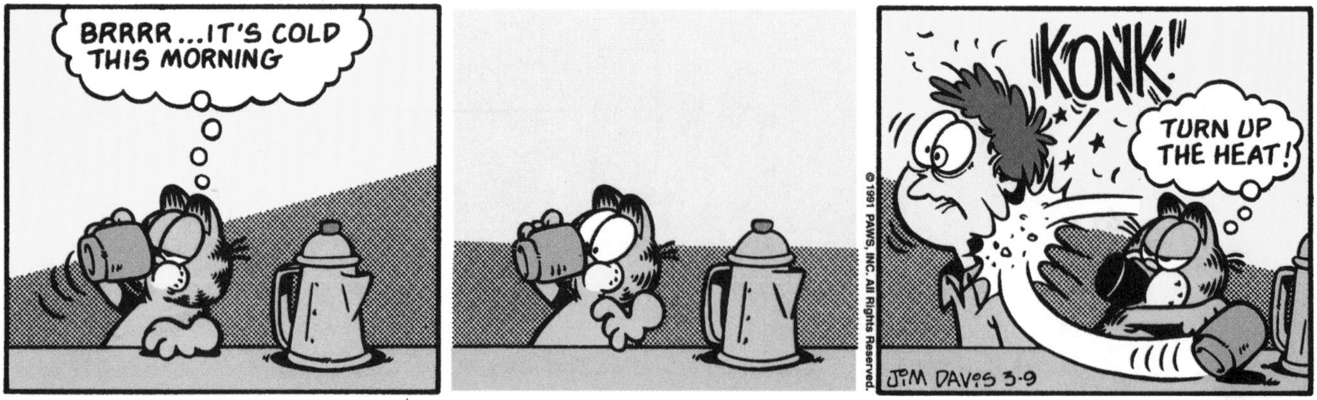
BRRRR...IT'S COLD THIS MORNING
© 1991 PAWS, INC. All Rights Reserved.
KONK!
TURN UP THE HEAT!
JIM DAVIS 3-9

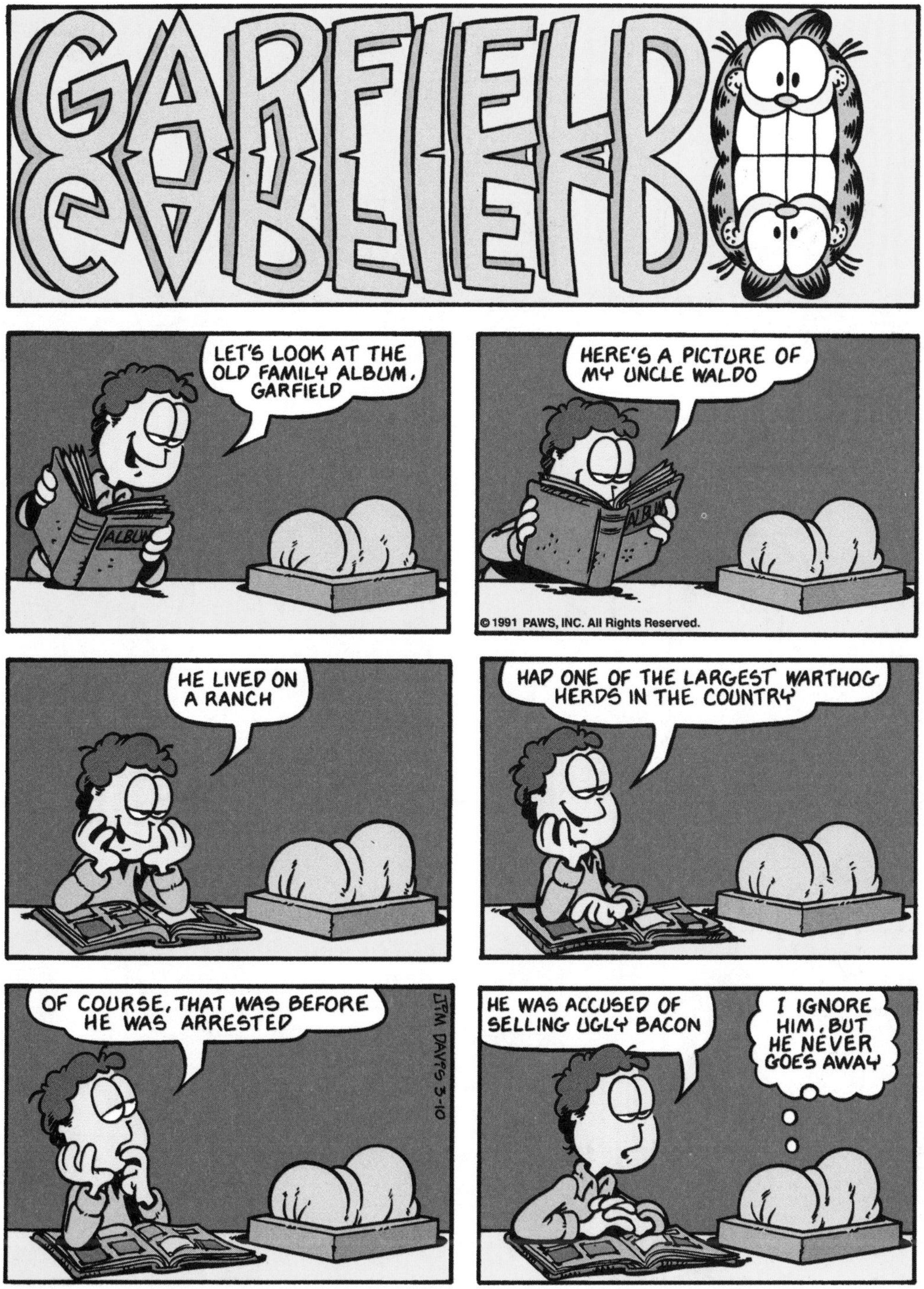
GARFIELD
LET'S LOOK AT THE OLD FAMILY ALBUM, GARFIELD
ALBUM
HERE'S A PICTURE OF MY UNCLE WALDO
ALBUM
© 1991 PAWS, INC. All Rights Reserved.
HE LIVED ON A RANCH
HAD ONE OF THE LARGEST WARTHOG HERDS IN THE COUNTRY
OF COURSE, THAT WAS BEFORE HE WAS ARRESTED
JIM DAVIS 3-10
HE WAS ACCUSED OF SELLING UGLY BACON
I IGNORE HIM, BUT HE NEVER GOES AWAY

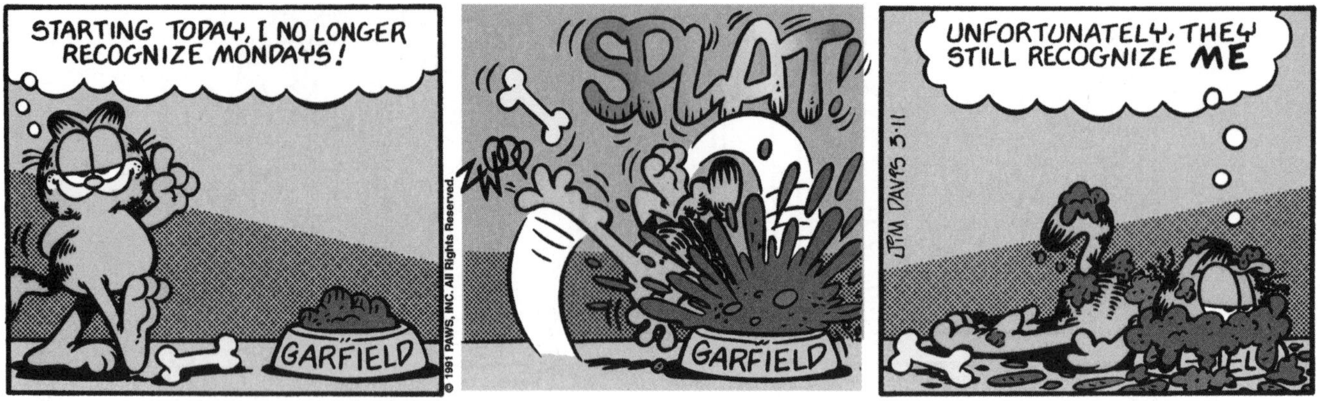
STARTING TODAY, I NO LONGER RECOGNIZE MONDAYS!
GARFIELD
© 1991 PAWS, INC. All Rights Reserved.
ZWOOP
SPLAT!
GARFIELD
UNFORTUNATELY, THEY STILL RECOGNIZE ME
JIM DAVIS 3-11

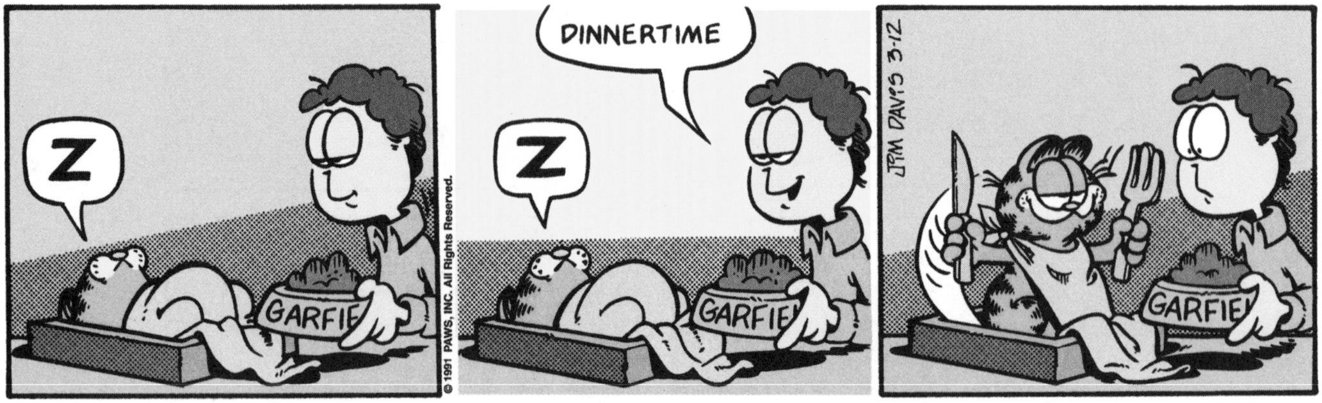
Z
GARFIE
© 1991 PAWS, INC. All Rights Reserved.
DINNERTIME
Z
GARFIE
JIM DAVIS 3-12
GARFIE

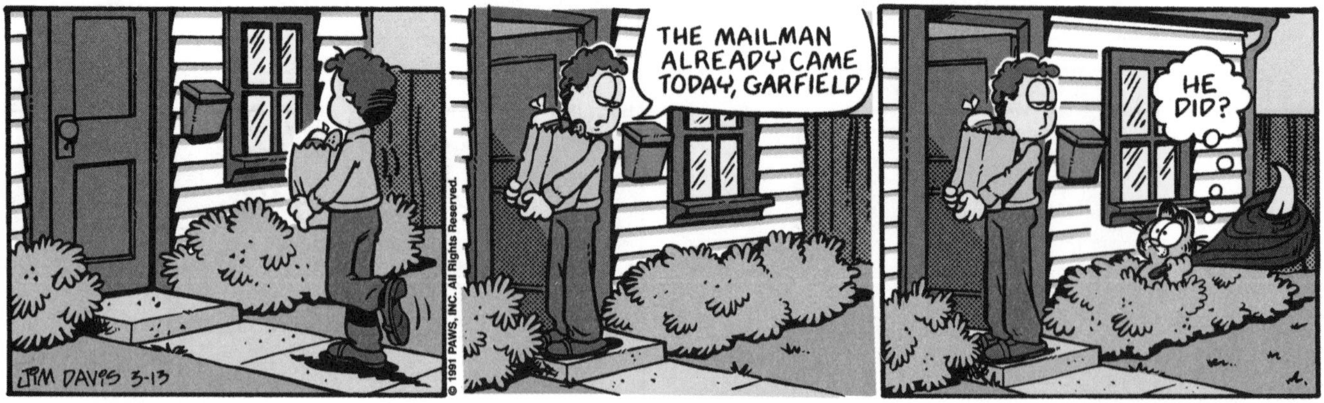
JIM DAVIS 3-13
© 1991 PAWS, INC. All Rights Reserved.
THE MAILMAN ALREADY CAME TODAY, GARFIELD
HE DID?

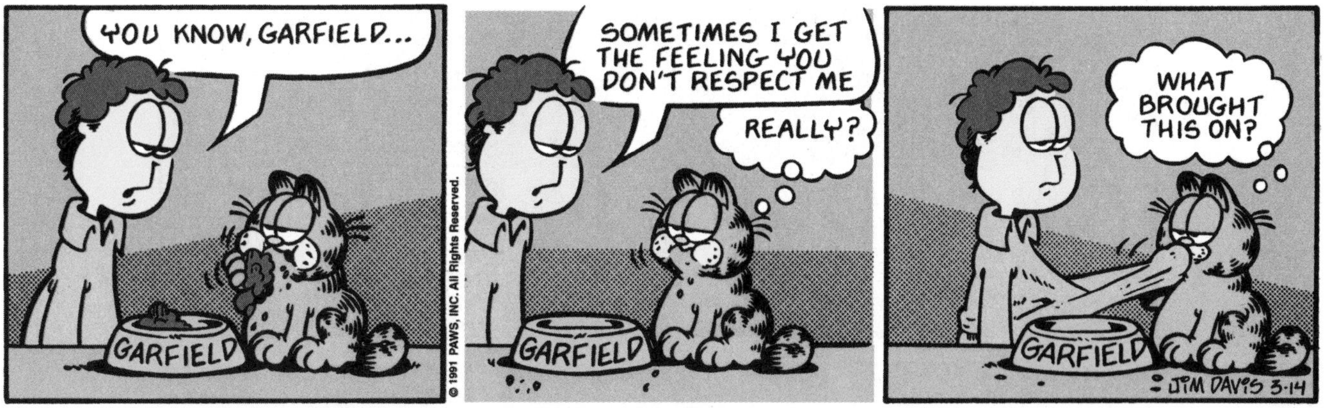
YOU KNOW, GARFIELD...
SOMETIMES I GET THE FEELING YOU DON'T RESPECT ME
REALLY?
WHAT BROUGHT THIS ON?
GARFIELD
GARFIELD
GARFIELD
© 1991 PAWS, INC. All Rights Reserved.
JIM DAVIS 3-14

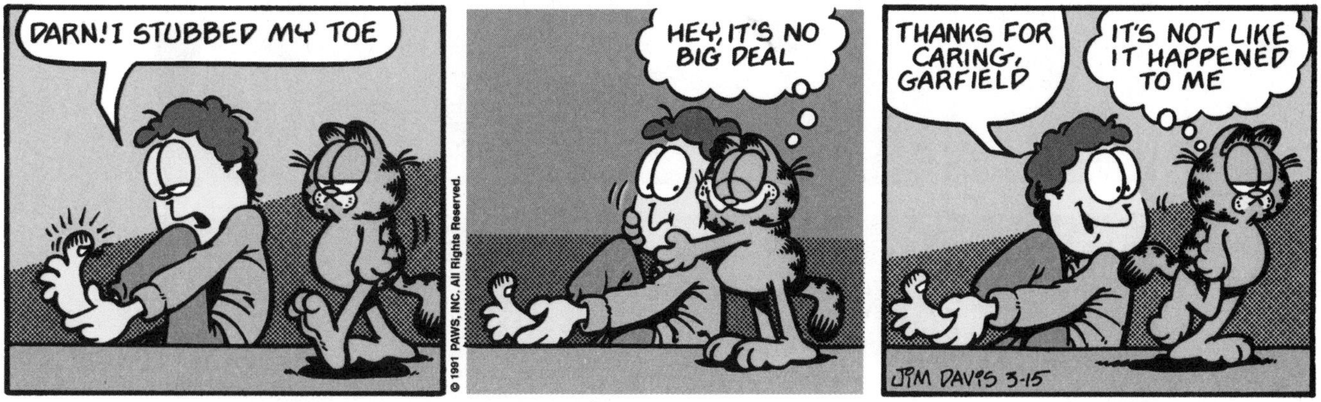
DARN! I STUBBED MY TOE
HEY, IT'S NO BIG DEAL
THANKS FOR CARING, GARFIELD
IT'S NOT LIKE IT HAPPENED TO ME
© 1991 PAWS, INC. All Rights Reserved.
JIM DAVIS 3-15

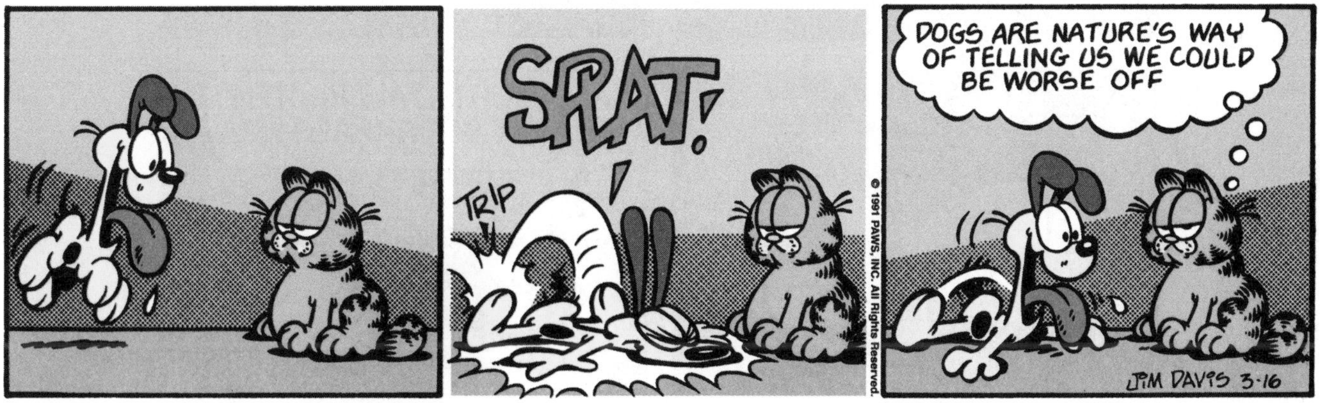
SPLAT!
TRIP
DOGS ARE NATURE'S WAY OF TELLING US WE COULD BE WORSE OFF
© 1991 PAWS, INC. All Rights Reserved.
JIM DAVIS 3-16

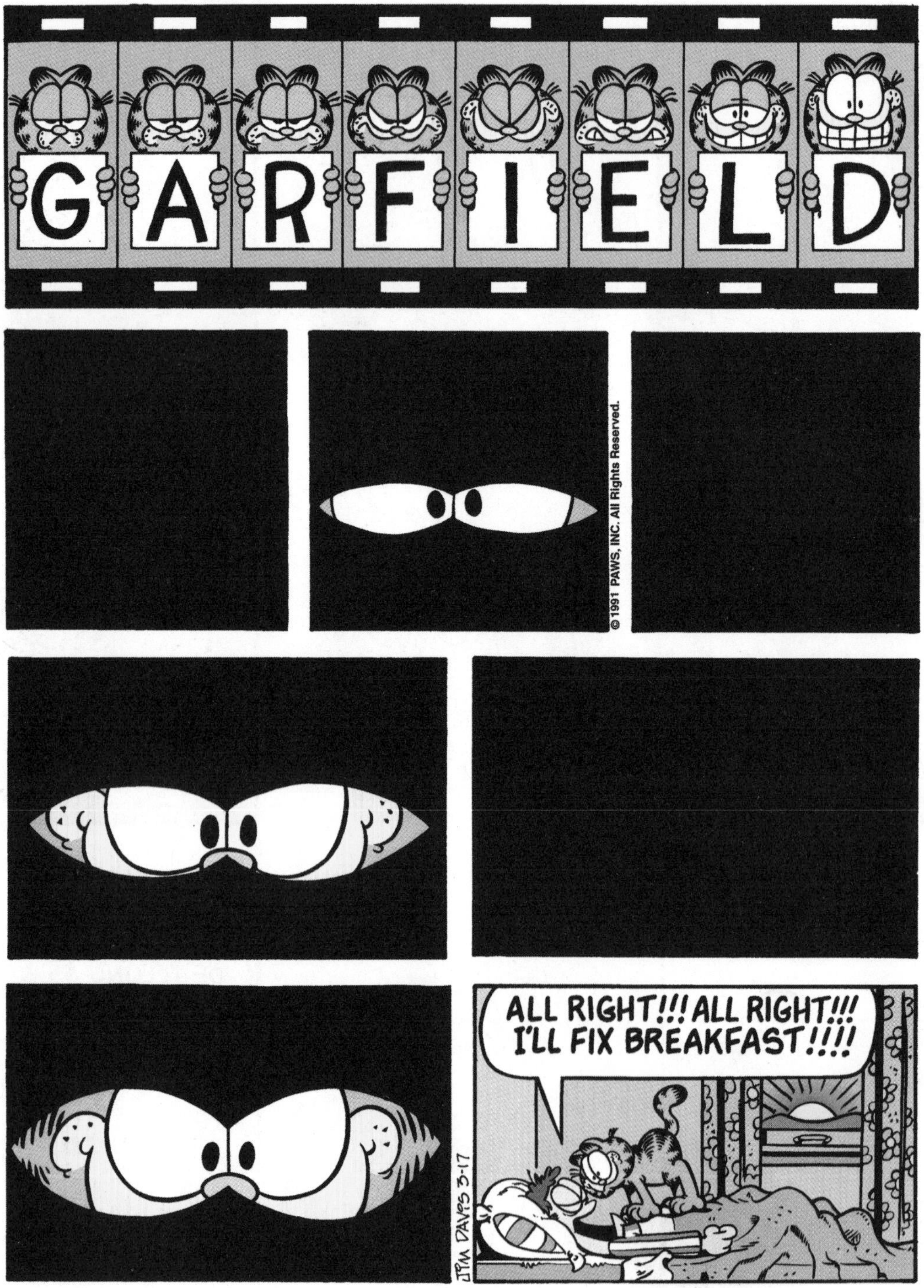
GARFIELD
© 1991 PAWS, INC. All Rights Reserved.
ALL RIGHT!!! ALL RIGHT!!! I'LL FIX BREAKFAST!!!!
JIM DAVIS 3-17

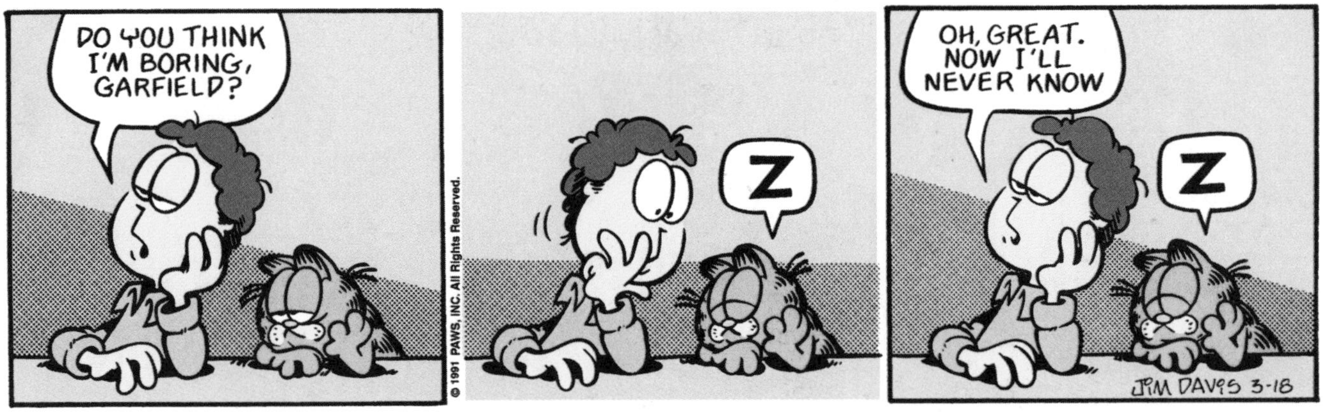
DO YOU THINK I'M BORING, GARFIELD?
© 1991 PAWS, INC. All Rights Reserved.
Z
OH, GREAT. NOW I'LL NEVER KNOW
Z
JIM DAVIS 3-18

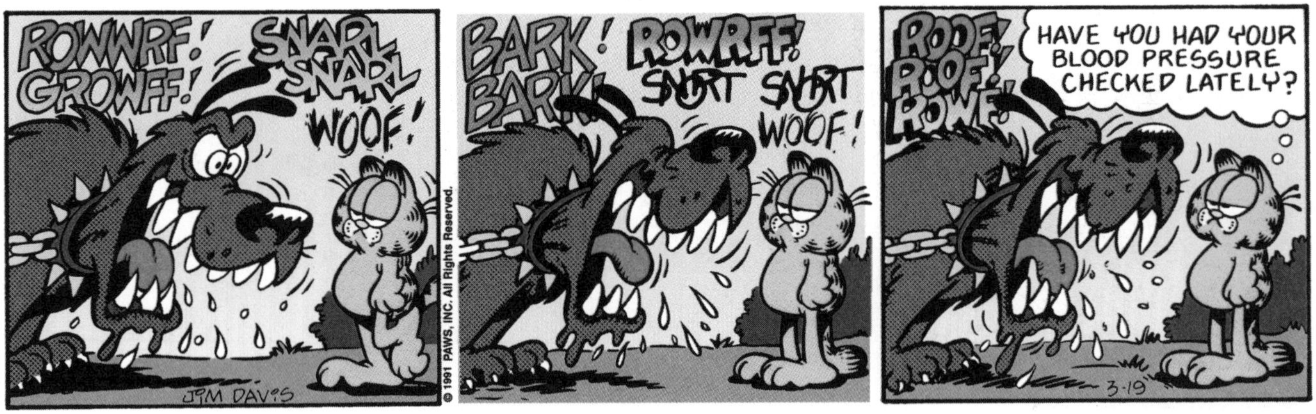
ROWWRF! GROWFF!
SNARL SNARL
WOOF!
JIM DAVIS
© 1991 PAWS, INC. All Rights Reserved.
BARK! BARK!
ROWRFF!
SNORT SNORT
WOOF!
ROOF! ROOF! ROWF!
HAVE YOU HAD YOUR BLOOD PRESSURE CHECKED LATELY?
3-19

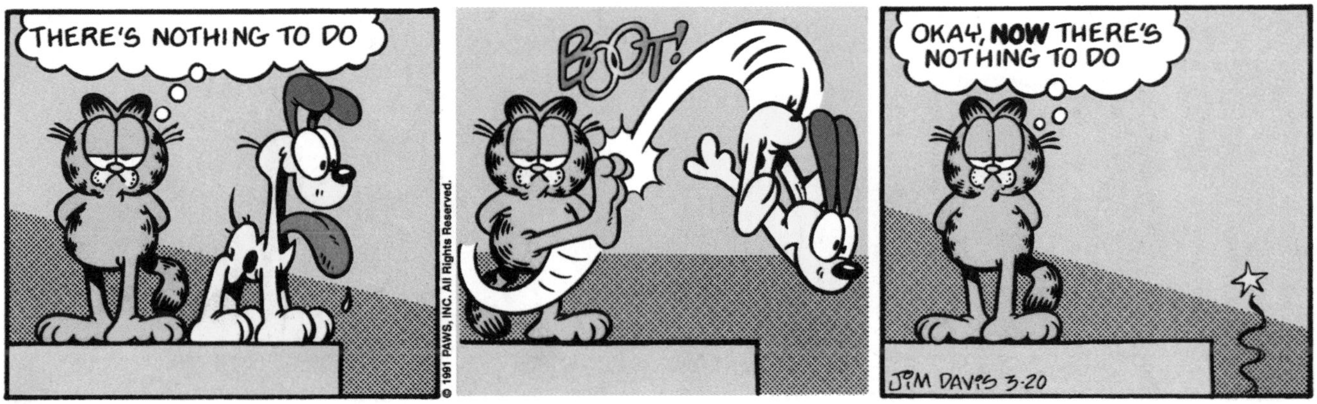
THERE'S NOTHING TO DO
© 1991 PAWS, INC. All Rights Reserved.
BOOT!
OKAY, NOW THERE'S NOTHING TO DO
JIM DAVIS 3-20

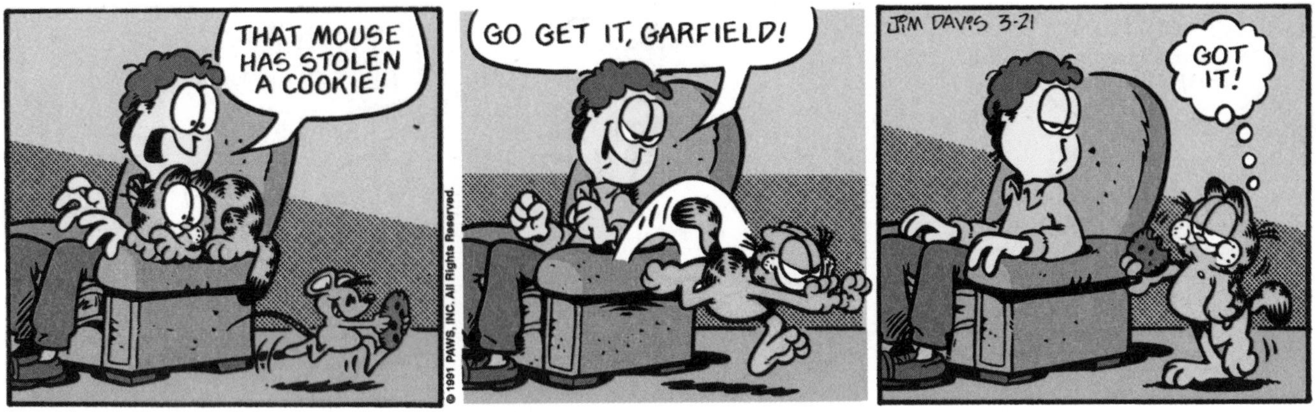
THAT MOUSE HAS STOLEN A COOKIE!
© 1991 PAWS, INC. All Rights Reserved.
GO GET IT, GARFIELD!
JIM DAVIS 3-21
GOT IT!

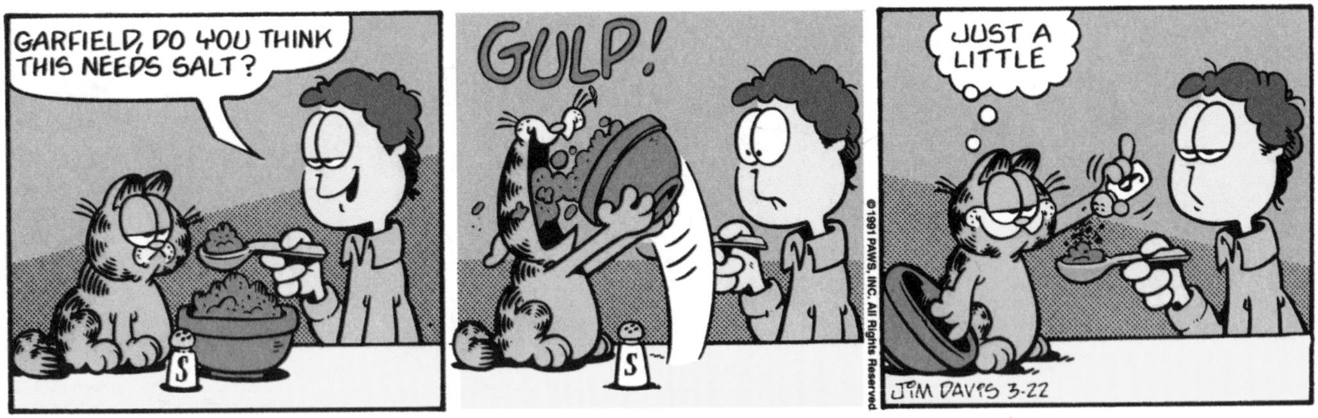
GARFIELD, DO YOU THINK THIS NEEDS SALT?
GULP!
© 1991 PAWS, INC. All Rights Reserved.
JUST A LITTLE
JIM DAVIS 3-22

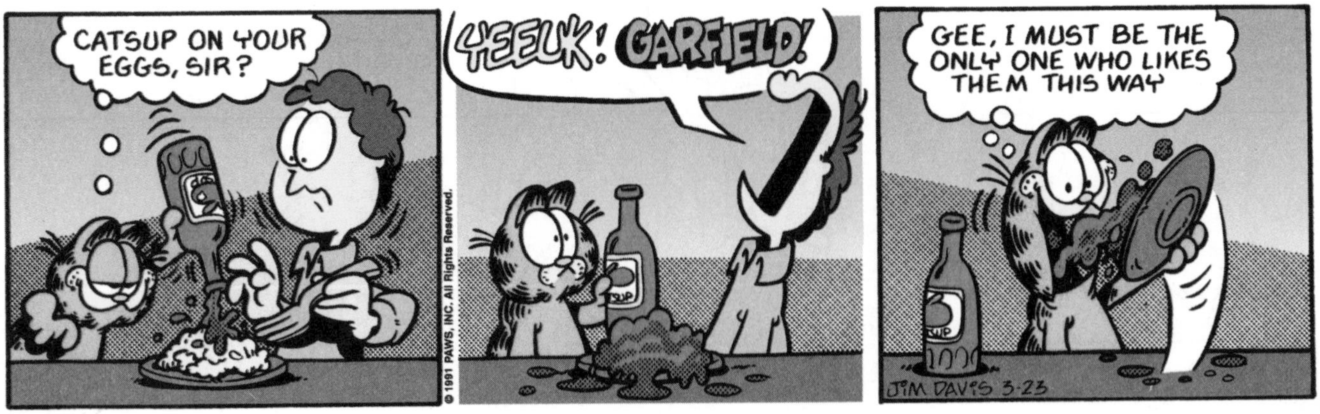
CATSUP ON YOUR EGGS, SIR?
© 1991 PAWS, INC. All Rights Reserved.
YEEUK! GARFIELD!
GEE, I MUST BE THE ONLY ONE WHO LIKES THEM THIS WAY
JIM DAVIS 3-23

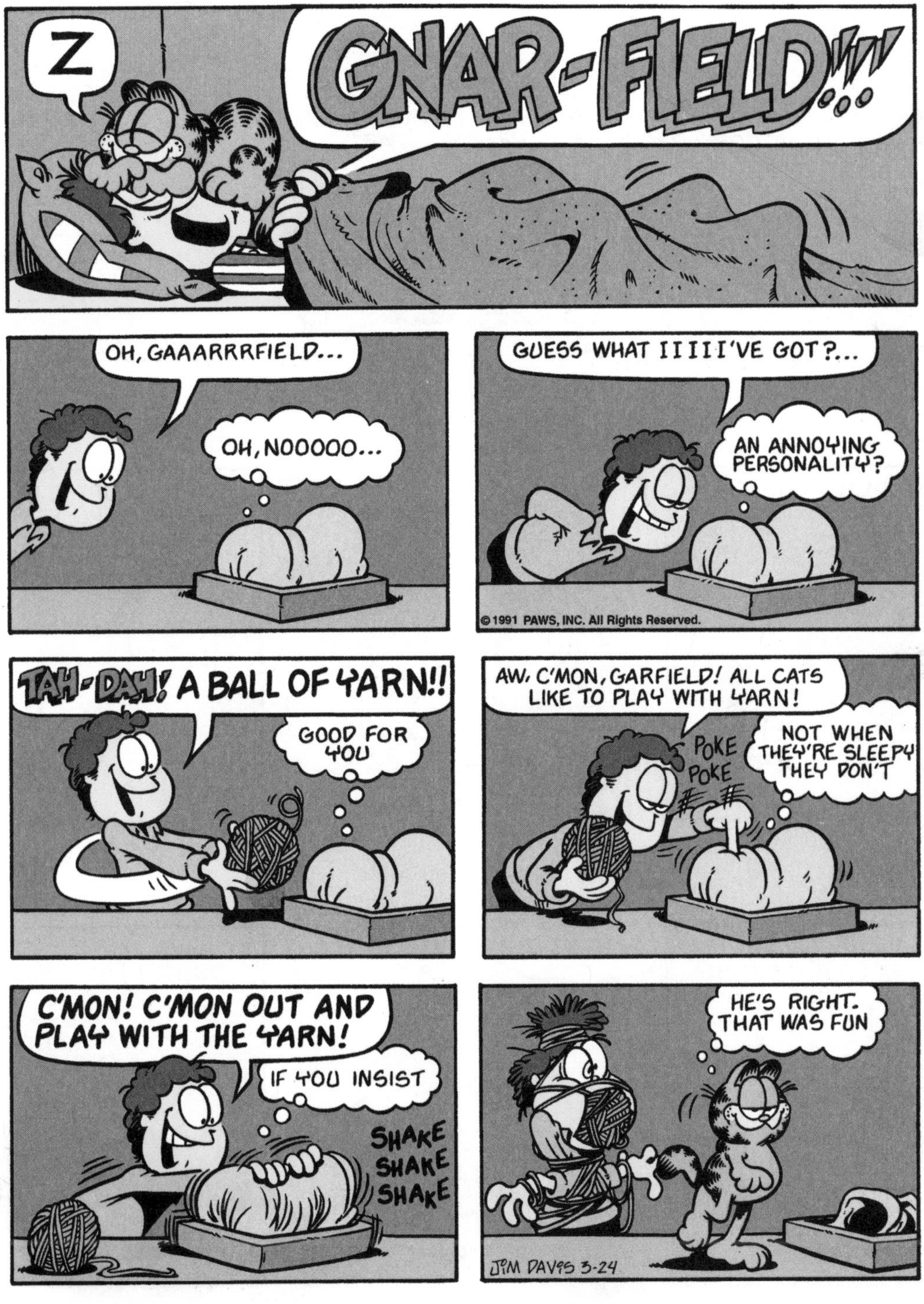
Z
GNAR-FIELD!!!
OH, GAAARRRFIELD...
OH, NOOOOO...
GUESS WHAT IIIII'VE GOT?...
AN ANNOYING PERSONALITY?
TAH-DAH! A BALL OF YARN!!
GOOD FOR YOU
AW, C'MON, GARFIELD! ALL CATS LIKE TO PLAY WITH YARN!
POKE POKE
NOT WHEN THEY'RE SLEEPY THEY DON'T
C'MON! C'MON OUT AND PLAY WITH THE YARN!
IF YOU INSIST
SHAKE SHAKE SHAKE
HE'S RIGHT. THAT WAS FUN
JIM DAVIS 3-24

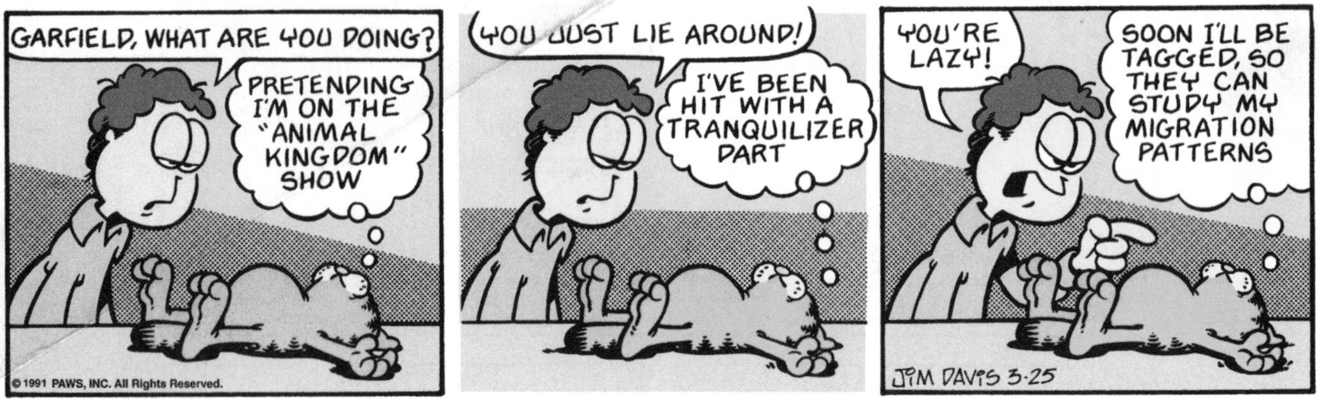
GARFIELD, WHAT ARE YOU DOING?
PRETENDING I'M ON THE "ANIMAL KINGDOM" SHOW
© 1991 PAWS, INC. All Rights Reserved.
YOU JUST LIE AROUND!
I'VE BEEN HIT WITH A TRANQUILIZER DART
YOU'RE LAZY!
SOON I'LL BE TAGGED, SO THEY CAN STUDY MY MIGRATION PATTERNS
JIM DAVIS 3-25

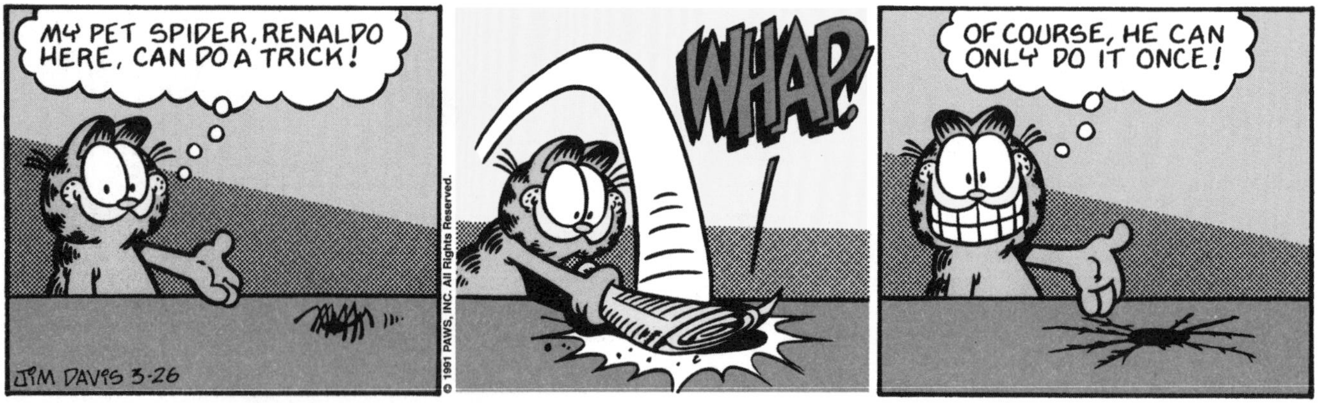
MY PET SPIDER, RENALDO HERE, CAN DO A TRICK!
JIM DAVIS 3-26
© 1991 PAWS, INC. All Rights Reserved.
WHAP!
OF COURSE, HE CAN ONLY DO IT ONCE!

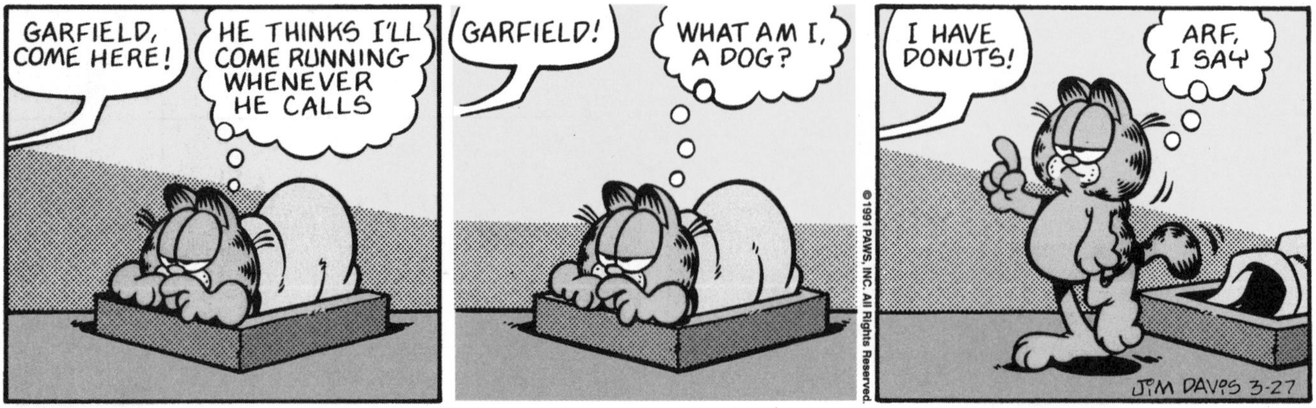
GARFIELD, COME HERE!
HE THINKS I'LL COME RUNNING WHENEVER HE CALLS
GARFIELD!
WHAT AM I, A DOG?
© 1991 PAWS, INC. All Rights Reserved.
I HAVE DONUTS!
ARF, I SAY
JIM DAVIS 3-27

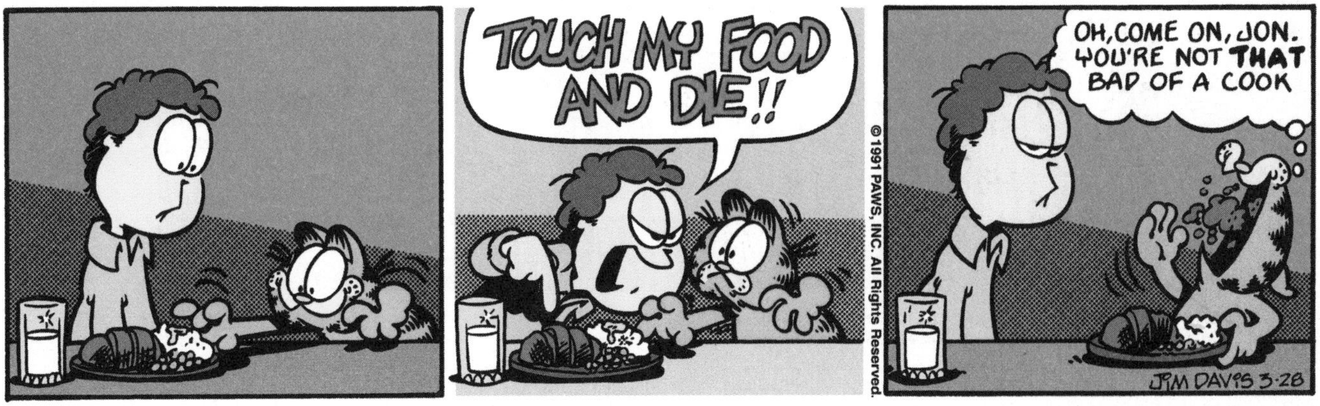
TOUCH MY FOOD AND DIE!!
© 1991 PAWS, INC. All Rights Reserved.
OH, COME ON, JON. YOU'RE NOT **THAT** BAD OF A COOK
JIM DAVIS 3-28

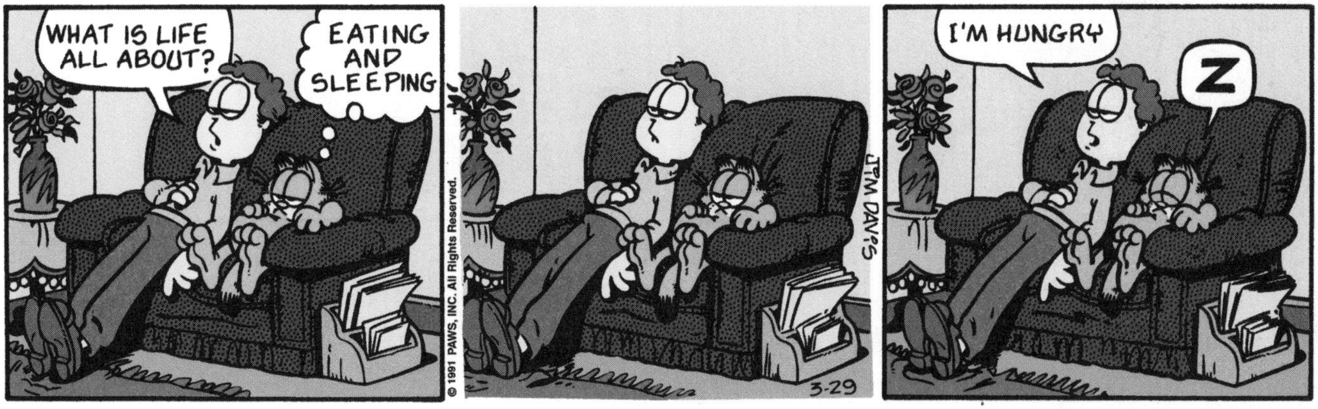
WHAT IS LIFE ALL ABOUT?
EATING AND SLEEPING
© 1991 PAWS, INC. All Rights Reserved.
JIM DAVIS
3-29
I'M HUNGRY
Z

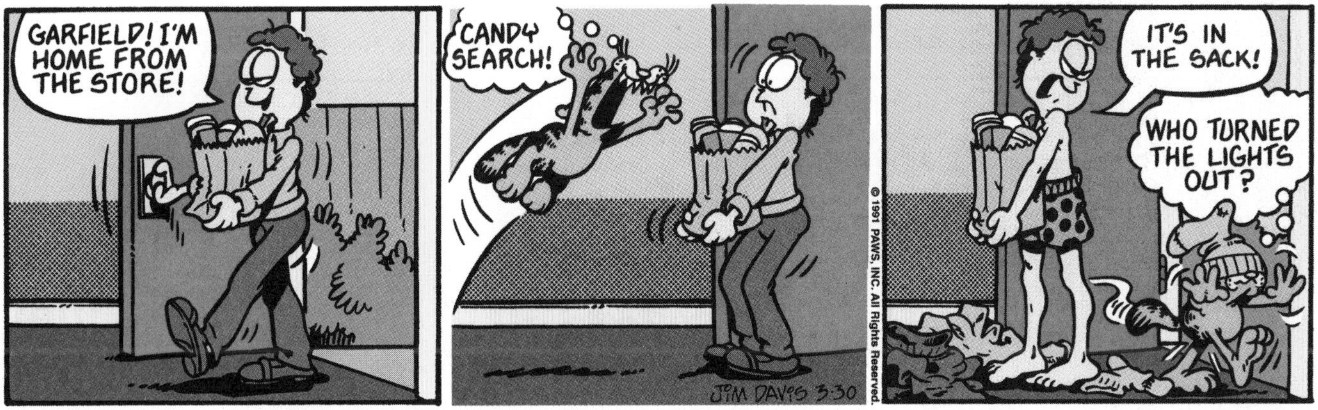
GARFIELD! I'M HOME FROM THE STORE!
CANDY SEARCH!
JIM DAVIS 3-30
© 1991 PAWS, INC. All Rights Reserved.
IT'S IN THE SACK!
WHO TURNED THE LIGHTS OUT?

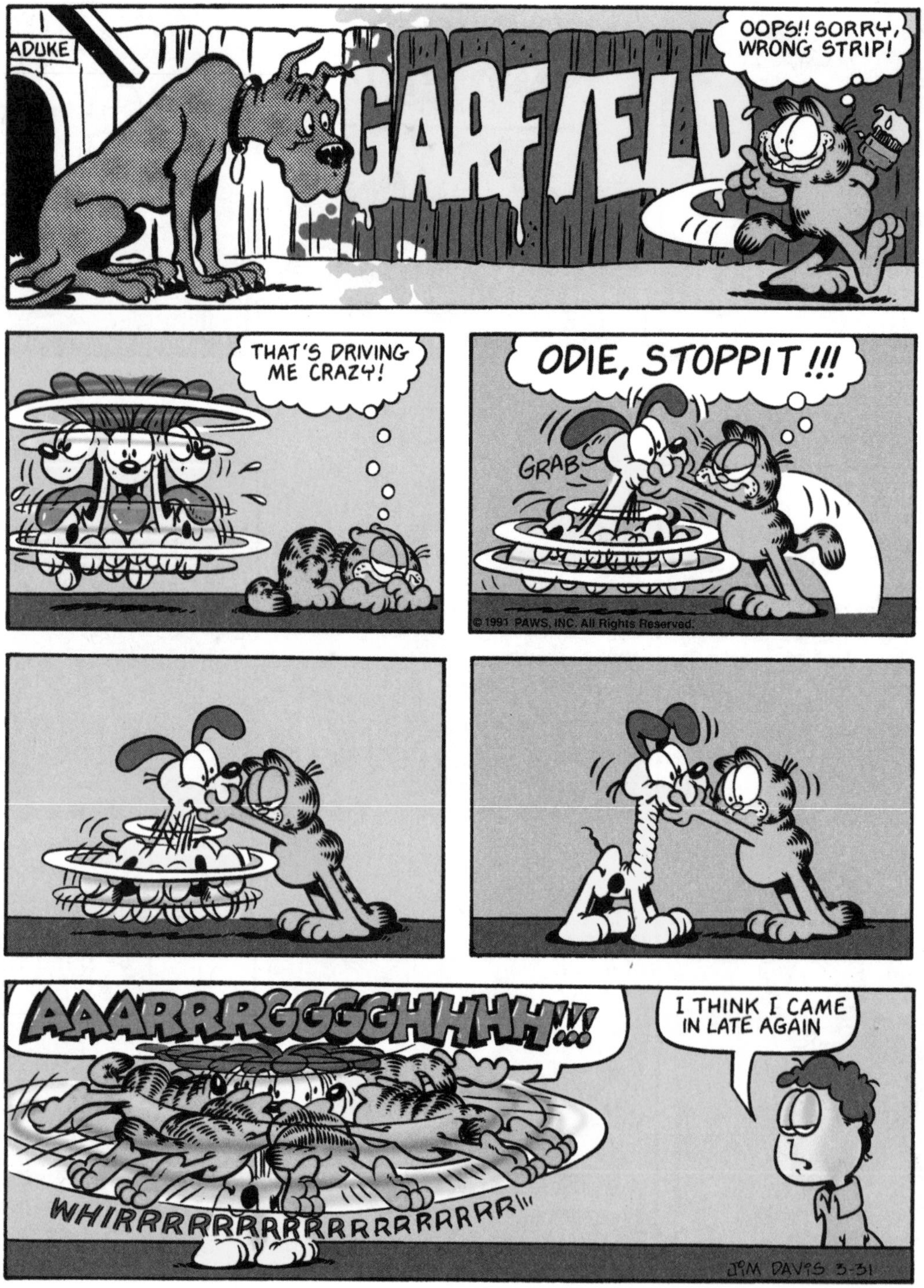
ADUKE
GARFIELD
OOPS!! SORRY, WRONG STRIP!
THAT'S DRIVING ME CRAZY!
ODIE, STOPPIT !!!
GRAB
© 1991 PAWS, INC. All Rights Reserved.
AAARRRGGGGHHHH!!!
I THINK I CAME IN LATE AGAIN
WHIRRRRRRRRRRRRRRRRRRR
JIM DAVIS 3-31

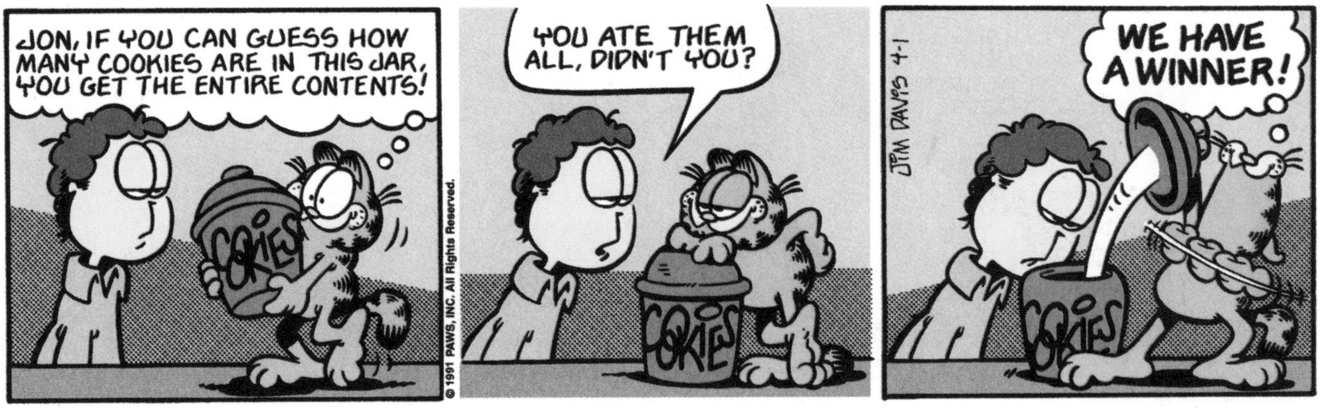
JON, IF YOU CAN GUESS HOW MANY COOKIES ARE IN THIS JAR, YOU GET THE ENTIRE CONTENTS!
COOKIES
© 1991 PAWS, INC. All Rights Reserved.
YOU ATE THEM ALL, DIDN'T YOU?
COOKIES
JIM DAVIS 4-1
WE HAVE A WINNER!
COOKIES

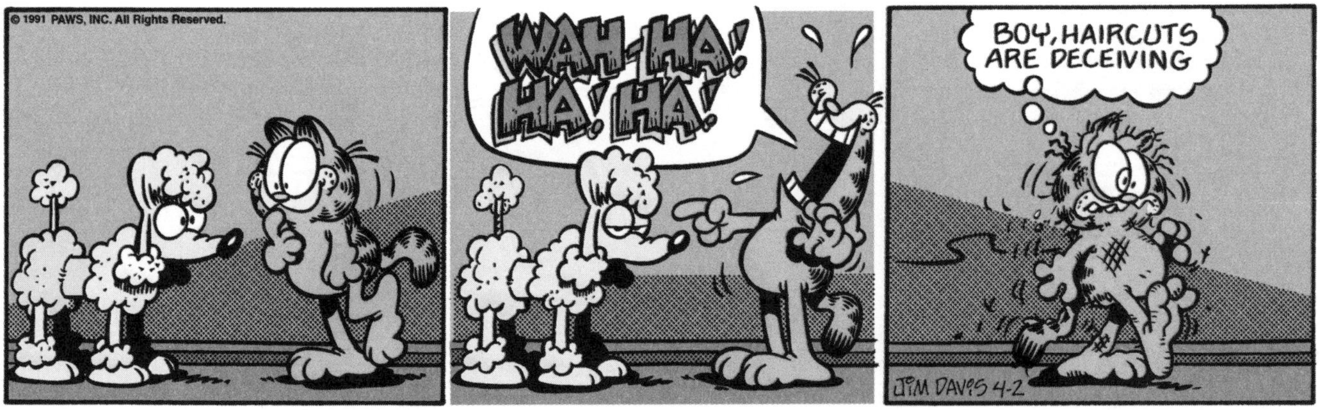
© 1991 PAWS, INC. All Rights Reserved.
WAH-HA! HA! HA!
BOY, HAIRCUTS ARE DECEIVING
JIM DAVIS 4-2

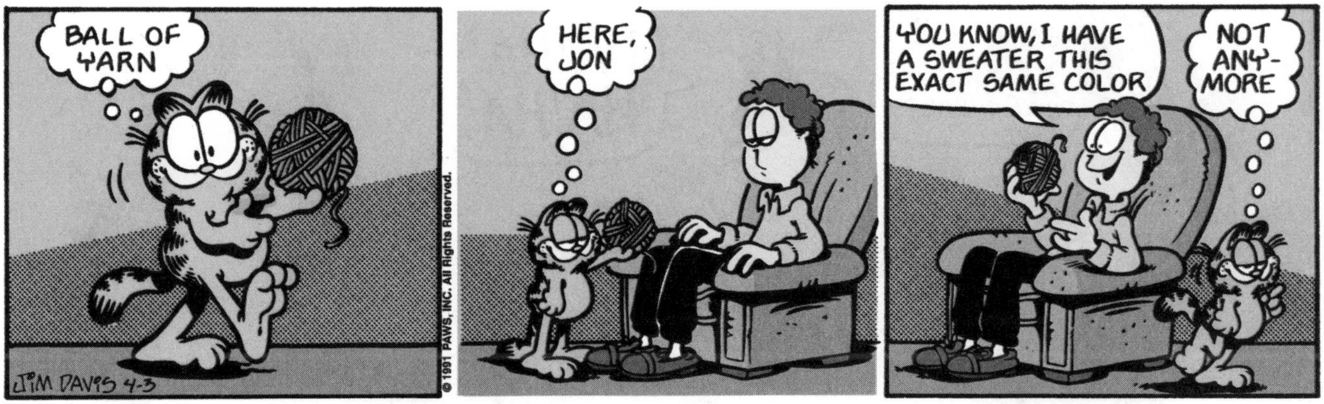
BALL OF YARN
JIM DAVIS 4-3
© 1991 PAWS, INC. All Rights Reserved.
HERE, JON
YOU KNOW, I HAVE A SWEATER THIS EXACT SAME COLOR
NOT ANY-MORE

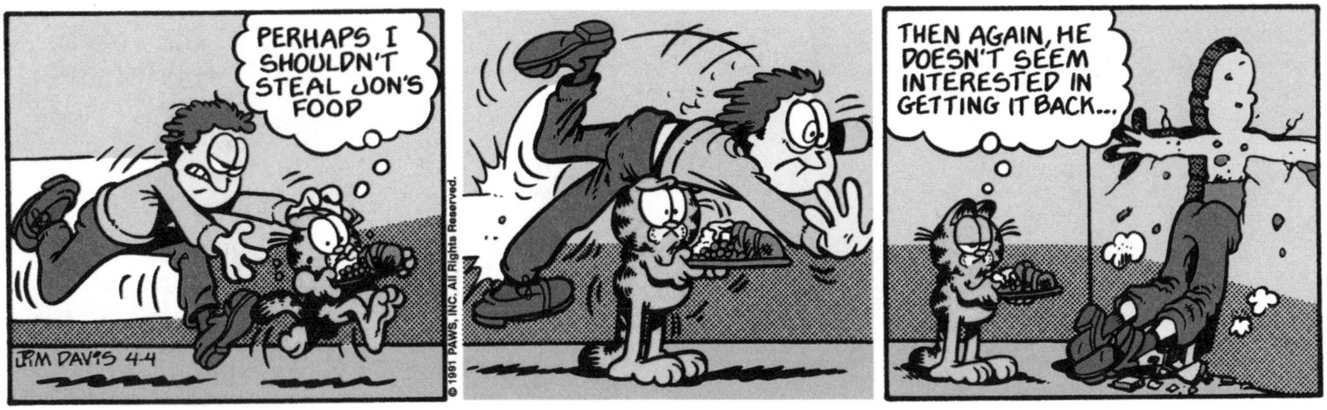
PERHAPS I SHOULDN'T STEAL JON'S FOOD
JIM DAVIS 4-4
© 1991 PAWS, INC. All Rights Reserved.
THEN AGAIN, HE DOESN'T SEEM INTERESTED IN GETTING IT BACK...

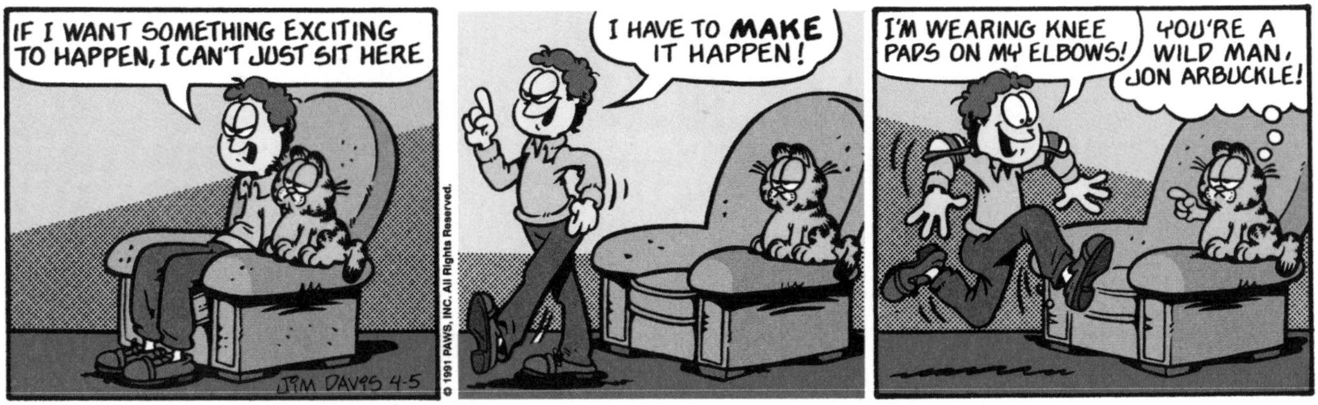
IF I WANT SOMETHING EXCITING TO HAPPEN, I CAN'T JUST SIT HERE
JIM DAVIS 4-5
© 1991 PAWS, INC. All Rights Reserved.
I HAVE TO MAKE IT HAPPEN!
I'M WEARING KNEE PADS ON MY ELBOWS!
YOU'RE A WILD MAN, JON ARBUCKLE!

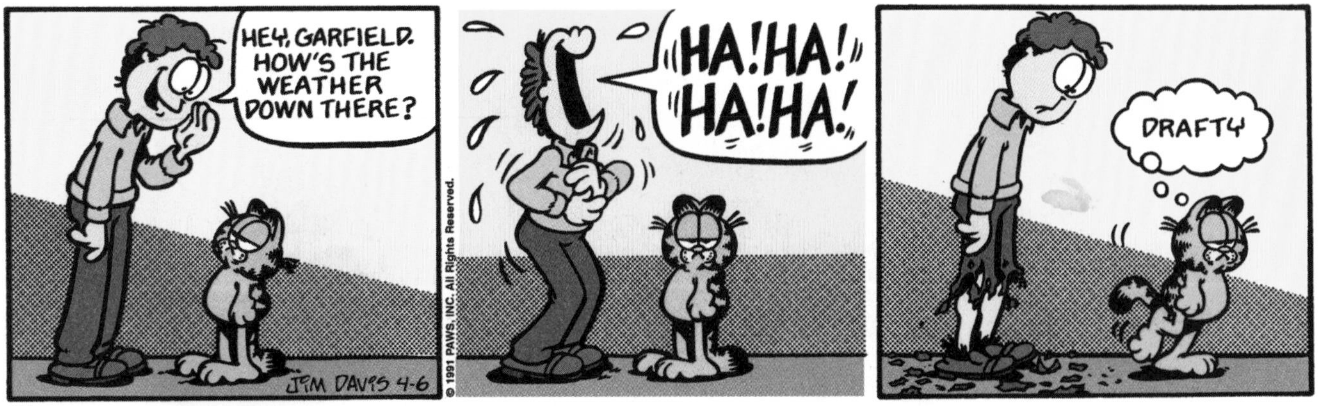
HEY, GARFIELD. HOW'S THE WEATHER DOWN THERE?
JIM DAVIS 4-6
© 1991 PAWS, INC. All Rights Reserved.
HA! HA! HA! HA!
DRAFTY

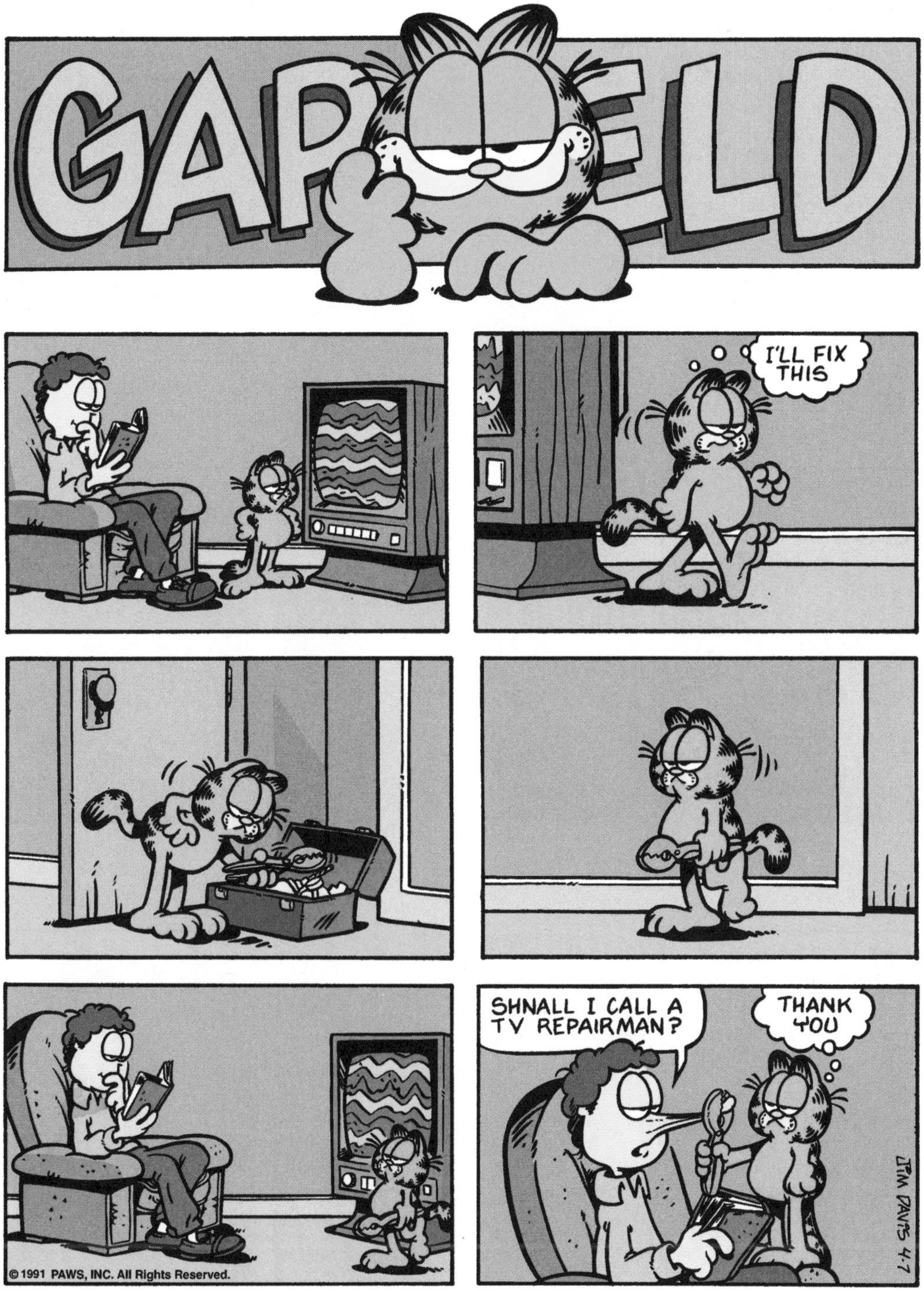
GARFIELD
I'LL FIX THIS
SHNALL I CALL A TV REPAIRMAN?
THANK YOU
JIM DAVIS 4-7

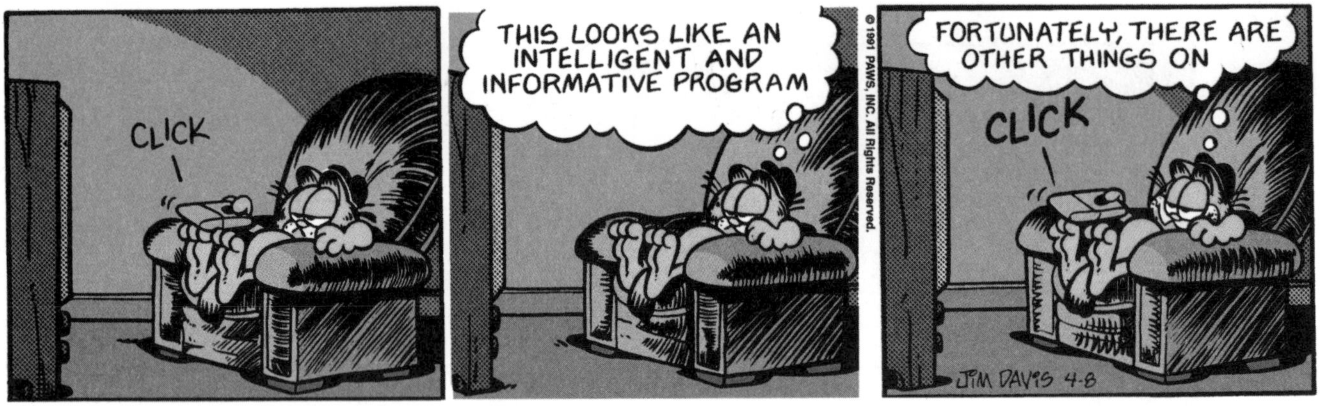
CLICK
THIS LOOKS LIKE AN INTELLIGENT AND INFORMATIVE PROGRAM
© 1991 PAWS, INC. All Rights Reserved.
FORTUNATELY, THERE ARE OTHER THINGS ON
CLICK
JIM DAVIS 4-8

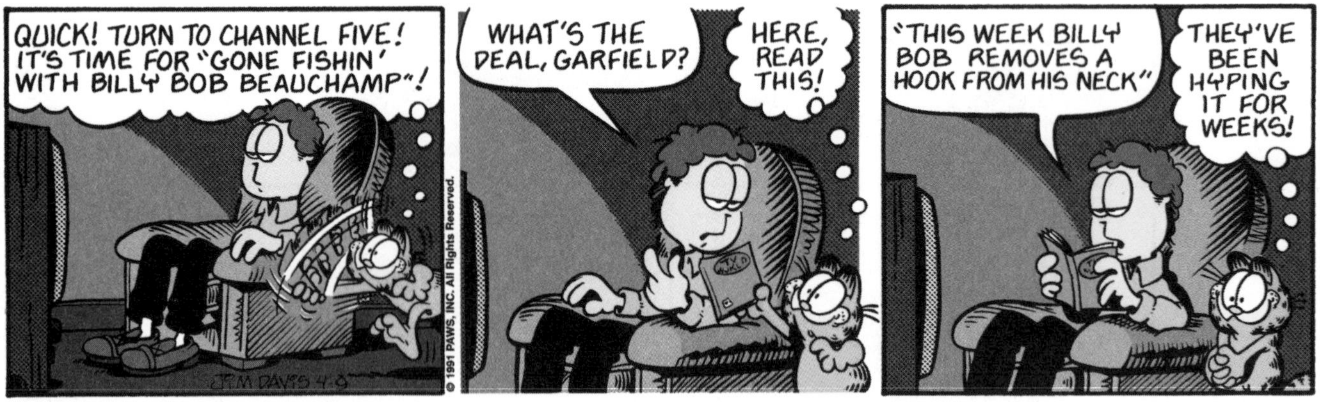
QUICK! TURN TO CHANNEL FIVE! IT'S TIME FOR "GONE FISHIN' WITH BILLY BOB BEAUCHAMP"!
JIM DAVIS 4-9
© 1991 PAWS, INC. All Rights Reserved.
WHAT'S THE DEAL, GARFIELD?
HERE, READ THIS!
"THIS WEEK BILLY BOB REMOVES A HOOK FROM HIS NECK"
THEY'VE BEEN HYPING IT FOR WEEKS!

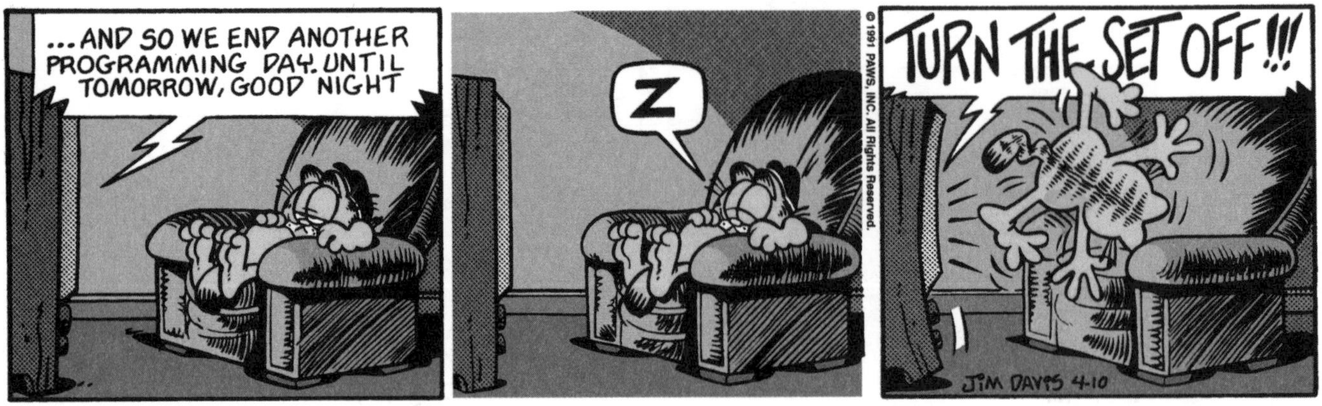
...AND SO WE END ANOTHER PROGRAMMING DAY. UNTIL TOMORROW, GOOD NIGHT
Z
© 1991 PAWS, INC. All Rights Reserved.
TURN THE SET OFF!!!
JIM DAVIS 4-10

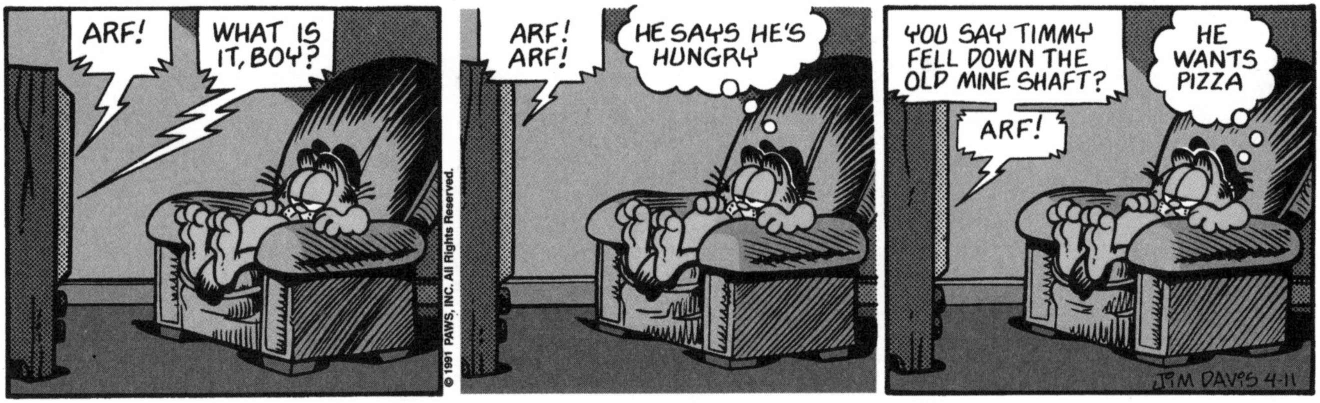
ARF!
WHAT IS IT, BOY?
© 1991 PAWS, INC. All Rights Reserved.
ARF! ARF!
HE SAYS HE'S HUNGRY
YOU SAY TIMMY FELL DOWN THE OLD MINE SHAFT?
ARF!
HE WANTS PIZZA
JIM DAVIS 4-11

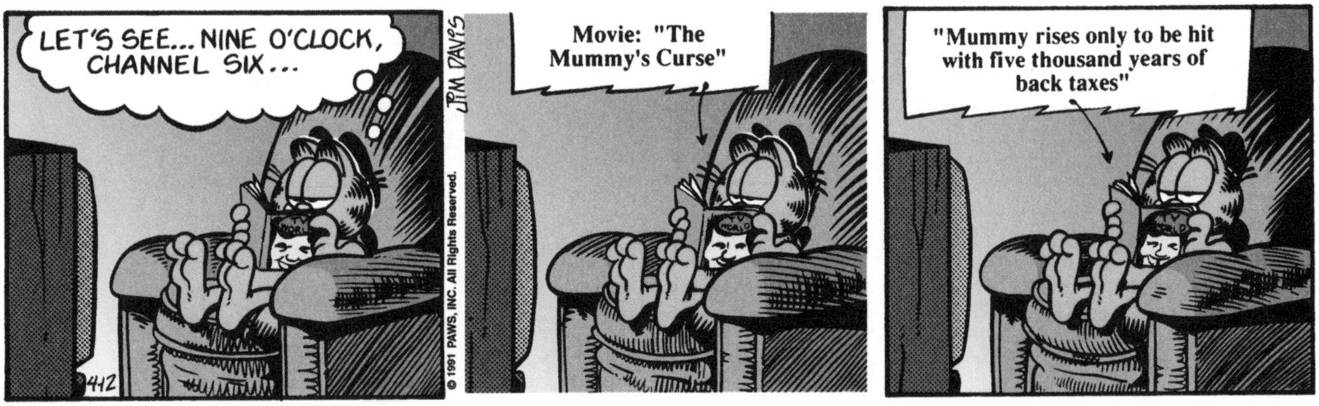
LET'S SEE... NINE O'CLOCK, CHANNEL SIX...
4-12
JIM DAVIS
© 1991 PAWS, INC. All Rights Reserved.
Movie: "The Mummy's Curse"
"Mummy rises only to be hit with five thousand years of back taxes"

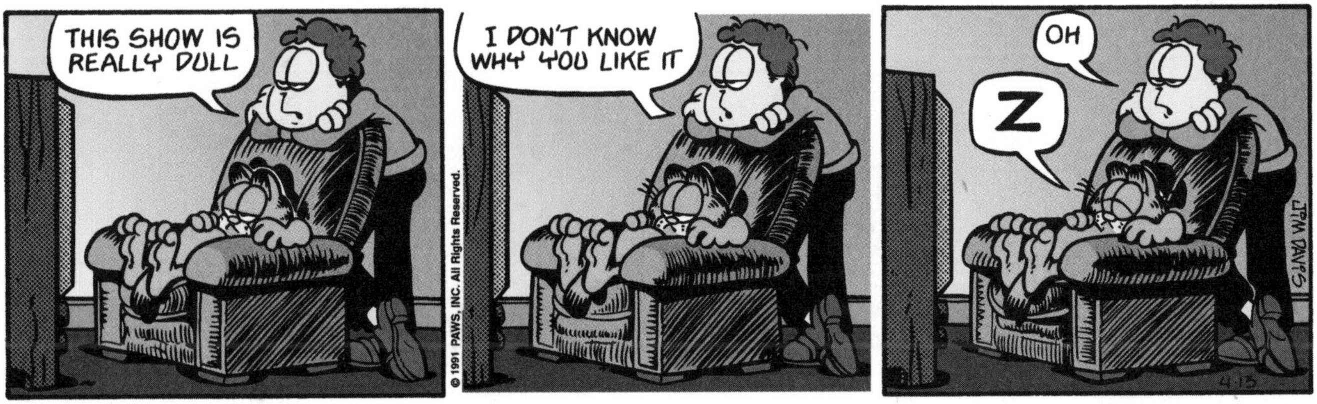
THIS SHOW IS REALLY DULL
© 1991 PAWS, INC. All Rights Reserved.
I DON'T KNOW WHY YOU LIKE IT
OH
Z
JIM DAVIS
4-13

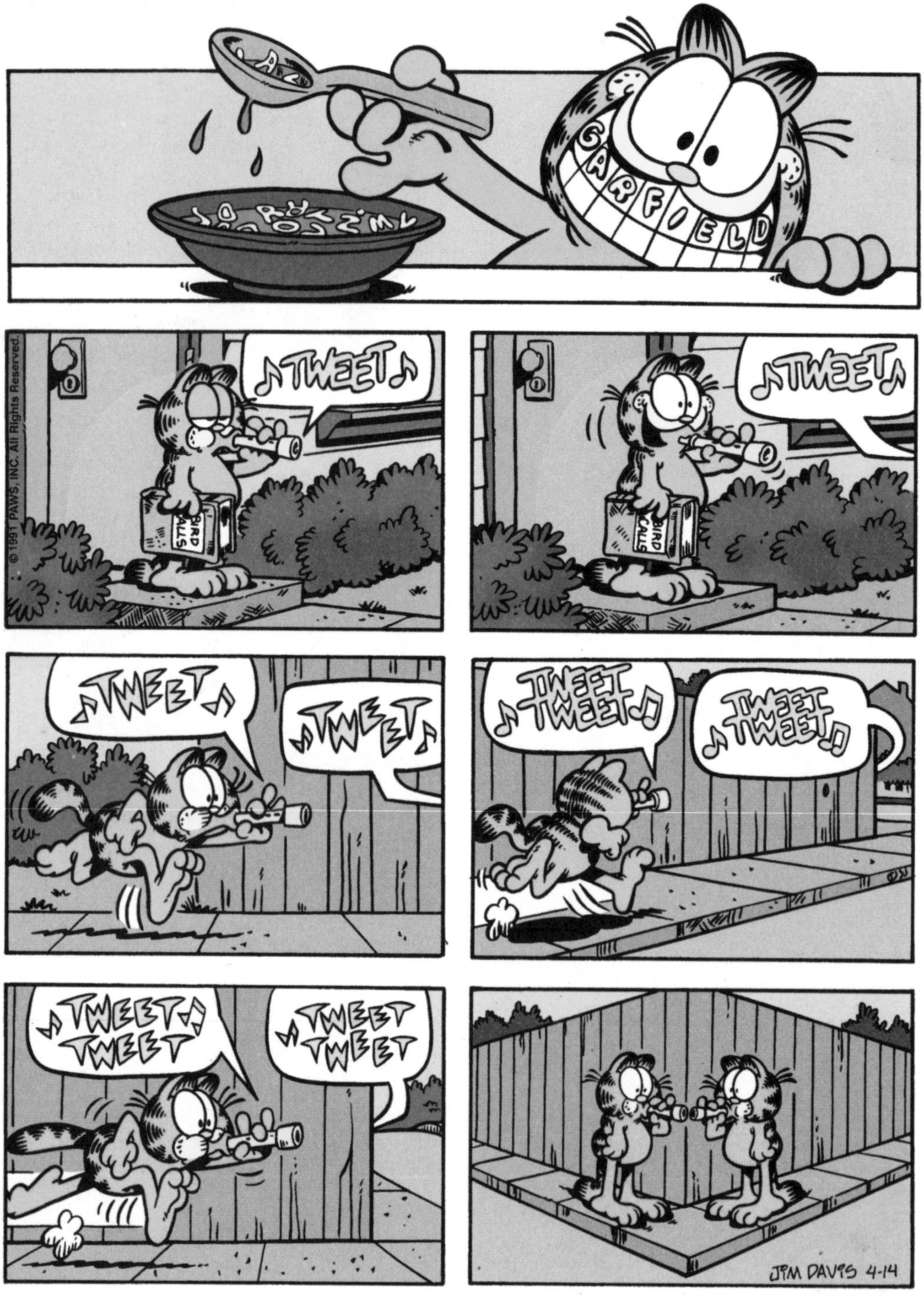
GARFIELD
© 1991 PAWS, INC. All Rights Reserved.
♪TWEET♪
♪TWEET♪
BIRD CALLS
♪TWEET♪
♪TWEET♪
♪TWEET TWEET♪
♪TWEET TWEET♪
♪TWEET TWEET♪
♪TWEET TWEET
JIM DAVIS 4-14

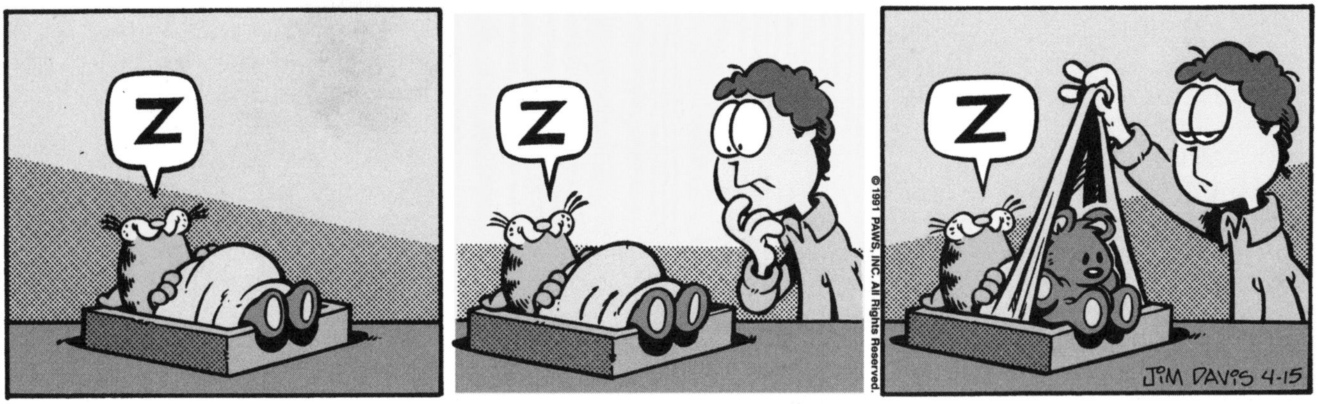
Z
Z
© 1991 PAWS, INC. All Rights Reserved.
Z
JIM DAVIS 4-15

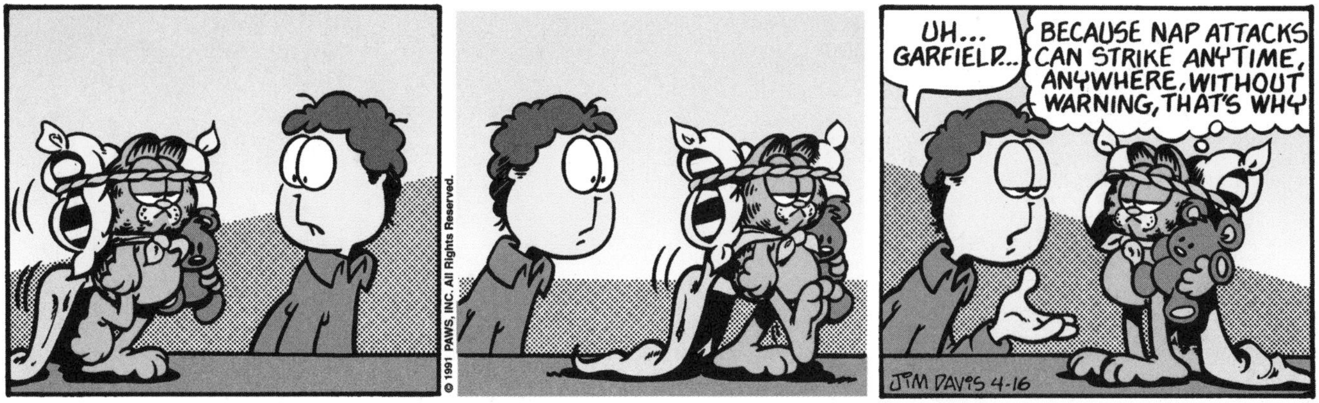
© 1991 PAWS, INC. All Rights Reserved.
UH... GARFIELD...
BECAUSE NAP ATTACKS CAN STRIKE ANYTIME, ANYWHERE, WITHOUT WARNING, THAT'S WHY
JIM DAVIS 4-16

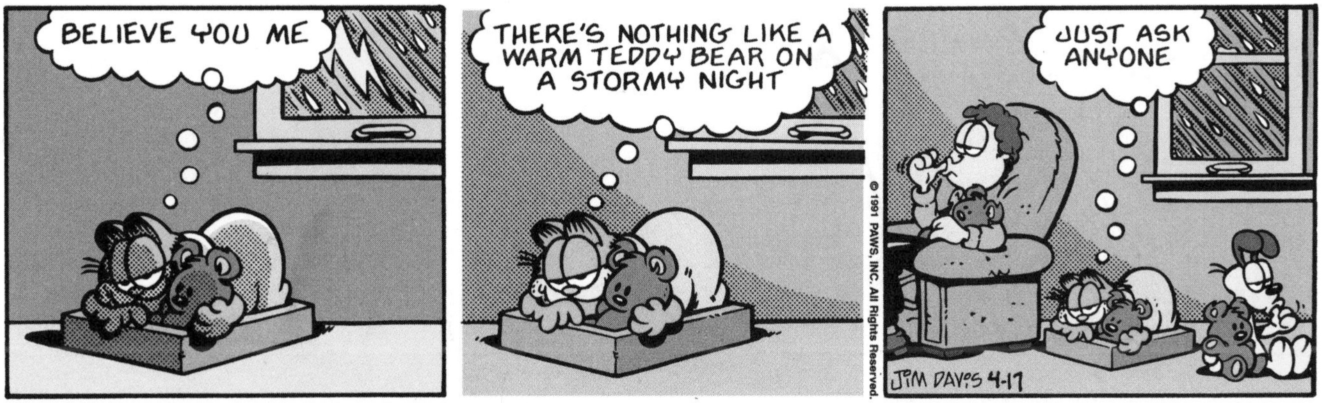
BELIEVE YOU ME
THERE'S NOTHING LIKE A WARM TEDDY BEAR ON A STORMY NIGHT
© 1991 PAWS, INC. All Rights Reserved.
JUST ASK ANYONE
JIM DAVIS 4-17

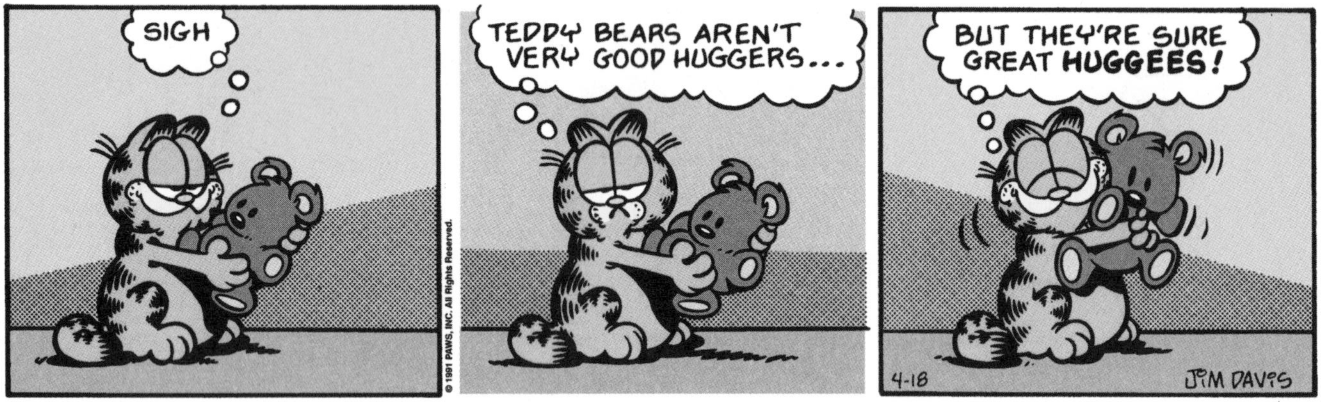
SIGH
TEDDY BEARS AREN'T VERY GOOD HUGGERS...
BUT THEY'RE SURE GREAT **HUGGEES!**
© 1991 PAWS, INC. All Rights Reserved.
4-18
JIM DAVIS

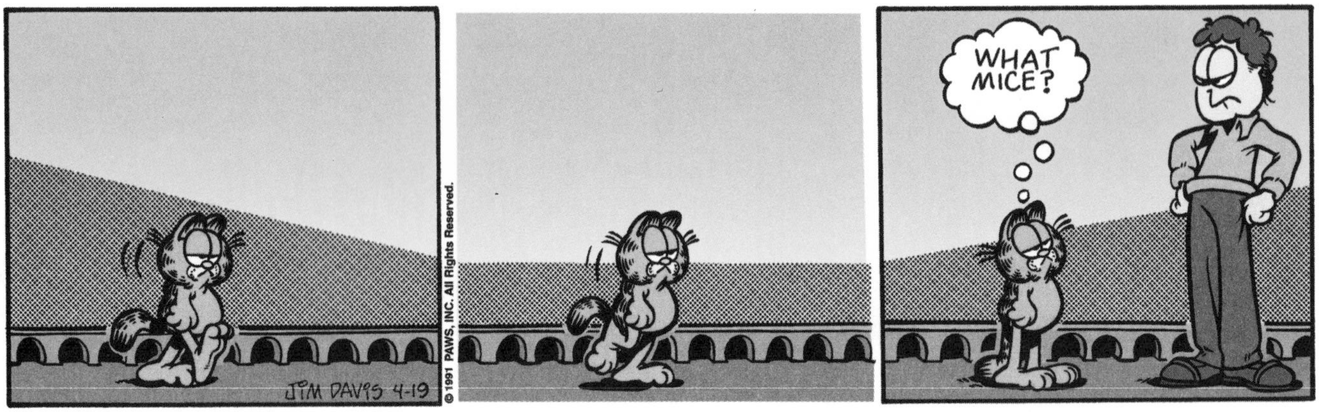
JIM DAVIS 4-19
© 1991 PAWS, INC. All Rights Reserved.
WHAT MICE?

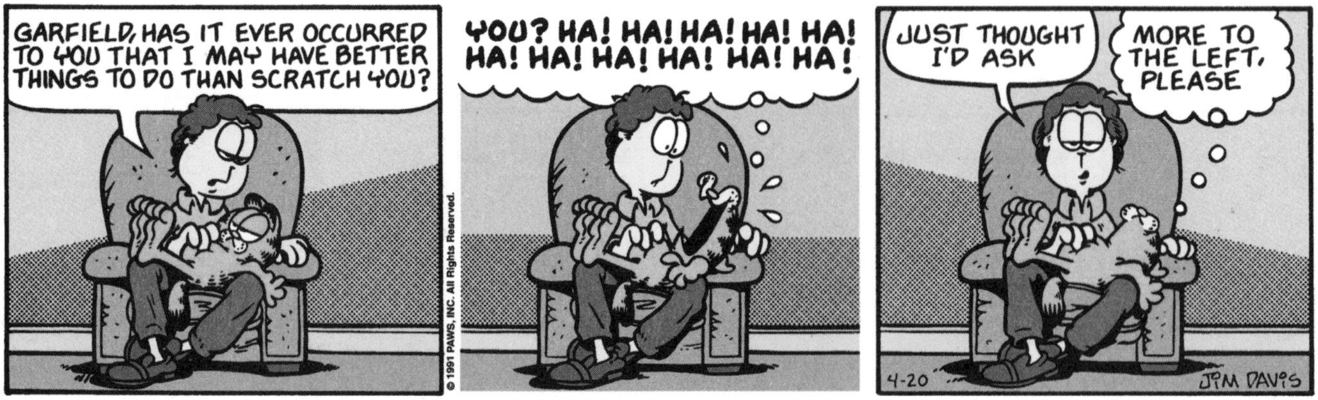
GARFIELD, HAS IT EVER OCCURRED TO YOU THAT I MAY HAVE BETTER THINGS TO DO THAN SCRATCH YOU?
© 1991 PAWS, INC. All Rights Reserved.
YOU? HA! HA! HA! HA! HA! HA! HA! HA! HA! HA! HA!
JUST THOUGHT I'D ASK
MORE TO THE LEFT, PLEASE
4-20
JIM DAVIS

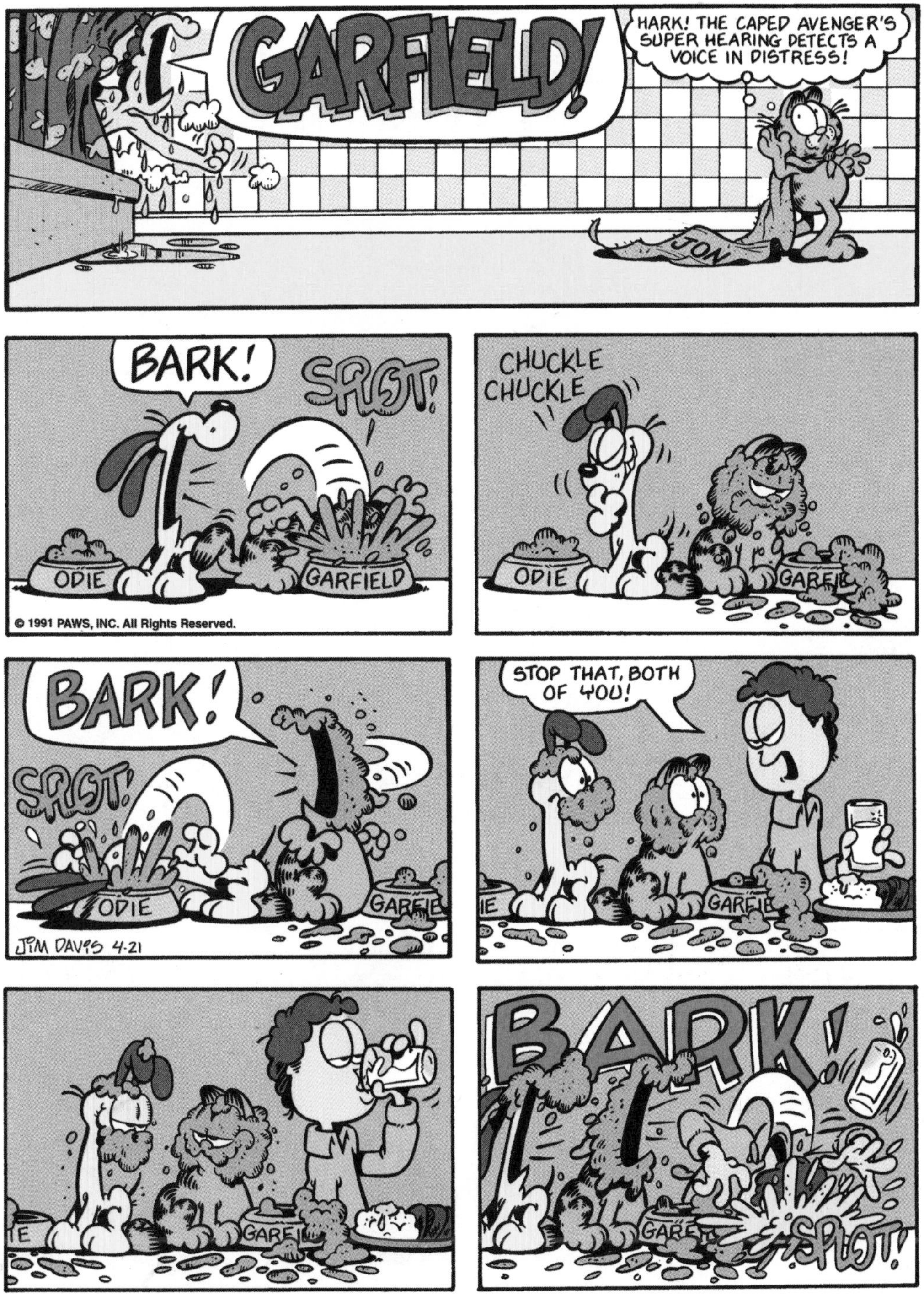
GARFIELD!
HARK! THE CAPED AVENGER'S SUPER HEARING DETECTS A VOICE IN DISTRESS!
JON
BARK!
SPLOT!
ODIE
GARFIELD
© 1991 PAWS, INC. All Rights Reserved.
CHUCKLE CHUCKLE
ODIE
BARK!
SPLOT!
ODIE
JIM DAVIS 4-21
STOP THAT, BOTH OF YOU!
BARK!
SPLOT!

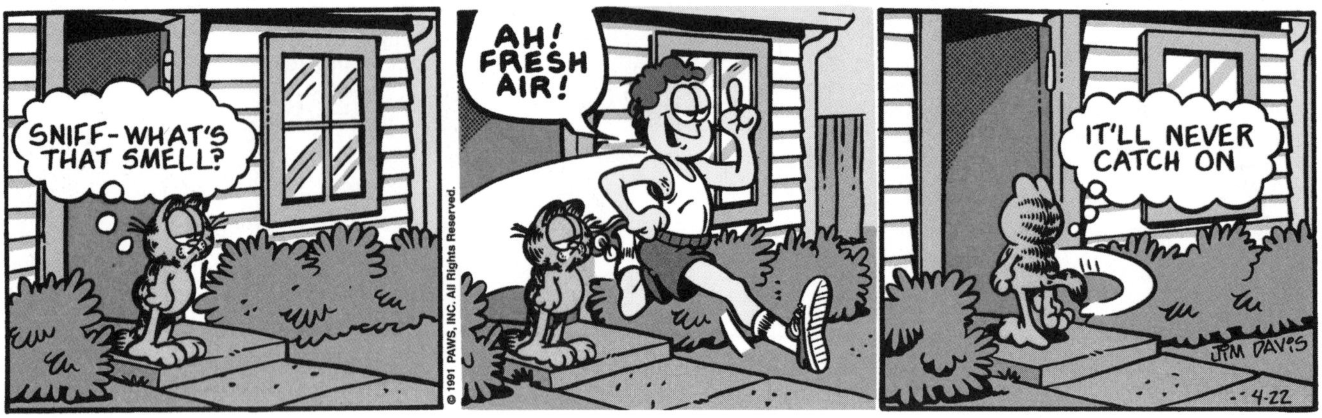
SNIFF-WHAT'S THAT SMELL?
© 1991 PAWS, INC. All Rights Reserved.
AH! FRESH AIR!
IT'LL NEVER CATCH ON
JIM DAVIS
4-22

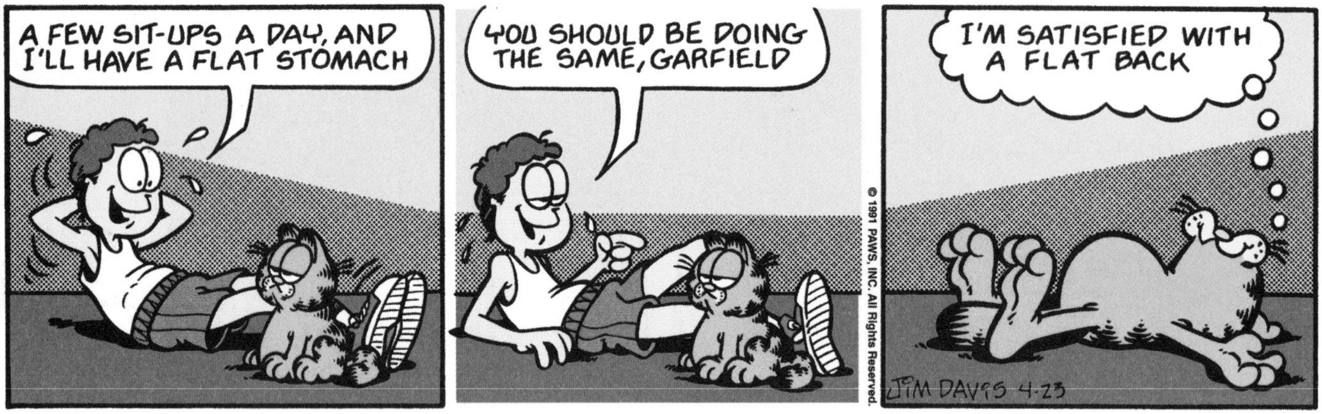
A FEW SIT-UPS A DAY, AND I'LL HAVE A FLAT STOMACH
YOU SHOULD BE DOING THE SAME, GARFIELD
© 1991 PAWS, INC. All Rights Reserved.
I'M SATISFIED WITH A FLAT BACK
JIM DAVIS 4-23

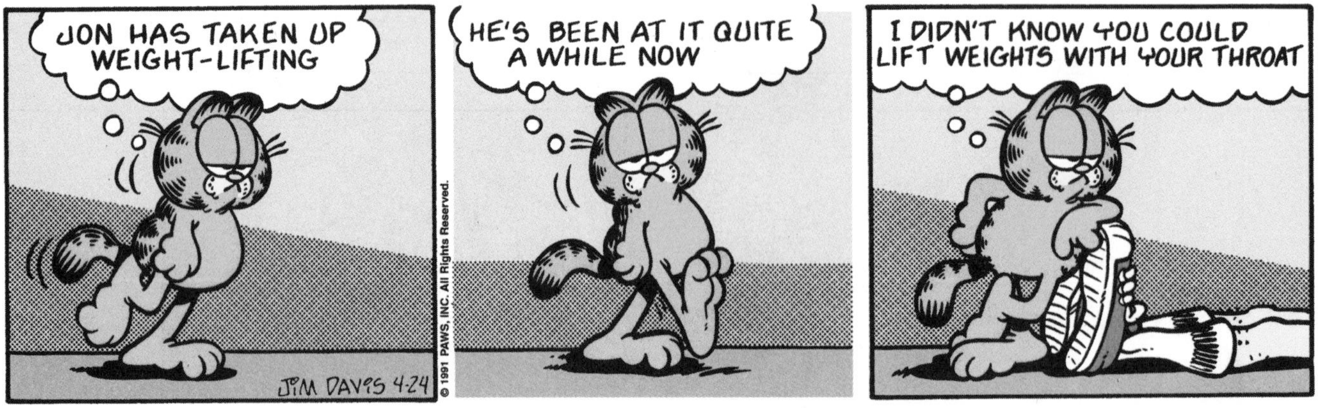
JON HAS TAKEN UP WEIGHT-LIFTING
JIM DAVIS 4-24
© 1991 PAWS, INC. All Rights Reserved.
HE'S BEEN AT IT QUITE A WHILE NOW
I DIDN'T KNOW YOU COULD LIFT WEIGHTS WITH YOUR THROAT

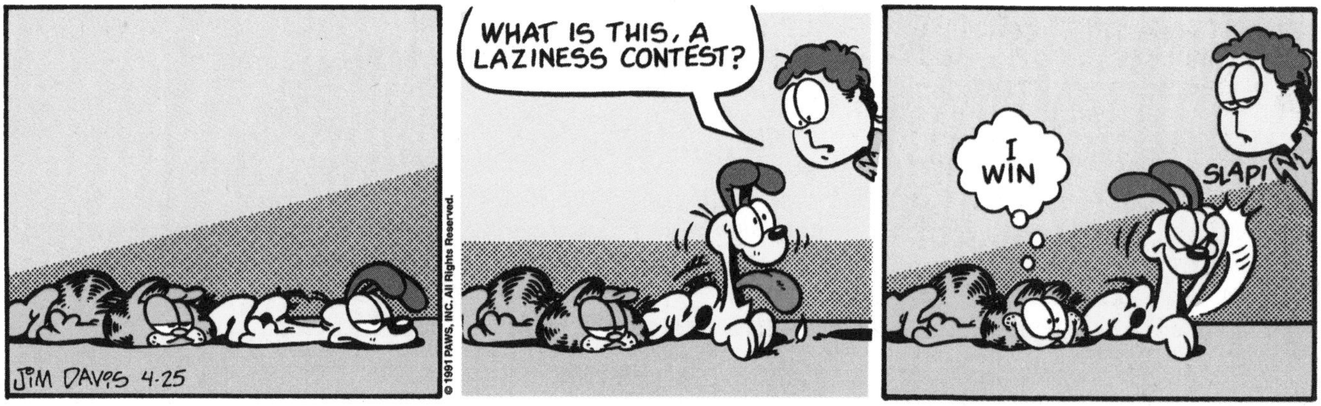
JIM DAVIS 4-25
© 1991 PAWS, INC. All Rights Reserved.
WHAT IS THIS, A LAZINESS CONTEST?
I WIN
SLAP!

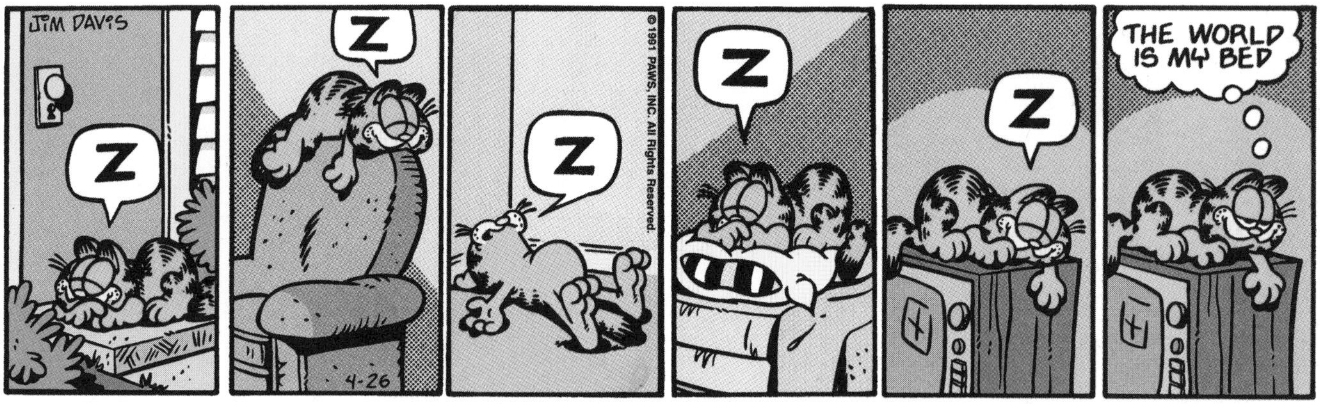
JIM DAVIS
Z
Z
4-26
© 1991 PAWS, INC. All Rights Reserved.
Z
Z
Z
THE WORLD IS MY BED

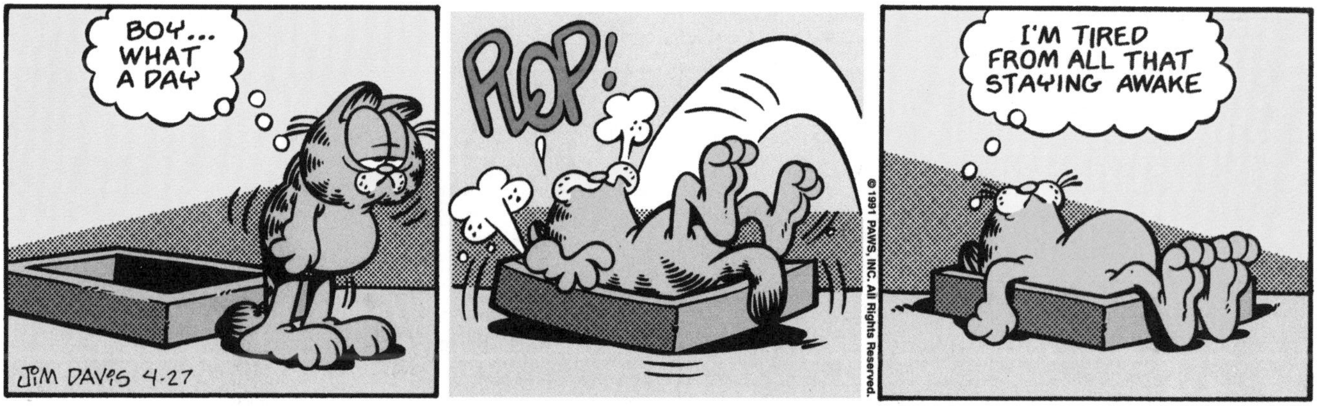
BOY... WHAT A DAY
JIM DAVIS 4-27
PLOP!
© 1991 PAWS, INC. All Rights Reserved.
I'M TIRED FROM ALL THAT STAYING AWAKE

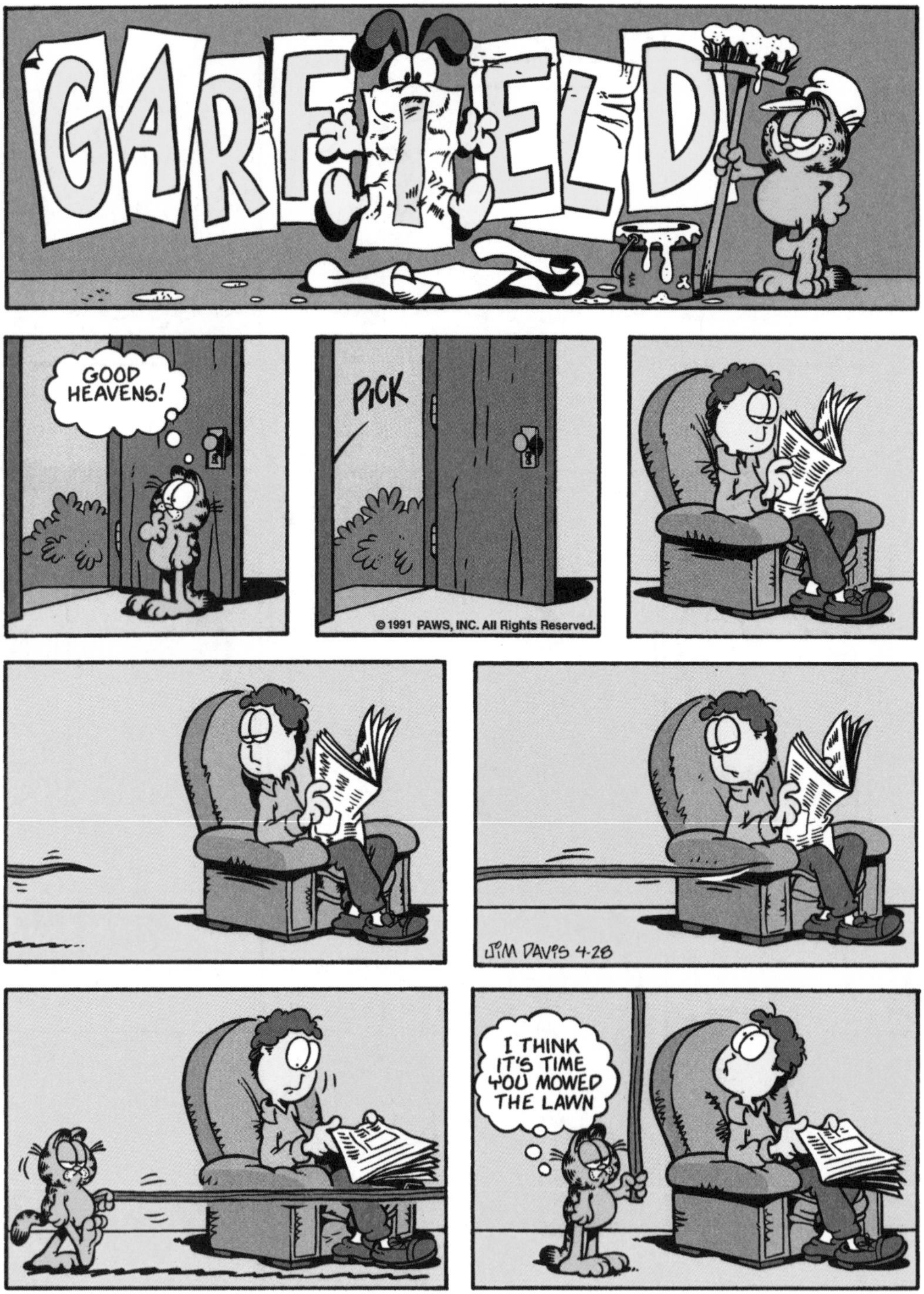
GARFIELD
GOOD HEAVENS!
PICK
© 1991 PAWS, INC. All Rights Reserved.
JIM DAVIS 4-28
I THINK IT'S TIME YOU MOWED THE LAWN

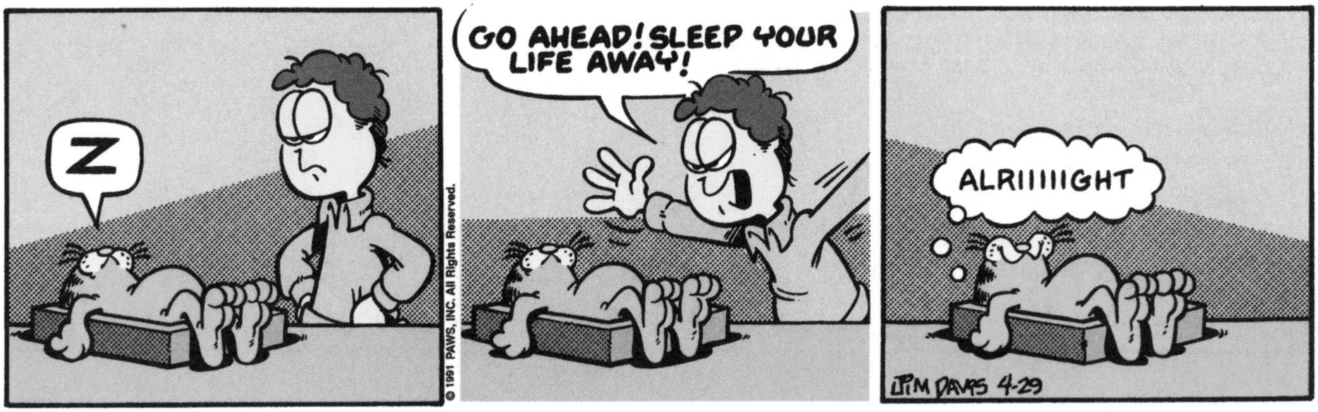
Z
GO AHEAD! SLEEP YOUR LIFE AWAY!
ALRIIIIIGHT
© 1991 PAWS, INC. All Rights Reserved.
JIM DAVIS 4-29

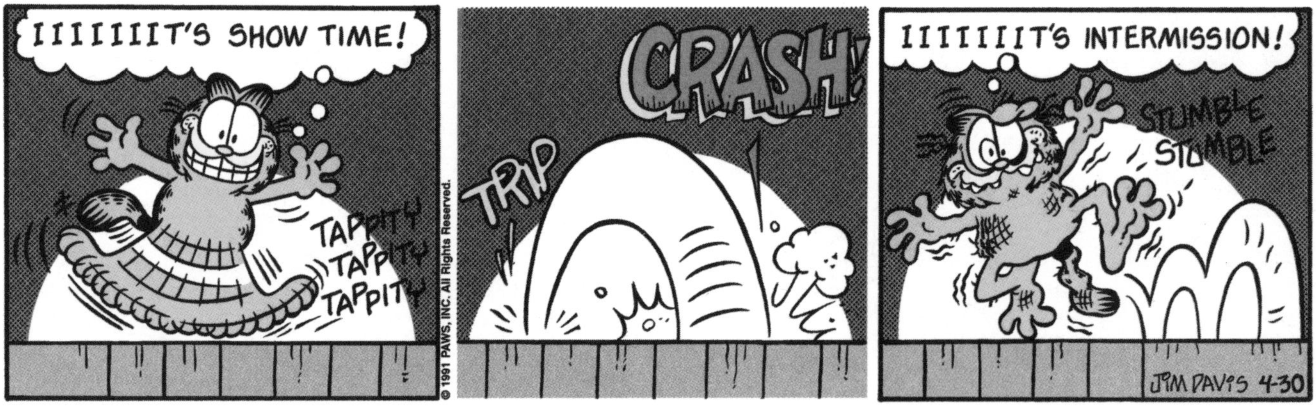
IIIIIIIT'S SHOW TIME!
TAPPITY TAPPITY TAPPITY
TRIP
CRASH!
IIIIIIIT'S INTERMISSION!
STUMBLE STUMBLE
© 1991 PAWS, INC. All Rights Reserved.
JIM DAVIS 4-30

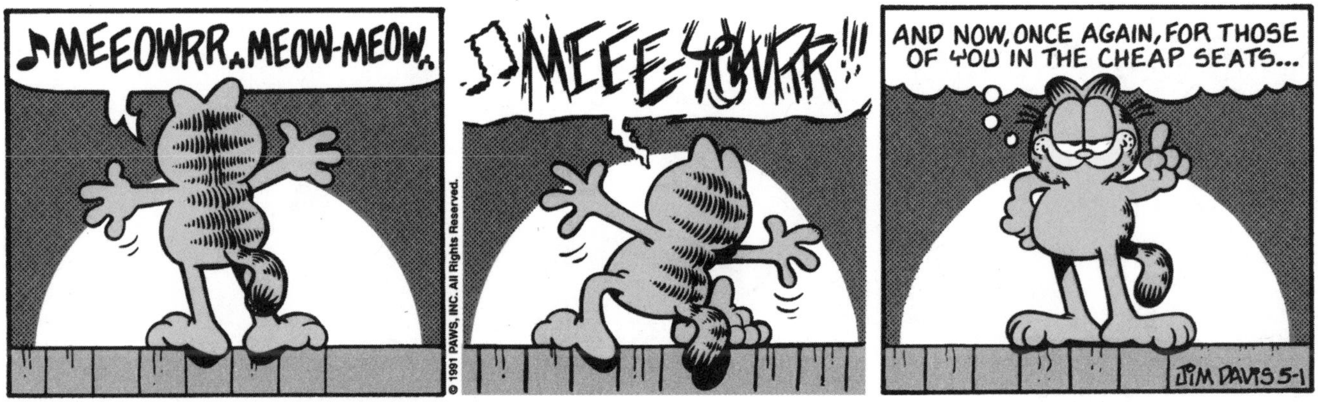
♪MEEOWRR MEOW-MEOW
♫MEEE-YOWRR!!!
AND NOW, ONCE AGAIN, FOR THOSE OF YOU IN THE CHEAP SEATS...
© 1991 PAWS, INC. All Rights Reserved.
JIM DAVIS 5-1

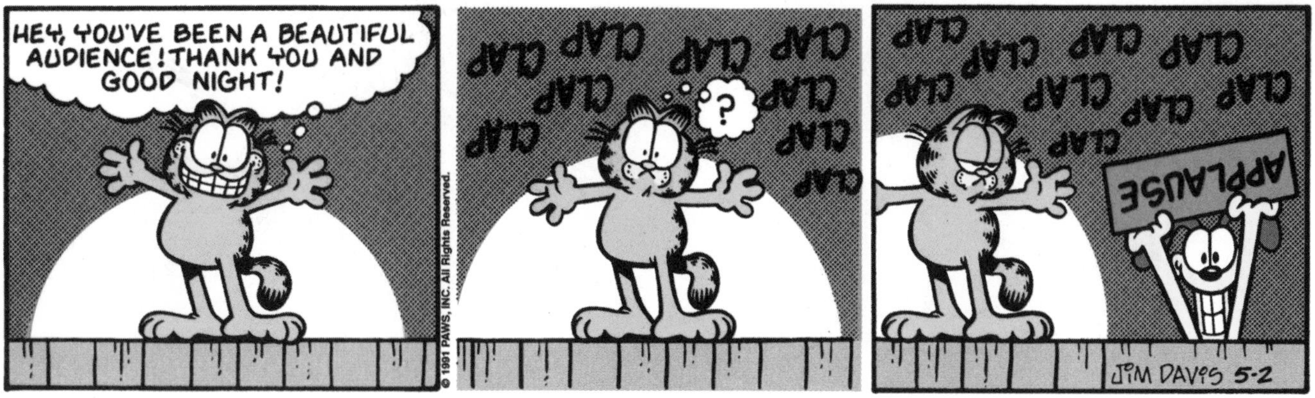
HEY, YOU'VE BEEN A BEAUTIFUL AUDIENCE! THANK YOU AND GOOD NIGHT!
© 1991 PAWS, INC. All Rights Reserved.
CLAP CLAP CLAP CLAP CLAP CLAP CLAP CLAP
?
CLAP CLAP CLAP CLAP CLAP CLAP CLAP CLAP CLAP CLAP CLAP
APPLAUSE
JIM DAVIS 5-2

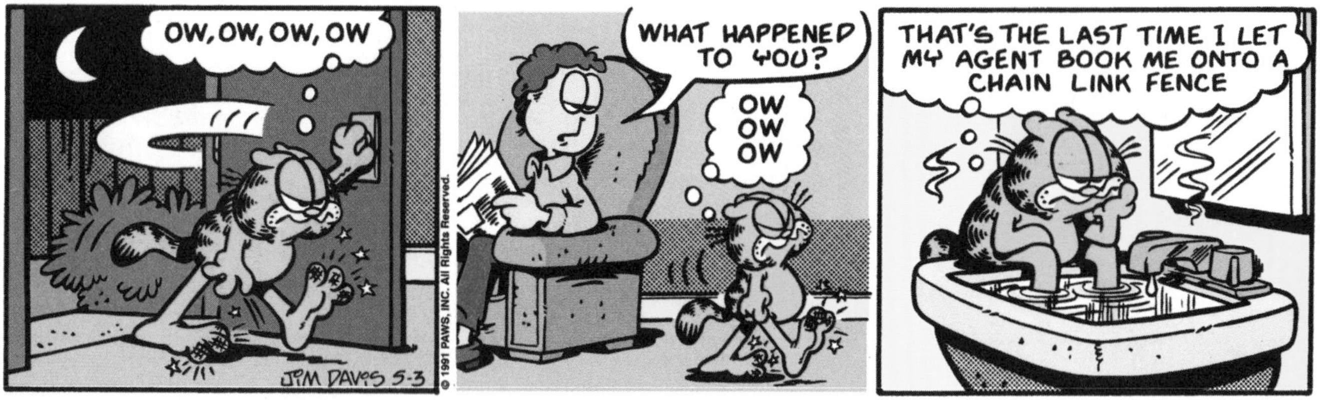
OW, OW, OW, OW
JIM DAVIS 5-3
© 1991 PAWS, INC. All Rights Reserved.
WHAT HAPPENED TO YOU?
OW OW OW
THAT'S THE LAST TIME I LET MY AGENT BOOK ME ONTO A CHAIN LINK FENCE

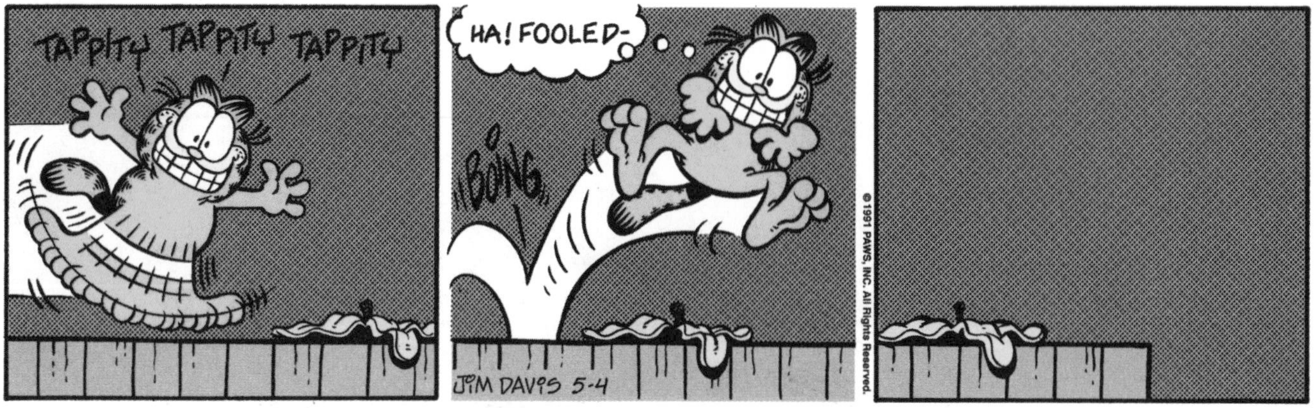
TAPPITY TAPPITY TAPPITY
HA! FOOLED-
BOING
JIM DAVIS 5-4
© 1991 PAWS, INC. All Rights Reserved.

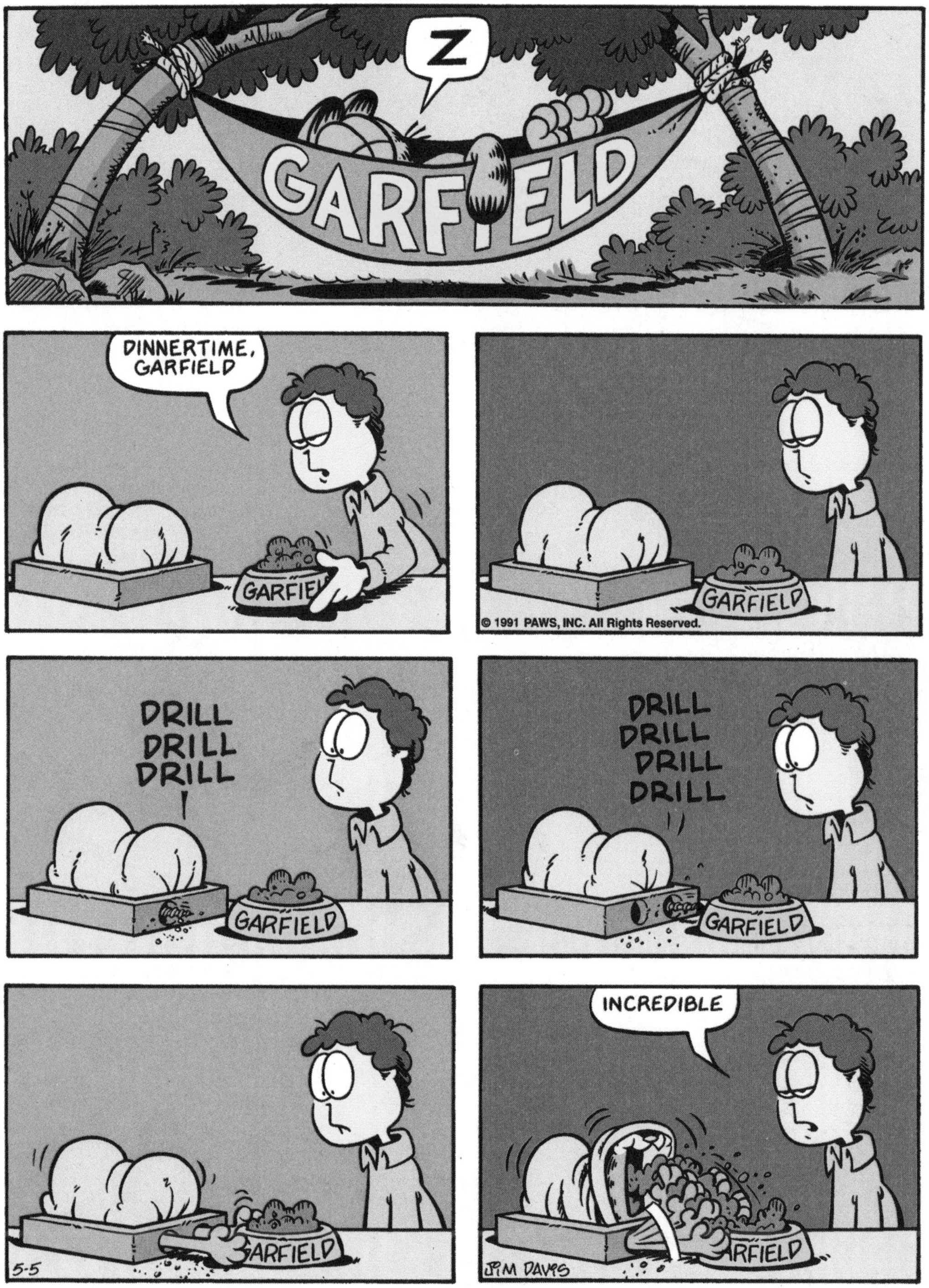
Z
GARFIELD
DINNERTIME, GARFIELD
GARFIELD
GARFIELD
© 1991 PAWS, INC. All Rights Reserved.
DRILL DRILL DRILL
GARFIELD
DRILL DRILL DRILL DRILL
GARFIELD
5-5
ARFIELD
INCREDIBLE
ARFIELD
JIM DAVIS

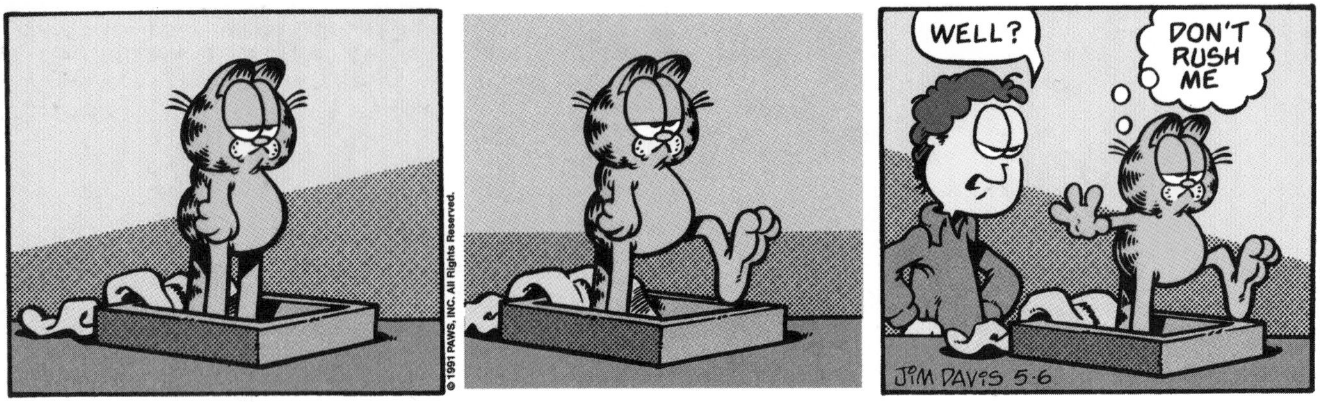
© 1991 PAWS, INC. All Rights Reserved.
WELL?
DON'T RUSH ME
JIM DAVIS 5-6

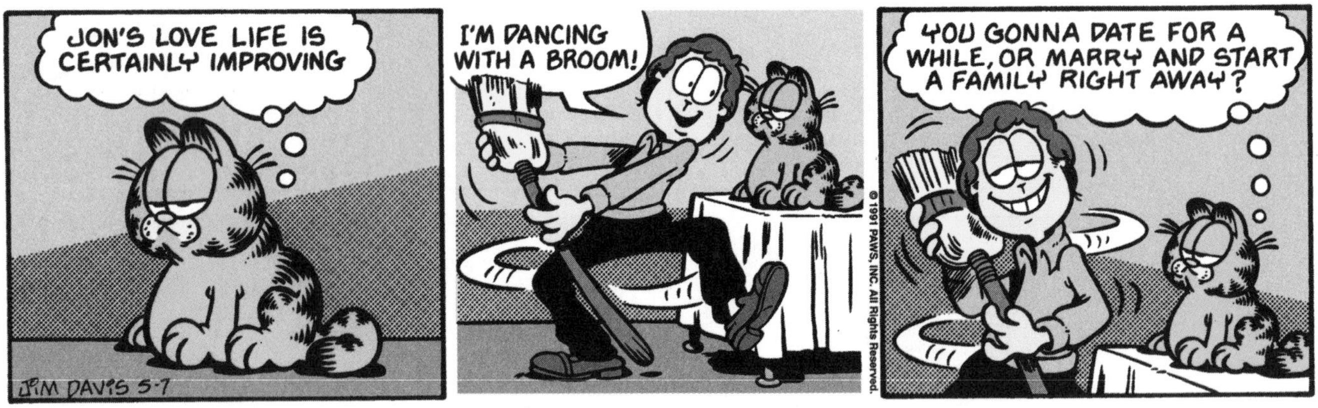
JON'S LOVE LIFE IS CERTAINLY IMPROVING
JIM DAVIS 5-7
I'M DANCING WITH A BROOM!
© 1991 PAWS, INC. All Rights Reserved.
YOU GONNA DATE FOR A WHILE, OR MARRY AND START A FAMILY RIGHT AWAY?

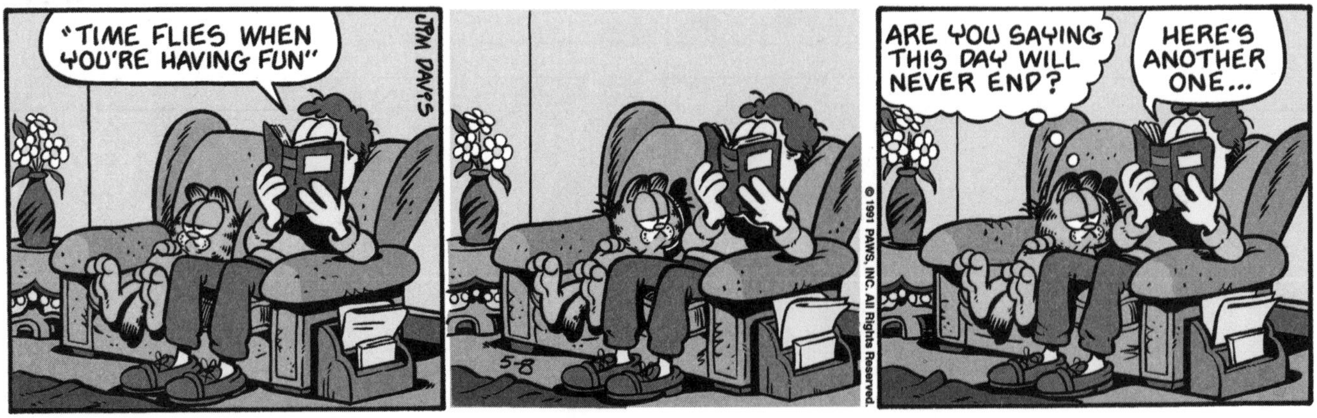
"TIME FLIES WHEN YOU'RE HAVING FUN"
JIM DAVIS
5-8
© 1991 PAWS, INC. All Rights Reserved.
ARE YOU SAYING THIS DAY WILL NEVER END?
HERE'S ANOTHER ONE...

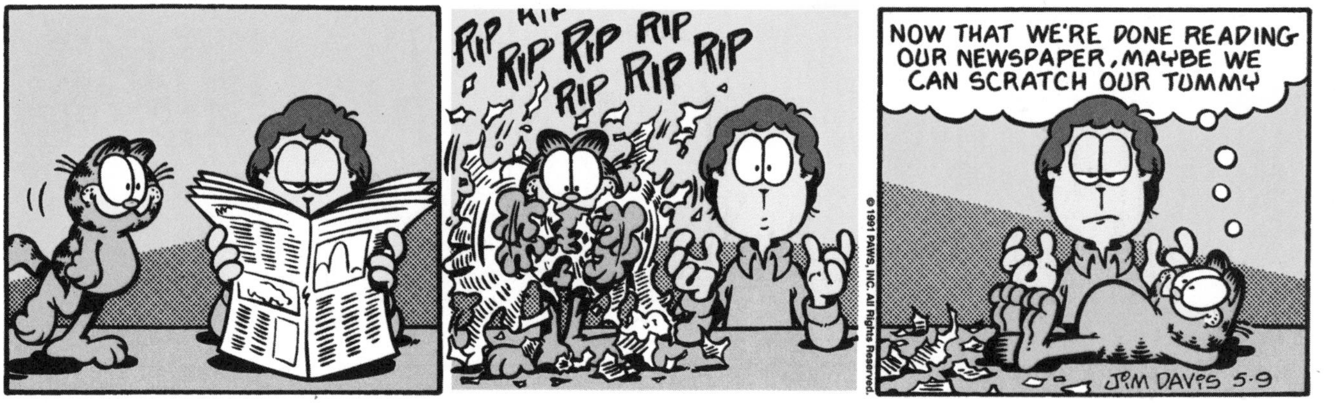
RIP RIP RIP RIP RIP RIP RIP RIP RIP
© 1991 PAWS, INC. All Rights Reserved.
NOW THAT WE'RE DONE READING OUR NEWSPAPER, MAYBE WE CAN SCRATCH OUR TUMMY
JIM DAVIS 5-9

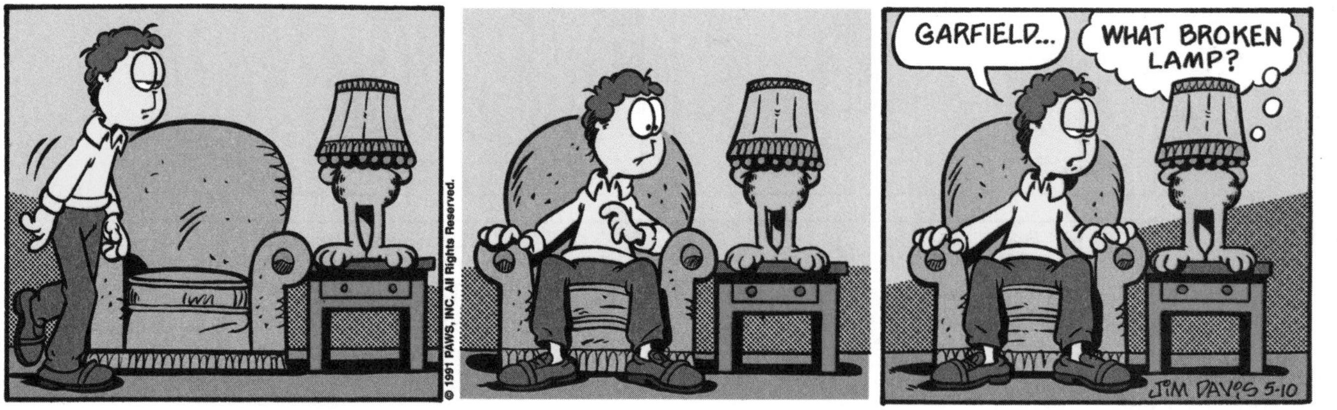
© 1991 PAWS, INC. All Rights Reserved.
GARFIELD...
WHAT BROKEN LAMP?
JIM DAVIS 5-10

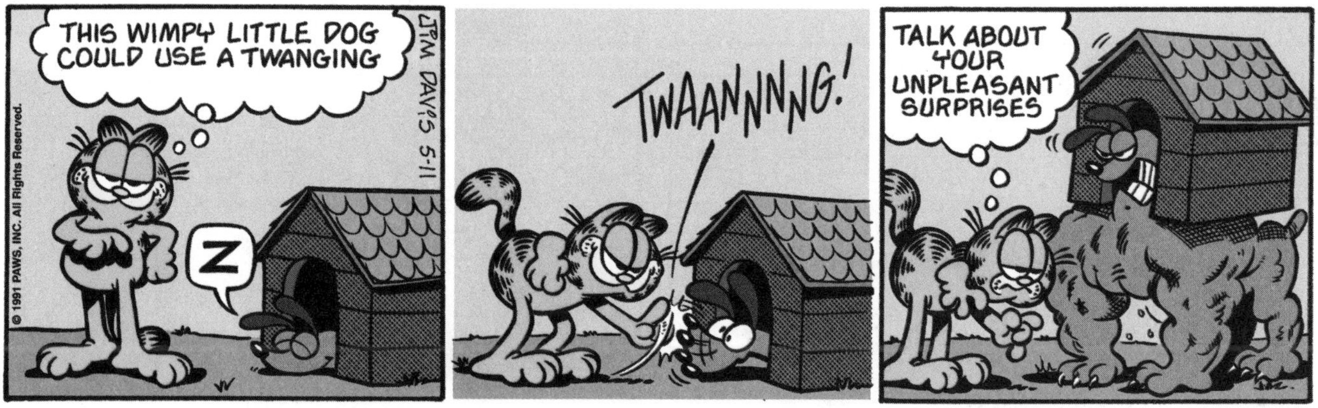
THIS WIMPY LITTLE DOG COULD USE A TWANGING
JIM DAVIS 5-11
© 1991 PAWS, INC. All Rights Reserved.
Z
TWAANNNNG!
TALK ABOUT YOUR UNPLEASANT SURPRISES

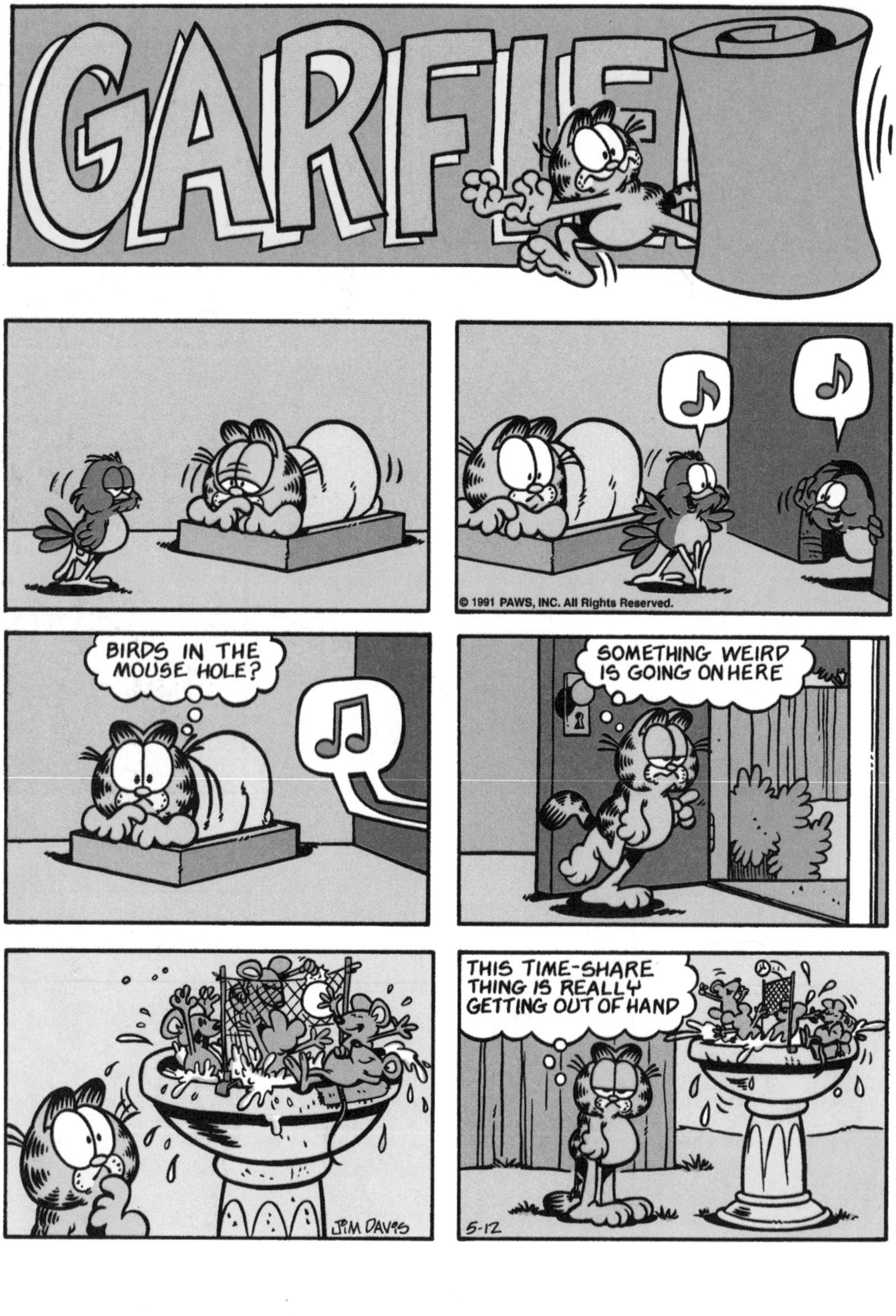
GARFIE
© 1991 PAWS, INC. All Rights Reserved.
BIRDS IN THE MOUSE HOLE?
SOMETHING WEIRD IS GOING ON HERE
THIS TIME-SHARE THING IS REALLY GETTING OUT OF HAND
JIM DAVIS
5-12

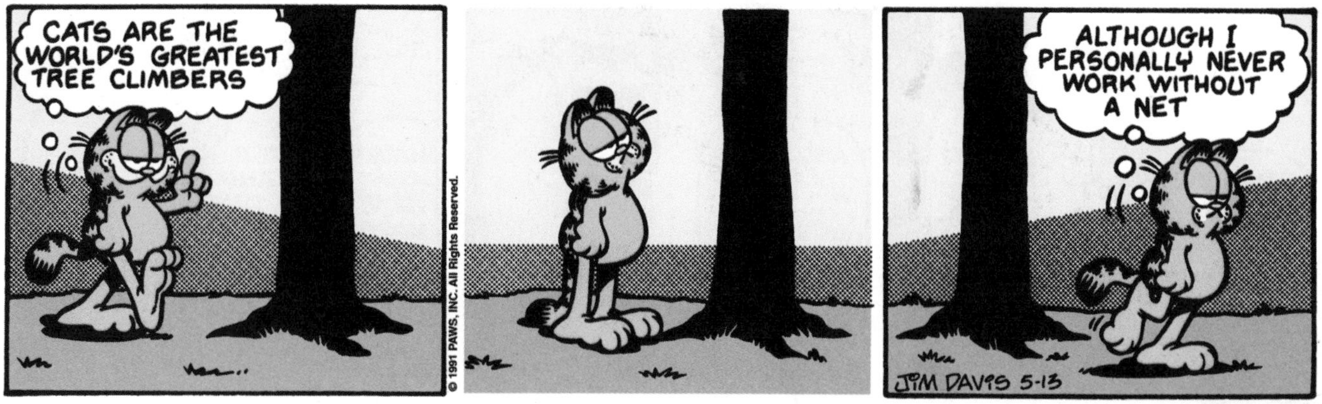
CATS ARE THE WORLD'S GREATEST TREE CLIMBERS
© 1991 PAWS, INC. All Rights Reserved.
ALTHOUGH I PERSONALLY NEVER WORK WITHOUT A NET
JIM DAVIS 5-13

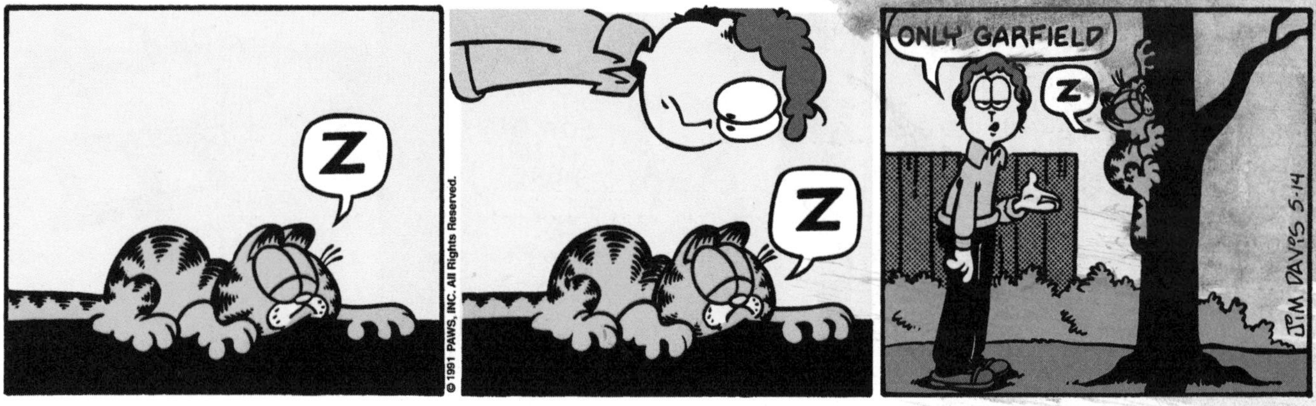
Z
© 1991 PAWS, INC. All Rights Reserved.
Z
ONLY GARFIELD
Z
JIM DAVIS 5-14

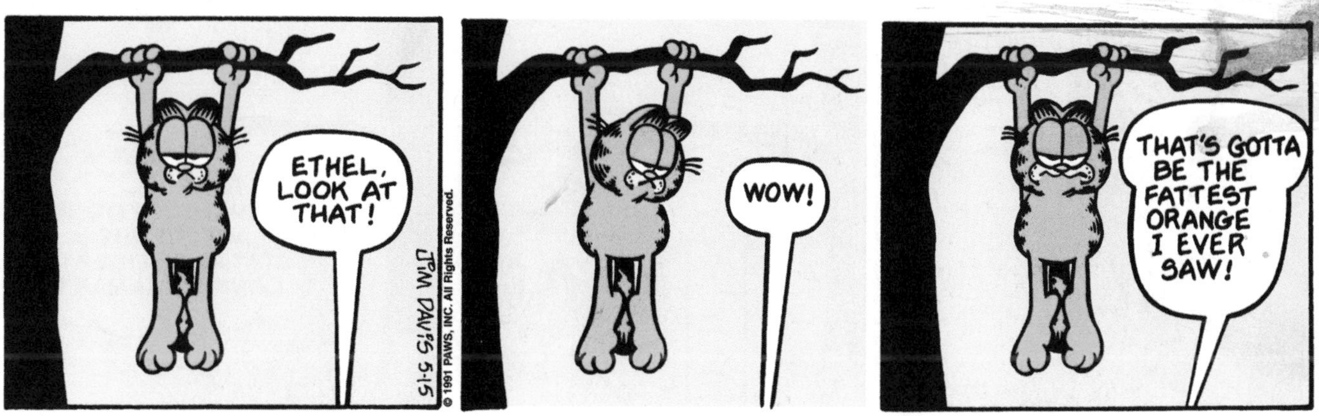
ETHEL, LOOK AT THAT!
JIM DAVIS 5-15
© 1991 PAWS, INC. All Rights Reserved.
WOW!
THAT'S GOTTA BE THE FATTEST ORANGE I EVER SAW!

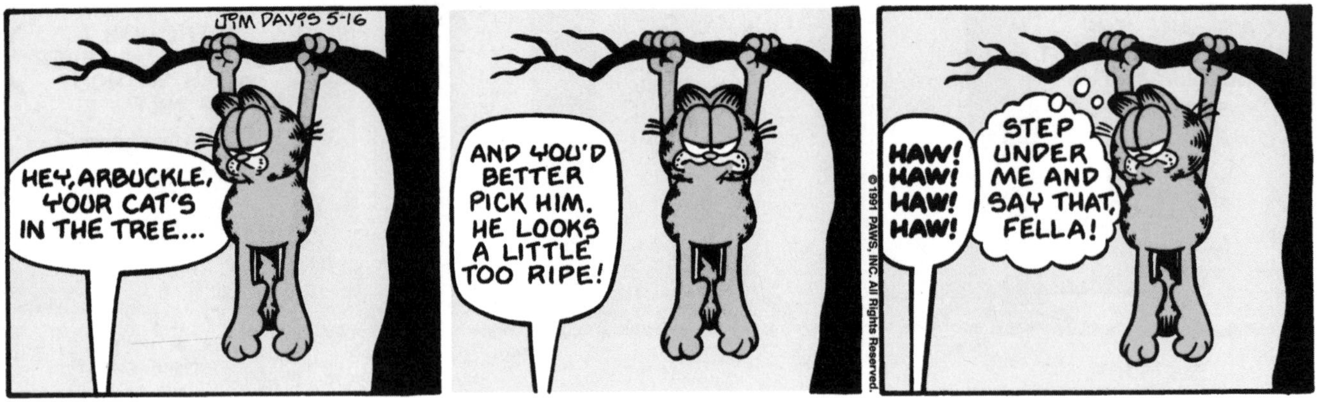
JIM DAVIS 5-16
HEY, ARBUCKLE, YOUR CAT'S IN THE TREE...
AND YOU'D BETTER PICK HIM. HE LOOKS A LITTLE TOO RIPE!
© 1991 PAWS, INC. All Rights Reserved.
HAW! HAW! HAW! HAW!
STEP UNDER ME AND SAY THAT, FELLA!

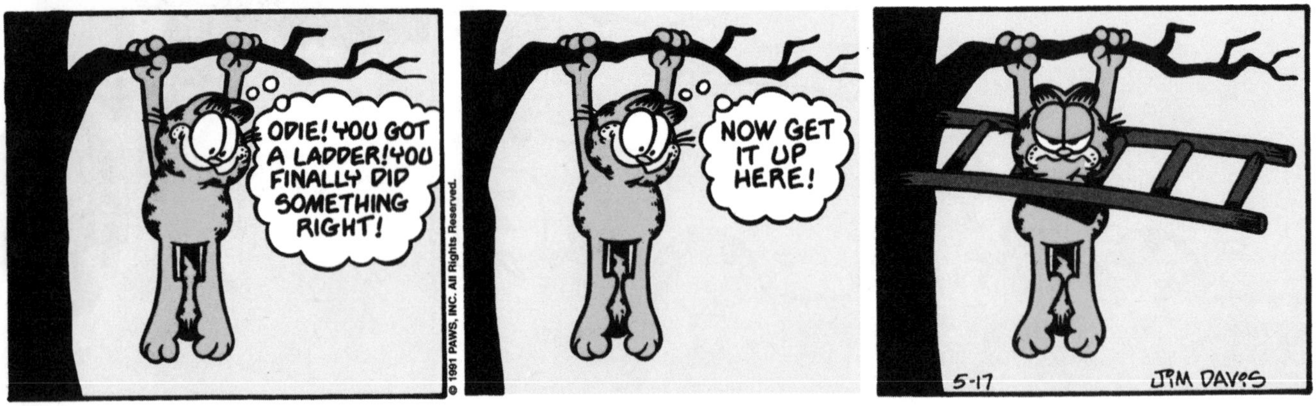
ODIE! YOU GOT A LADDER! YOU FINALLY DID SOMETHING RIGHT!
© 1991 PAWS, INC. All Rights Reserved.
NOW GET IT UP HERE!
5-17
JIM DAVIS

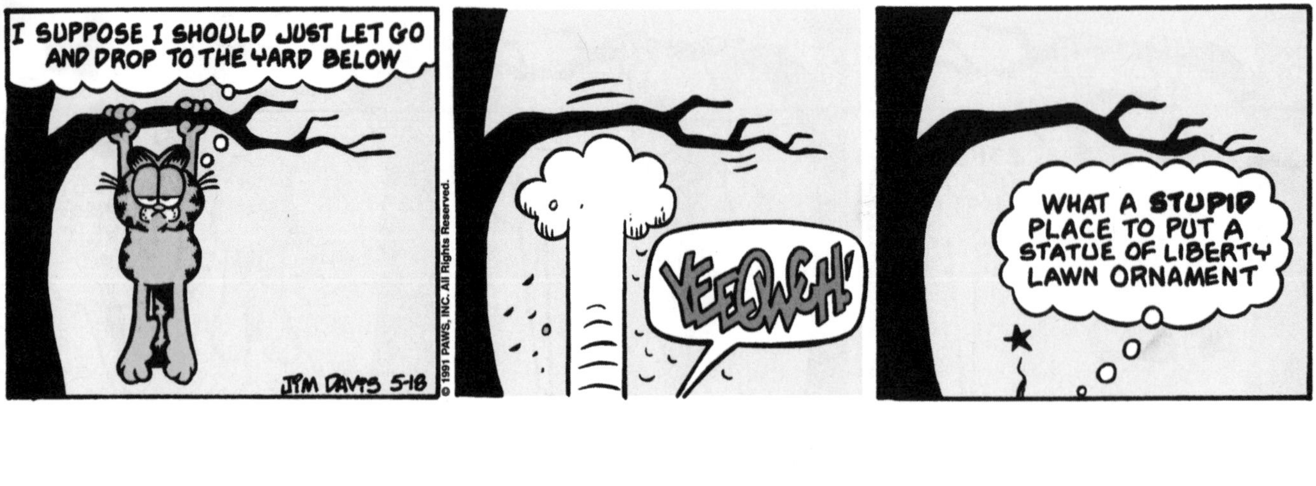
I SUPPOSE I SHOULD JUST LET GO AND DROP TO THE YARD BELOW
JIM DAVIS 5-18
© 1991 PAWS, INC. All Rights Reserved.
YEEOWCH!
WHAT A STUPID PLACE TO PUT A STATUE OF LIBERTY LAWN ORNAMENT

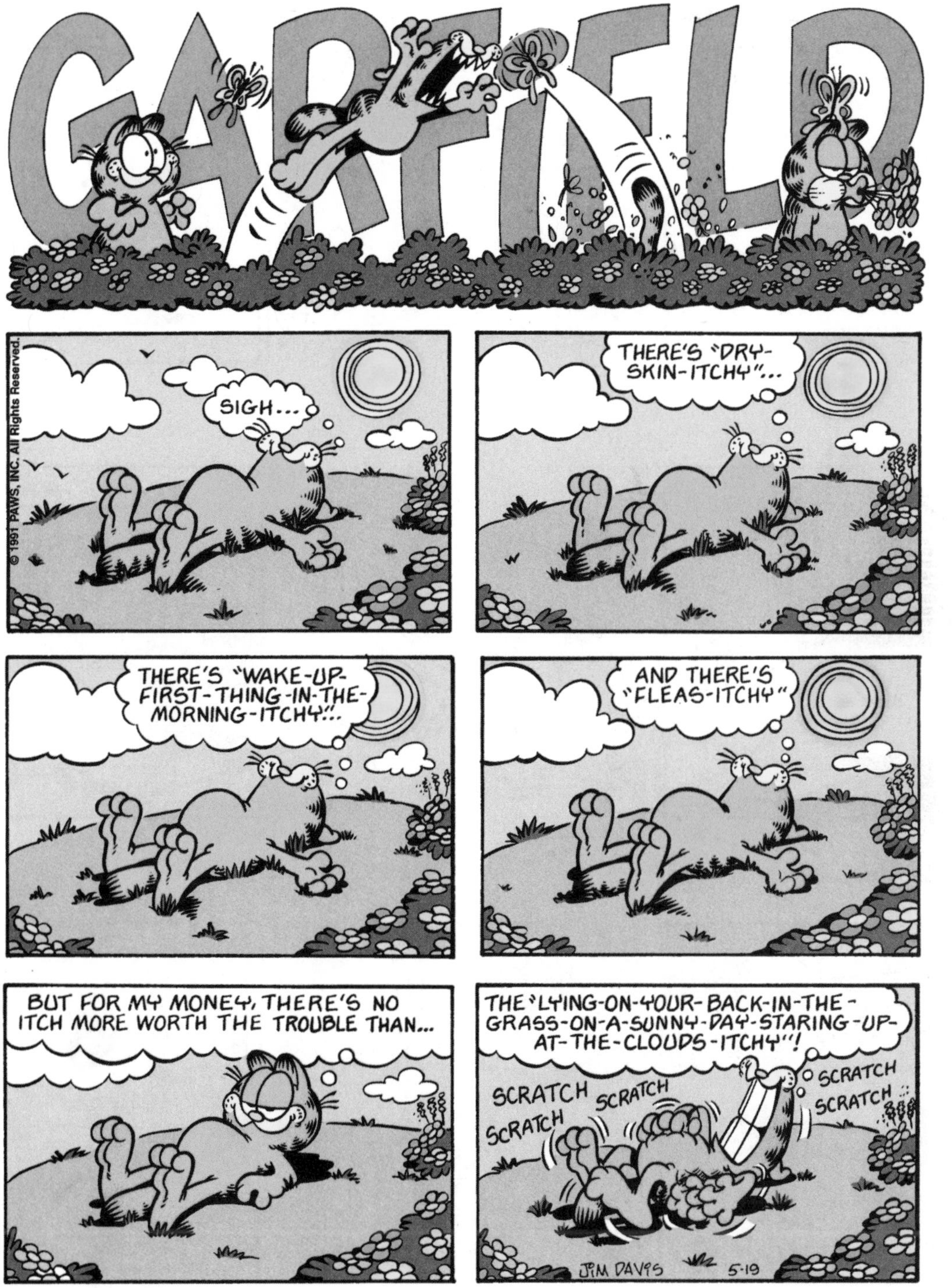
GARFIELD
© 1991 PAWS, INC. All Rights Reserved.
SIGH...
THERE'S "DRY-SKIN-ITCHY"...
THERE'S "WAKE-UP-FIRST-THING-IN-THE-MORNING-ITCHY"...
AND THERE'S "FLEAS-ITCHY"
BUT FOR MY MONEY, THERE'S NO ITCH MORE WORTH THE TROUBLE THAN...
THE "LYING-ON-YOUR-BACK-IN-THE-GRASS-ON-A-SUNNY-DAY-STARING-UP-AT-THE-CLOUDS-ITCHY"!
SCRATCH SCRATCH SCRATCH SCRATCH SCRATCH
JIM DAVIS 5-19

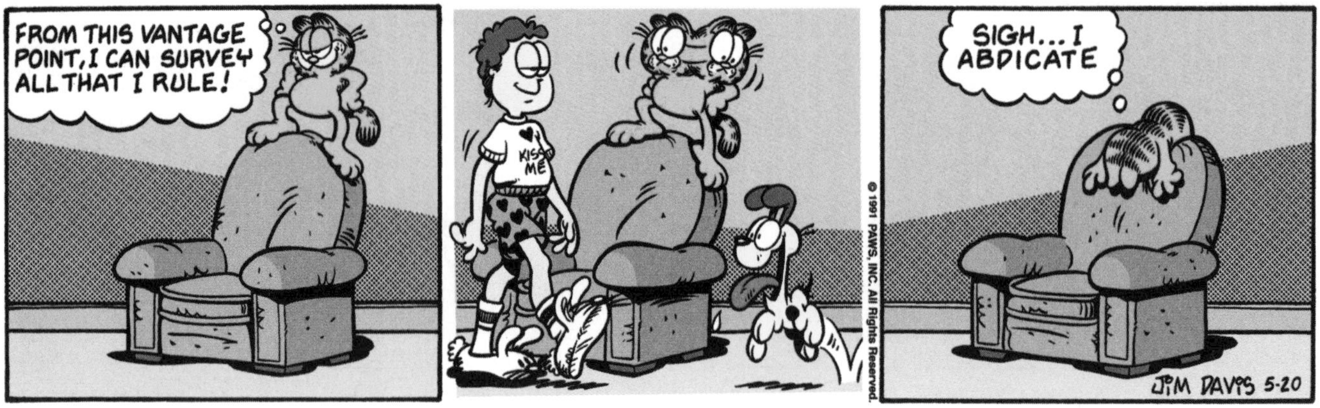
FROM THIS VANTAGE POINT, I CAN SURVEY ALL THAT I RULE!
KISS ME
© 1991 PAWS, INC. All Rights Reserved.
SIGH... I ABDICATE
JIM DAVIS 5-20

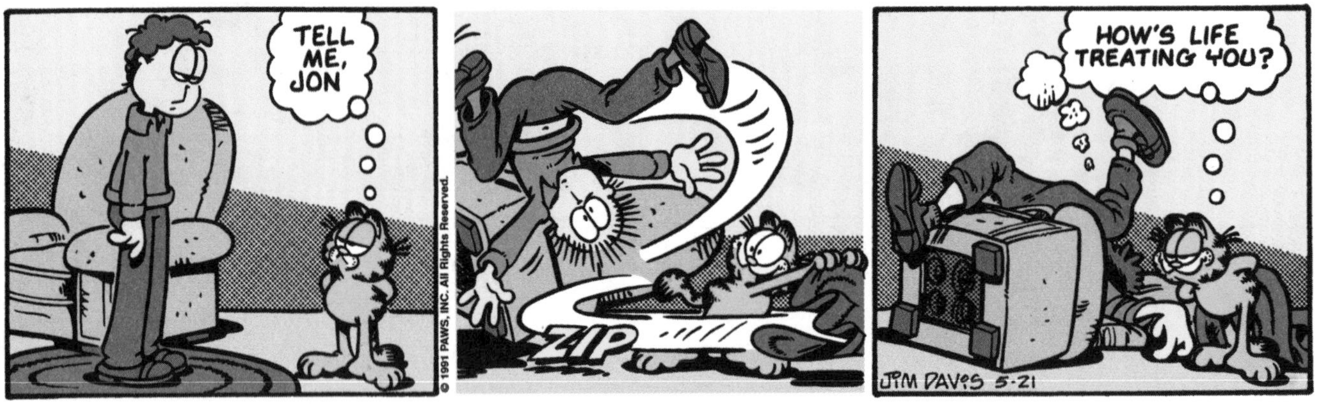
TELL ME, JON
© 1991 PAWS, INC. All Rights Reserved.
ZIP
HOW'S LIFE TREATING YOU?
JIM DAVIS 5-21

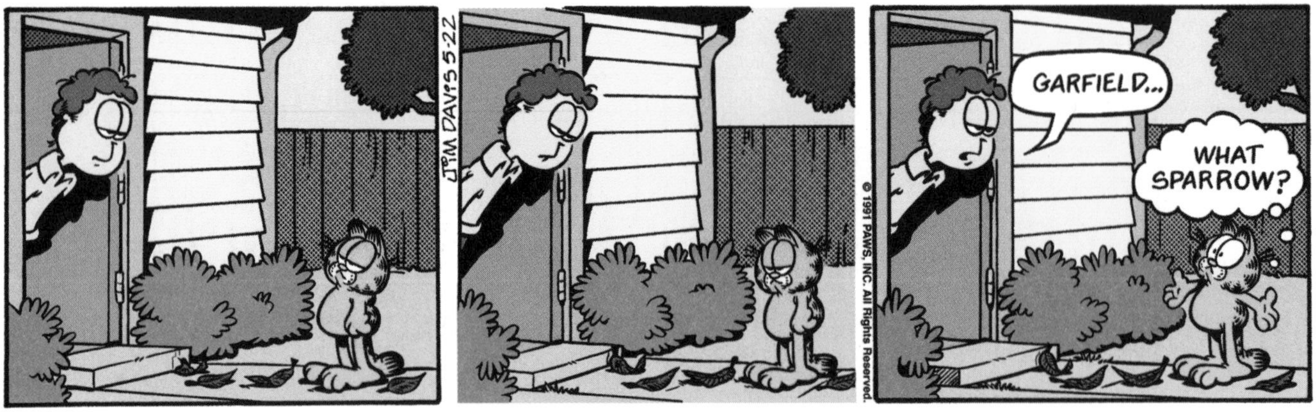
JIM DAVIS 5-22
© 1991 PAWS, INC. All Rights Reserved.
GARFIELD...
WHAT SPARROW?

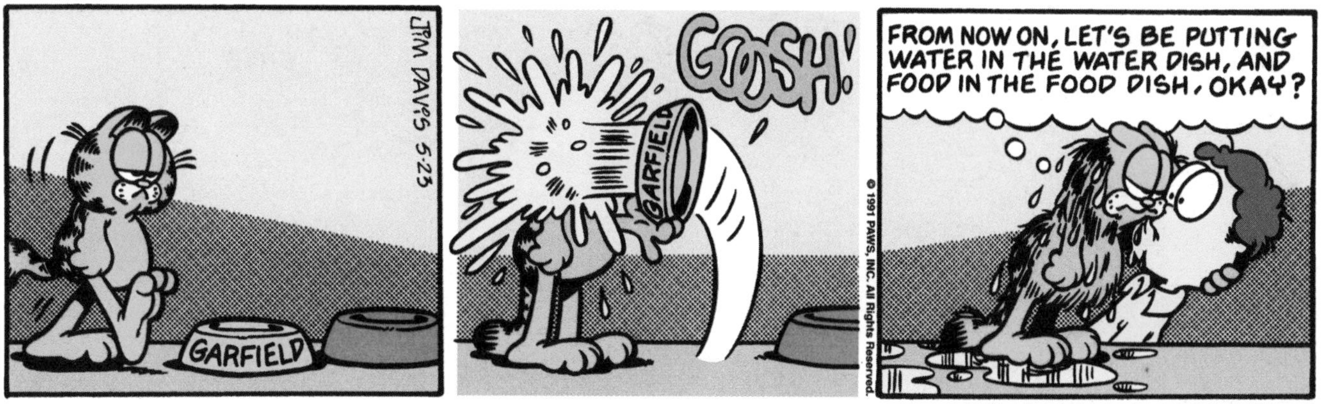
JIM DAVIS 5-23
GOOSH!
GARFIELD
© 1991 PAWS, INC. All Rights Reserved.
FROM NOW ON, LET'S BE PUTTING WATER IN THE WATER DISH, AND FOOD IN THE FOOD DISH, OKAY?

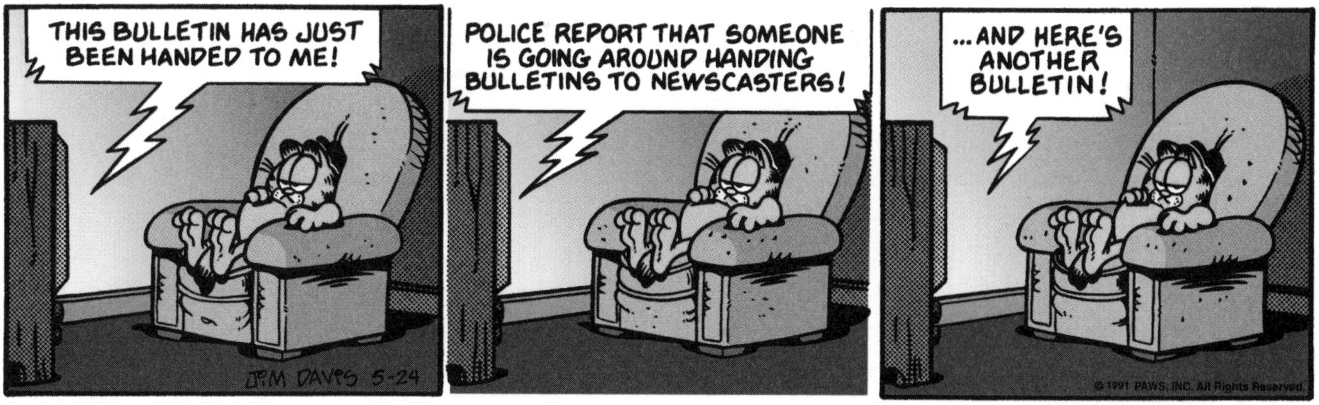
THIS BULLETIN HAS JUST BEEN HANDED TO ME!
JIM DAVIS 5-24
POLICE REPORT THAT SOMEONE IS GOING AROUND HANDING BULLETINS TO NEWSCASTERS!
...AND HERE'S ANOTHER BULLETIN!
© 1991 PAWS, INC. All Rights Reserved.

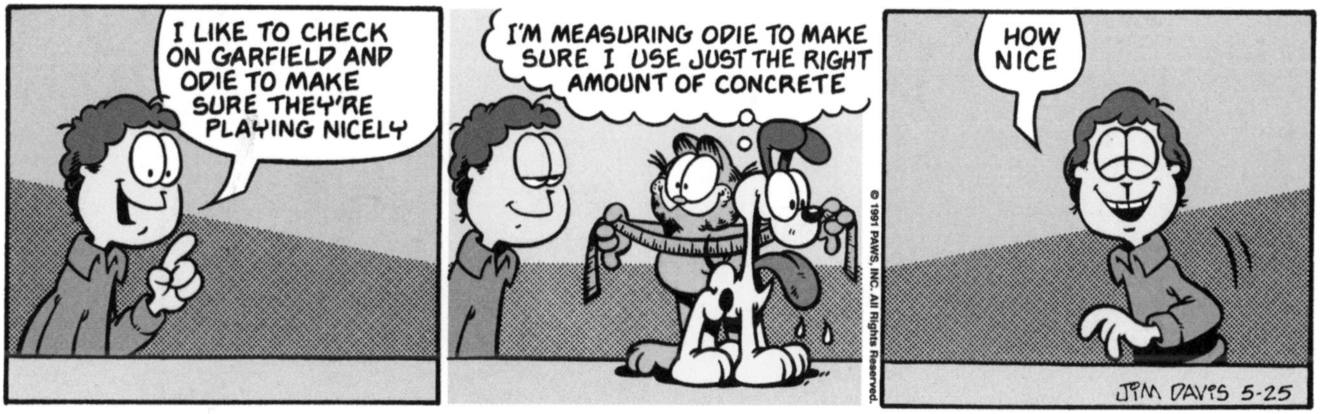
I LIKE TO CHECK ON GARFIELD AND ODIE TO MAKE SURE THEY'RE PLAYING NICELY
I'M MEASURING ODIE TO MAKE SURE I USE JUST THE RIGHT AMOUNT OF CONCRETE
© 1991 PAWS, INC. All Rights Reserved.
HOW NICE
JIM DAVIS 5-25

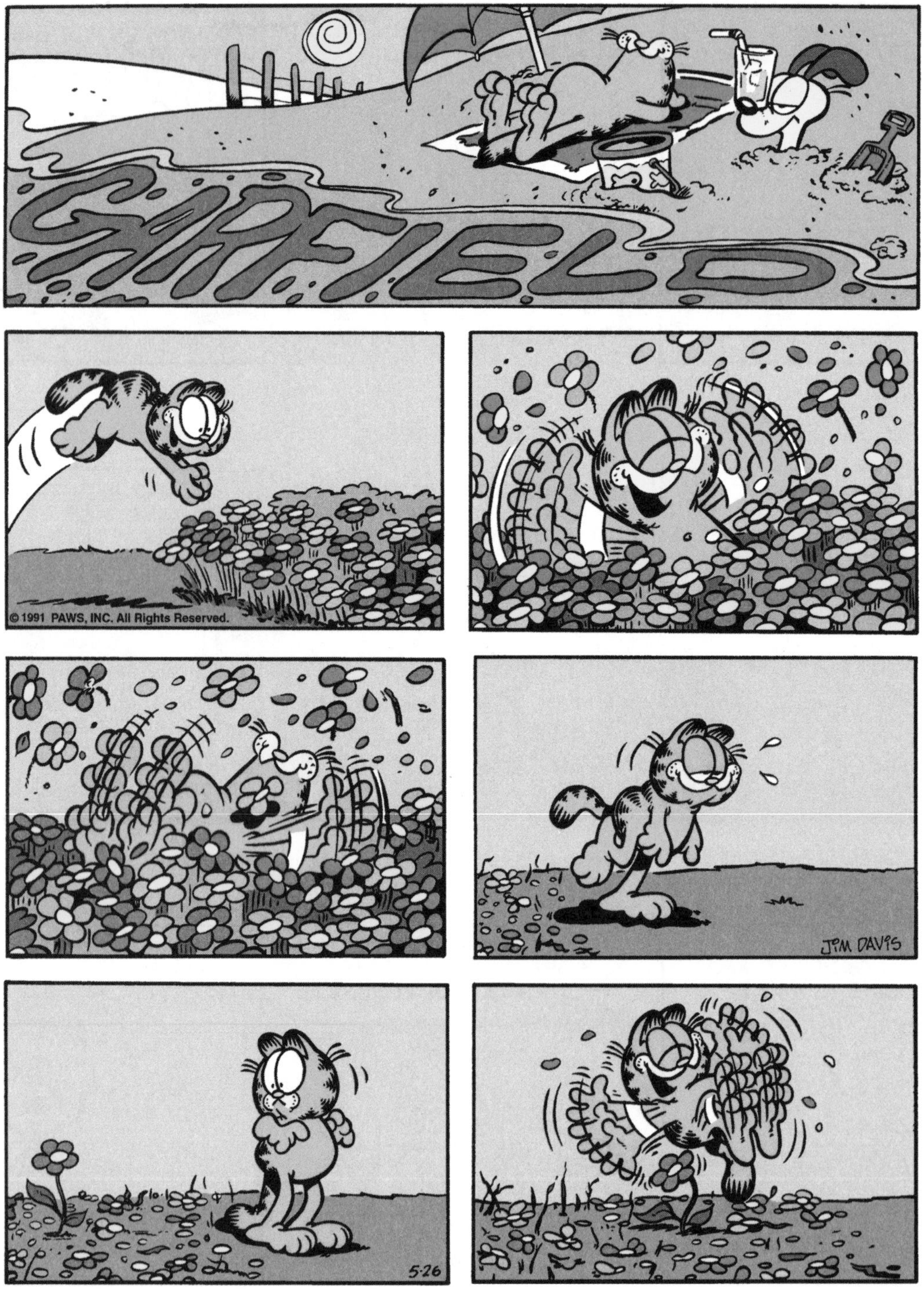
GARFIELD
© 1991 PAWS, INC. All Rights Reserved.
JIM DAVIS
5-26

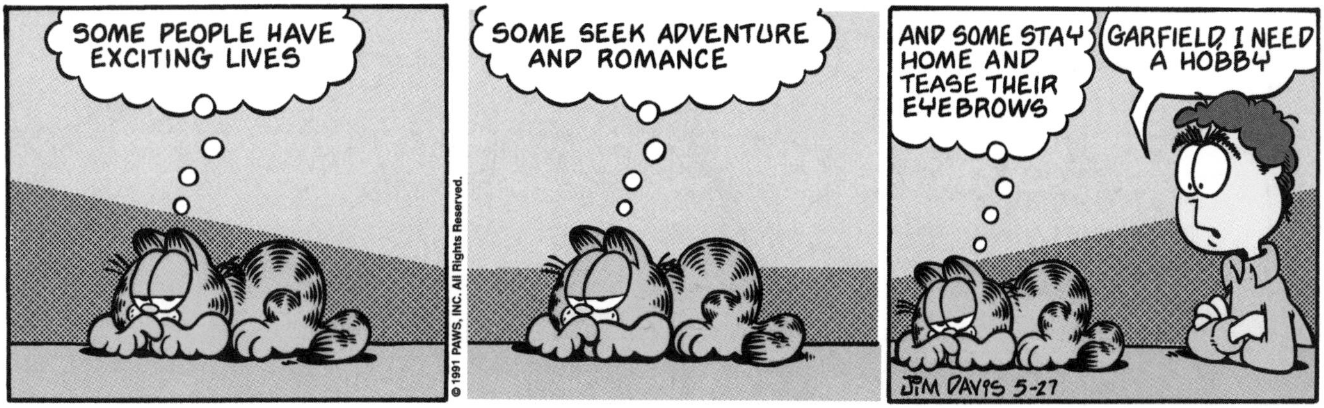
SOME PEOPLE HAVE EXCITING LIVES
SOME SEEK ADVENTURE AND ROMANCE
AND SOME STAY HOME AND TEASE THEIR EYEBROWS
GARFIELD, I NEED A HOBBY
© 1991 PAWS, INC. All Rights Reserved.
JIM DAVIS 5-27

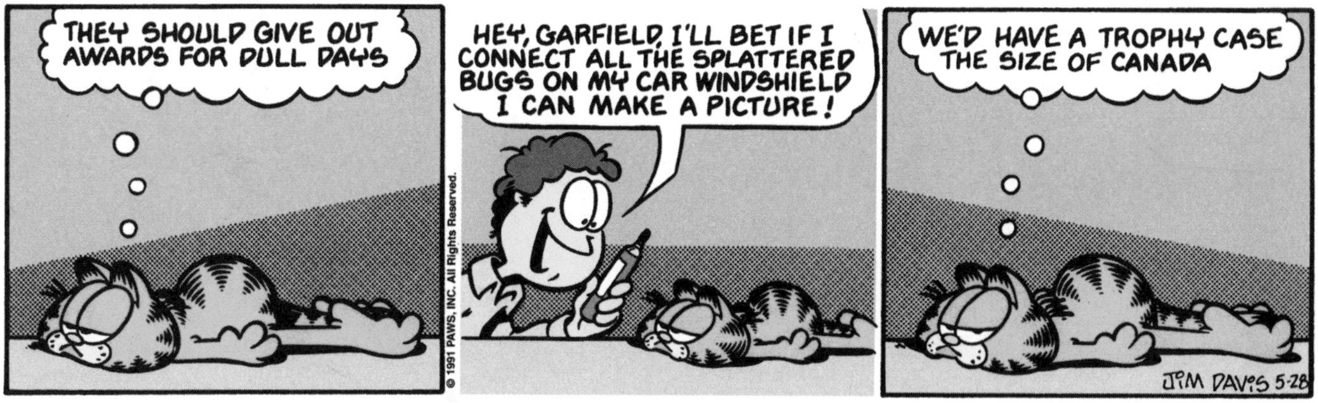
THEY SHOULD GIVE OUT AWARDS FOR DULL DAYS
HEY, GARFIELD, I'LL BET IF I CONNECT ALL THE SPLATTERED BUGS ON MY CAR WINDSHIELD I CAN MAKE A PICTURE!
WE'D HAVE A TROPHY CASE THE SIZE OF CANADA
© 1991 PAWS, INC. All Rights Reserved.
JIM DAVIS 5-28

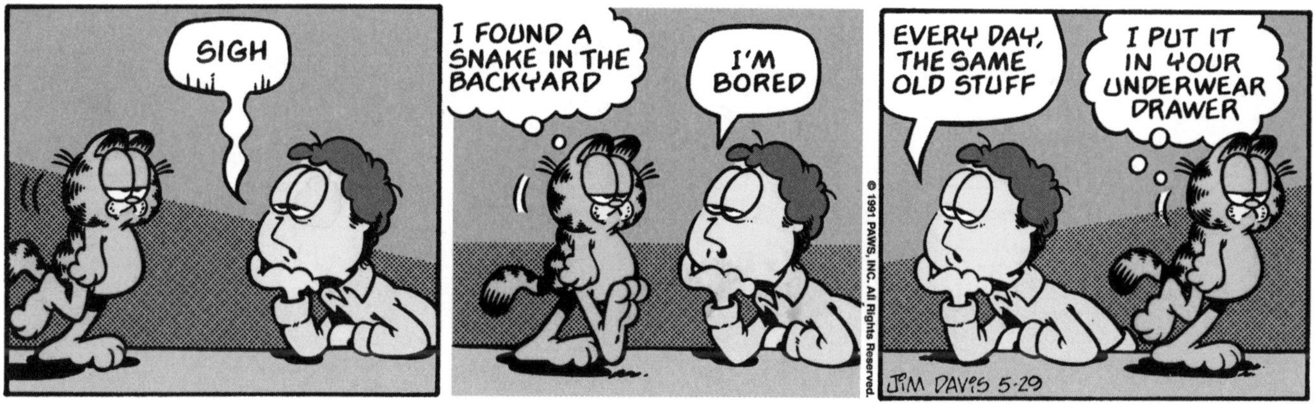
SIGH
I FOUND A SNAKE IN THE BACKYARD
I'M BORED
EVERY DAY, THE SAME OLD STUFF
I PUT IT IN YOUR UNDERWEAR DRAWER
© 1991 PAWS, INC. All Rights Reserved.
JIM DAVIS 5-29

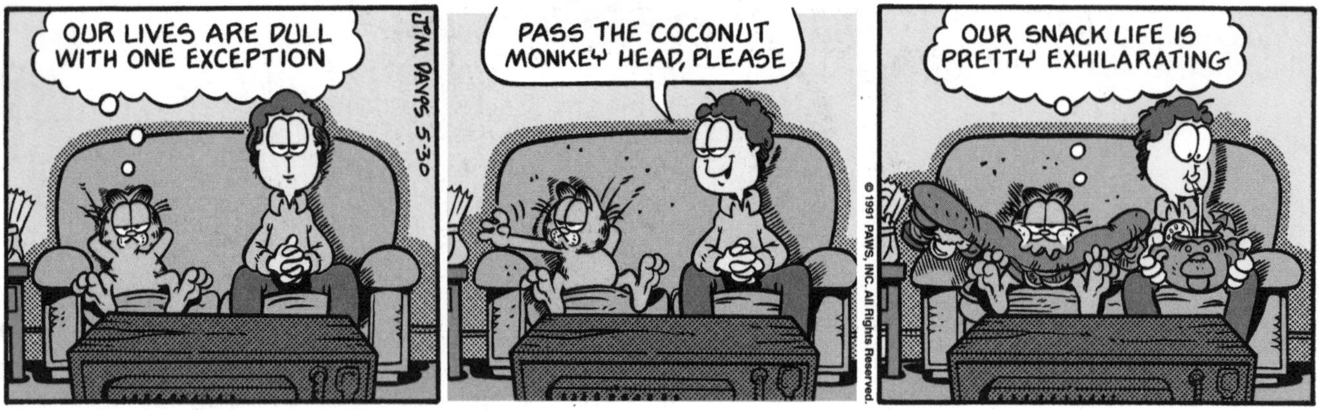
OUR LIVES ARE DULL WITH ONE EXCEPTION
JIM DAVIS 5-30
PASS THE COCONUT MONKEY HEAD, PLEASE
© 1991 PAWS, INC. All Rights Reserved.
OUR SNACK LIFE IS PRETTY EXHILARATING

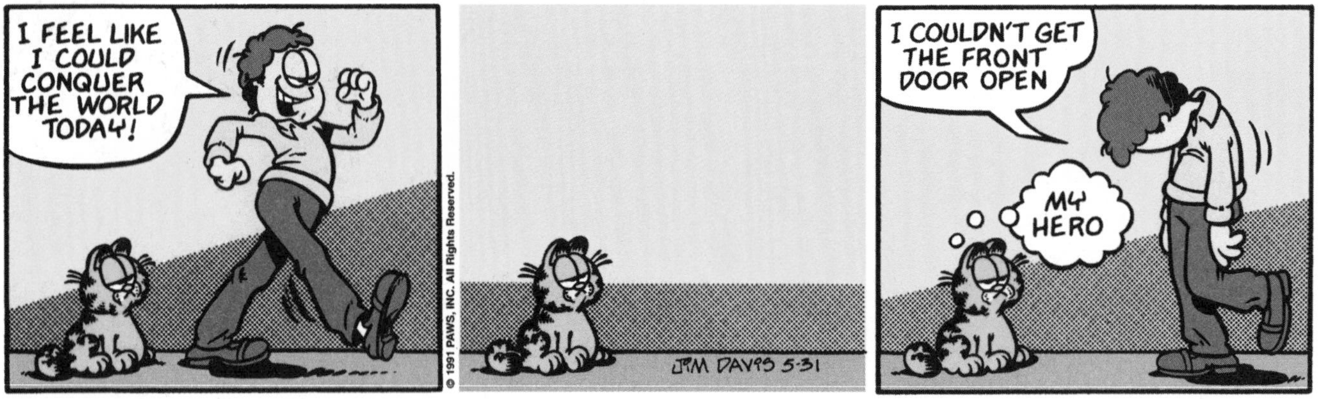
I FEEL LIKE I COULD CONQUER THE WORLD TODAY!
© 1991 PAWS, INC. All Rights Reserved.
JIM DAVIS 5-31
I COULDN'T GET THE FRONT DOOR OPEN
MY HERO

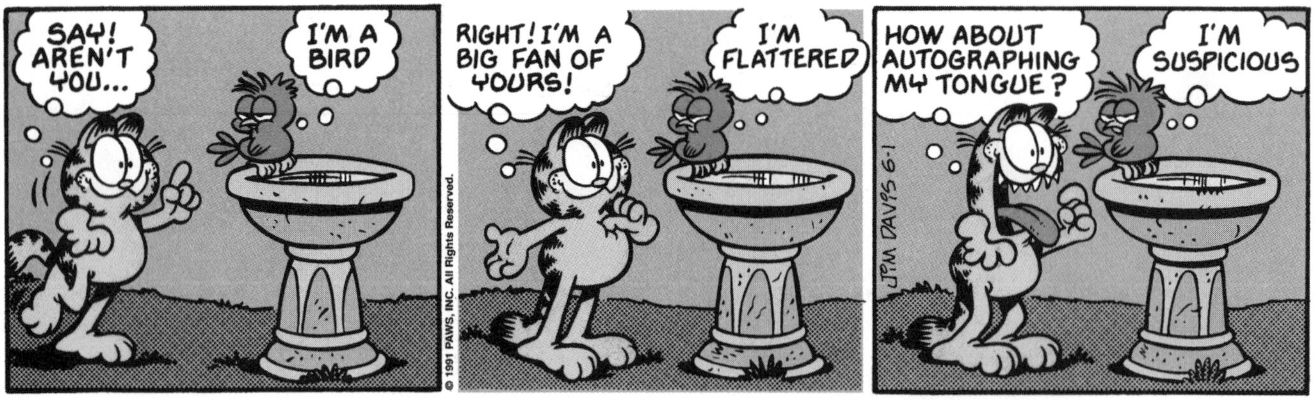
SAY! AREN'T YOU...
I'M A BIRD
© 1991 PAWS, INC. All Rights Reserved.
RIGHT! I'M A BIG FAN OF YOURS!
I'M FLATTERED
HOW ABOUT AUTOGRAPHING MY TONGUE?
I'M SUSPICIOUS
JIM DAVIS 6-1

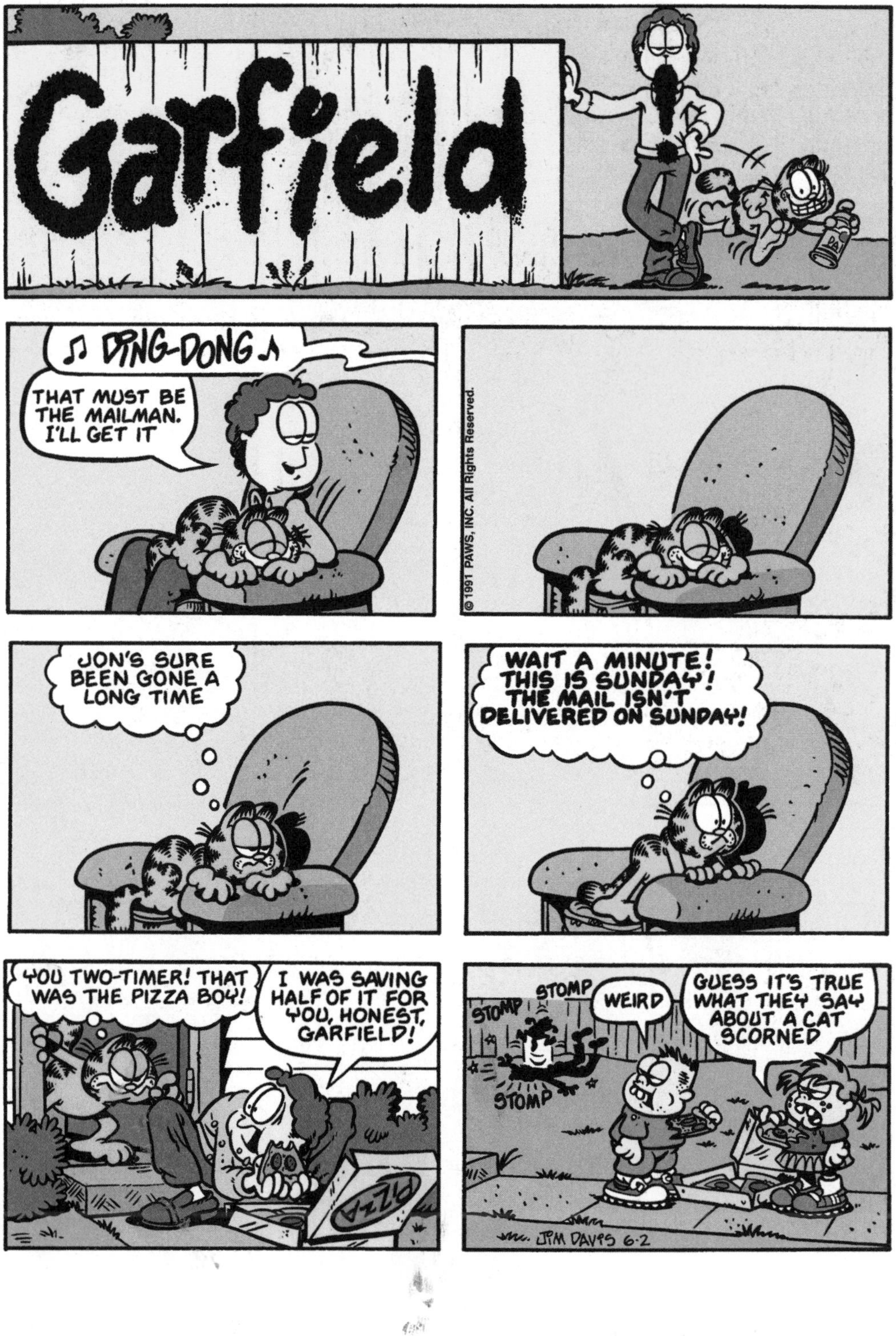
Garfield
♫ DING-DONG ♪
THAT MUST BE THE MAILMAN. I'LL GET IT
© 1991 PAWS, INC. All Rights Reserved.
JON'S SURE BEEN GONE A LONG TIME
WAIT A MINUTE! THIS IS SUNDAY! THE MAIL ISN'T DELIVERED ON SUNDAY!
YOU TWO-TIMER! THAT WAS THE PIZZA BOY!
I WAS SAVING HALF OF IT FOR YOU, HONEST, GARFIELD!
PIZZA
STOMP
STOMP
STOMP
WEIRD
GUESS IT'S TRUE WHAT THEY SAY ABOUT A CAT SCORNED
JIM DAVIS 6-2

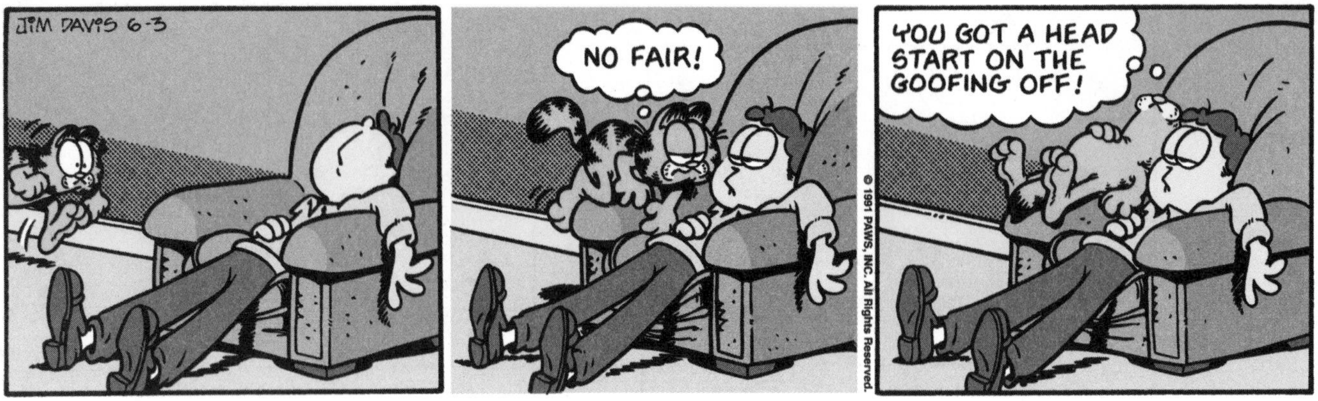
JIM DAVIS 6-3
NO FAIR!
© 1991 PAWS, INC. All Rights Reserved.
YOU GOT A HEAD START ON THE GOOFING OFF!

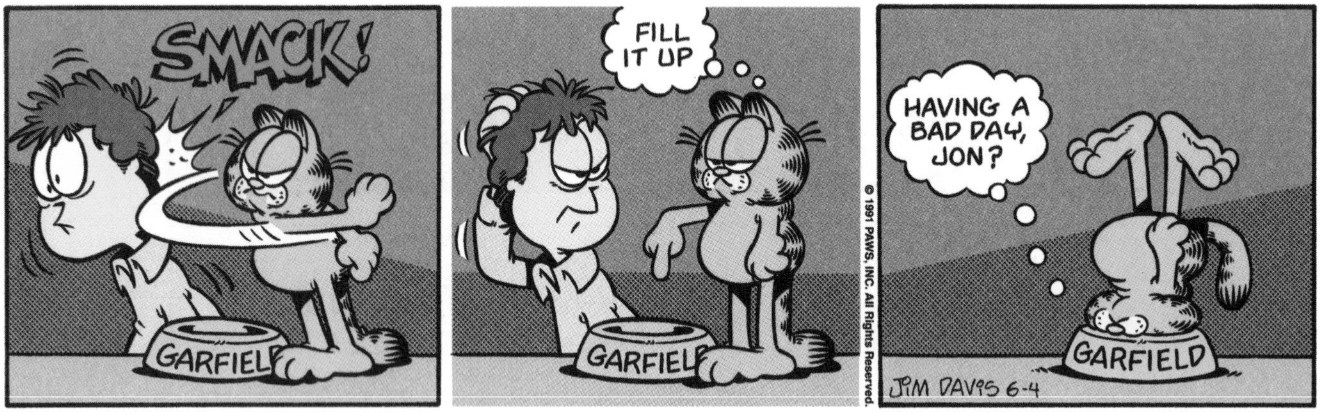
SMACK!
GARFIELD
FILL IT UP
GARFIELD
© 1991 PAWS, INC. All Rights Reserved.
HAVING A BAD DAY, JON?
GARFIELD
JIM DAVIS 6-4

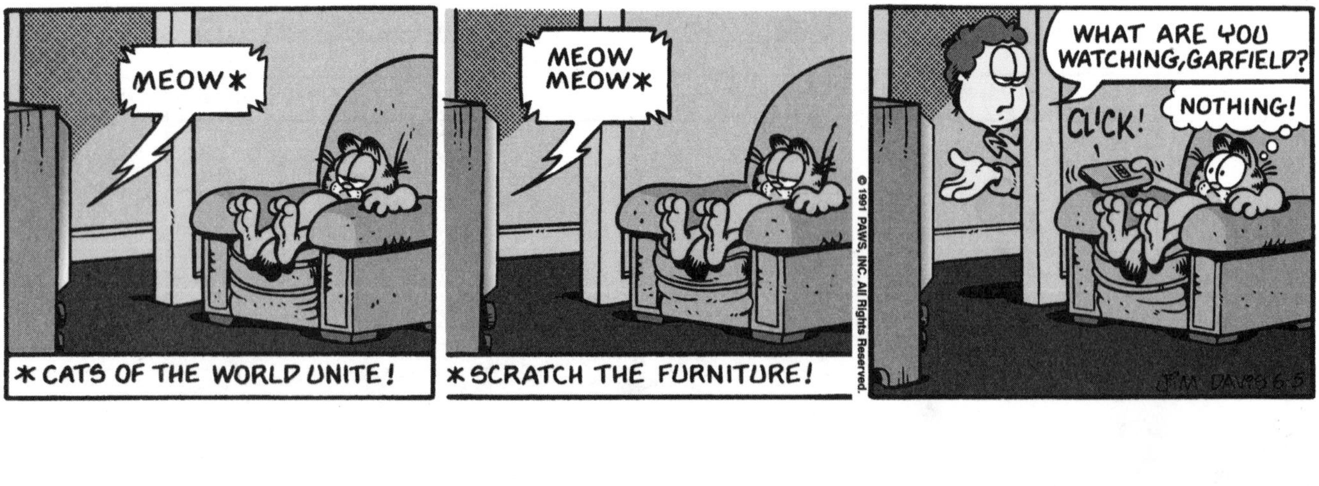
MEOW*
*CATS OF THE WORLD UNITE!
MEOW MEOW*
*SCRATCH THE FURNITURE!
© 1991 PAWS, INC. All Rights Reserved.
WHAT ARE YOU WATCHING, GARFIELD?
CLICK!
NOTHING!
JIM DAVIS 6-5

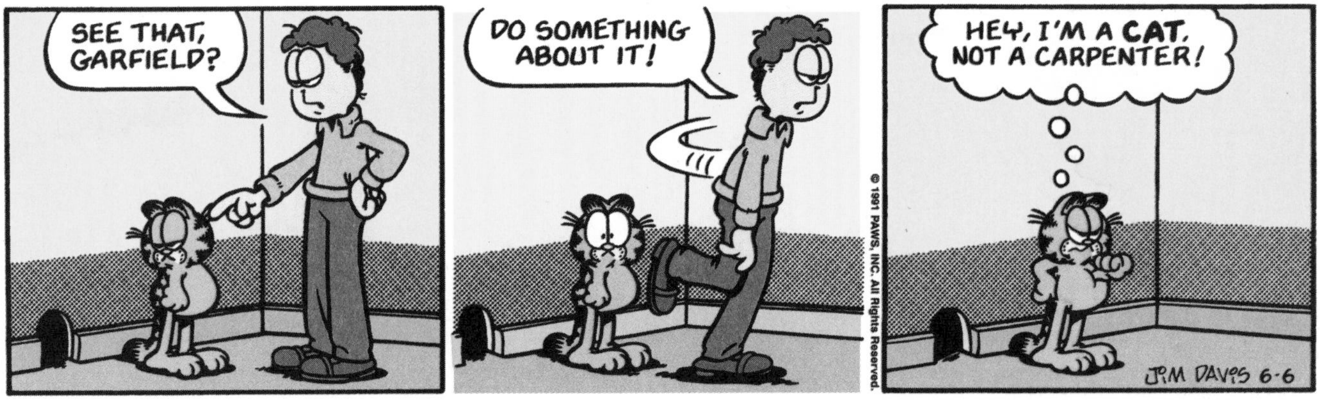
SEE THAT, GARFIELD?
DO SOMETHING ABOUT IT!
HEY, I'M A **CAT**, NOT A CARPENTER!
© 1991 PAWS, INC. All Rights Reserved.
JIM DAVIS 6-6

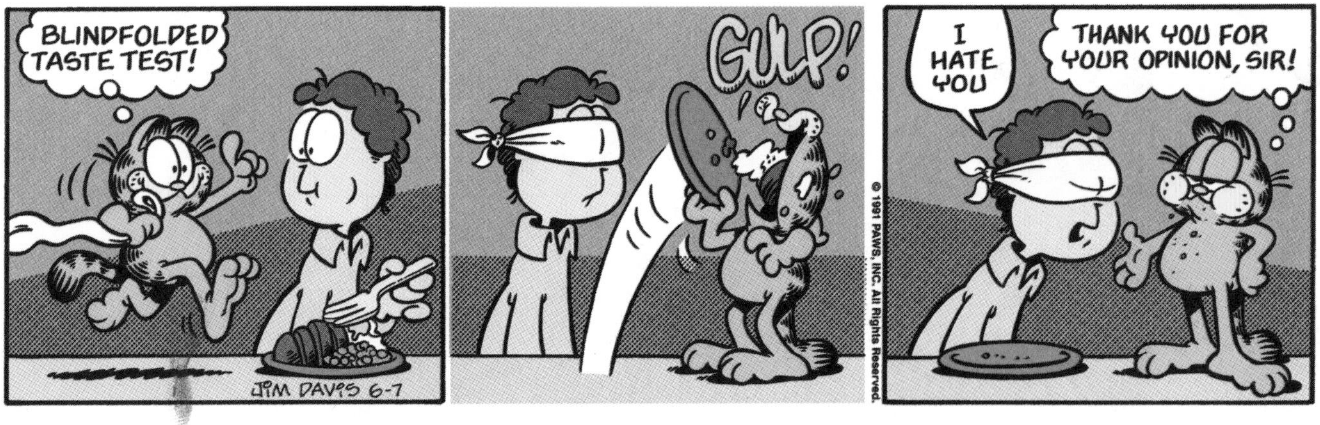
BLINDFOLDED TASTE TEST!
JIM DAVIS 6-7
GULP!
© 1991 PAWS, INC. All Rights Reserved.
I HATE YOU
THANK YOU FOR YOUR OPINION, SIR!

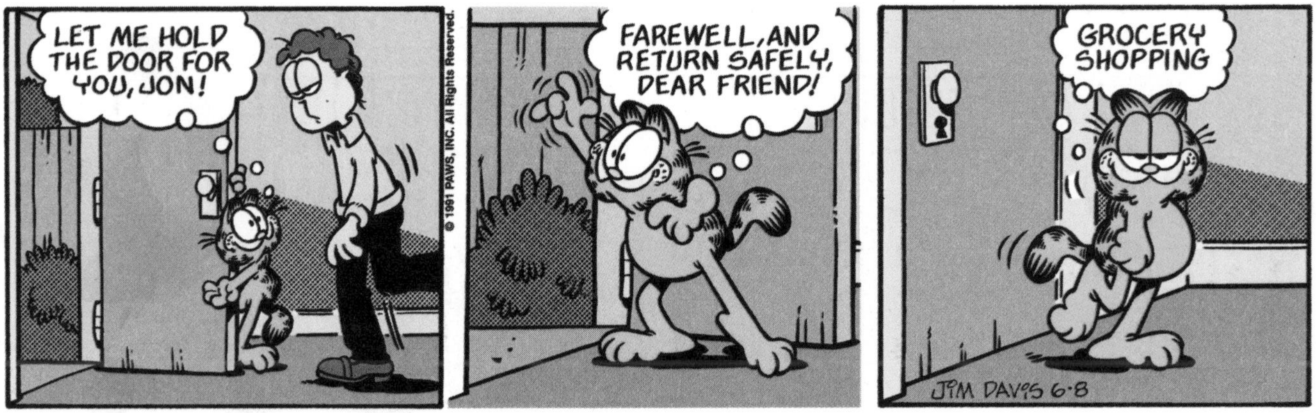
LET ME HOLD THE DOOR FOR YOU, JON!
© 1991 PAWS, INC. All Rights Reserved.
FAREWELL, AND RETURN SAFELY, DEAR FRIEND!
GROCERY SHOPPING
JIM DAVIS 6-8

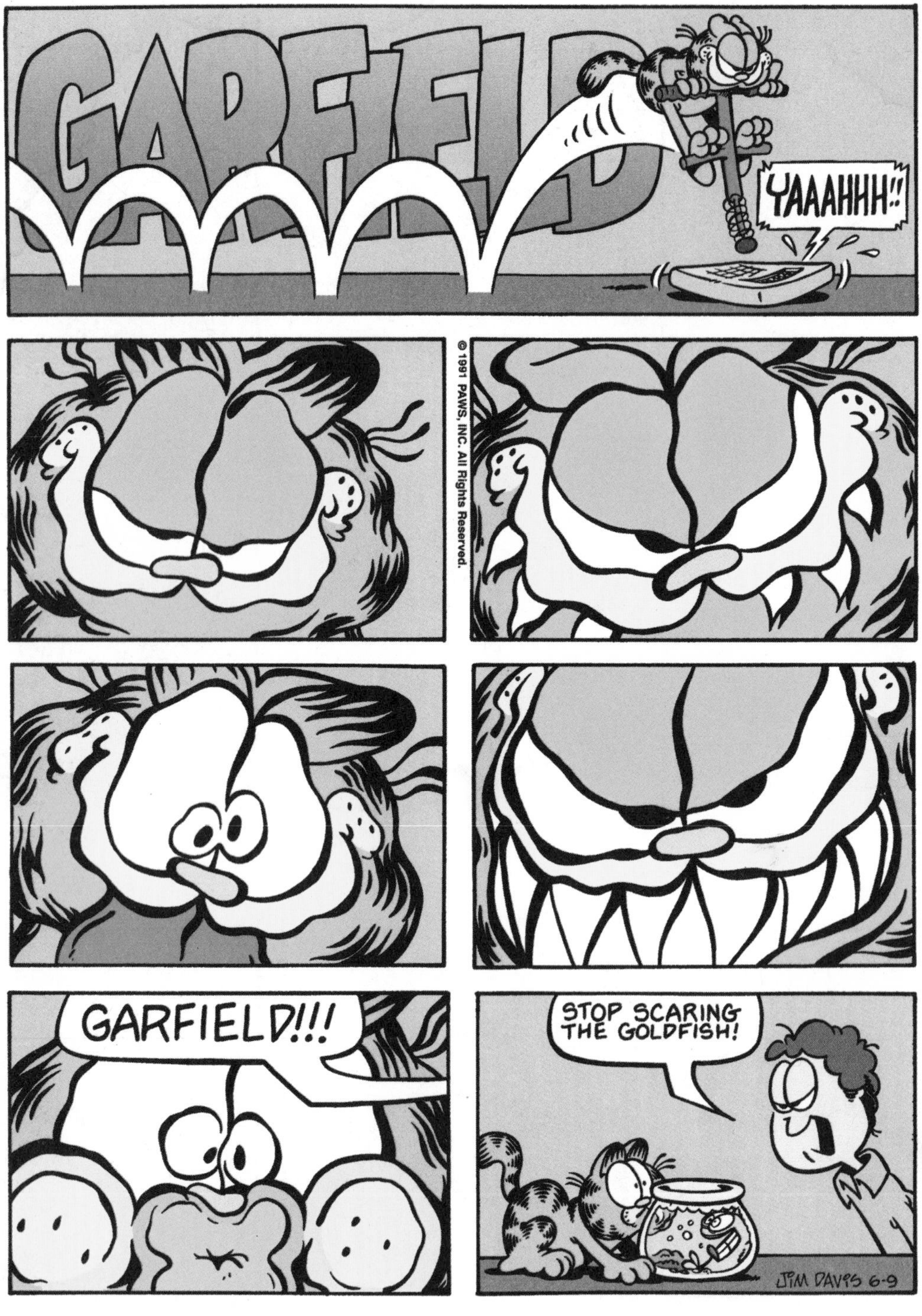
GARFIELD
YAAAHHH!!
© 1991 PAWS, INC. All Rights Reserved.
GARFIELD!!!
STOP SCARING THE GOLDFISH!
JIM DAVIS 6-9

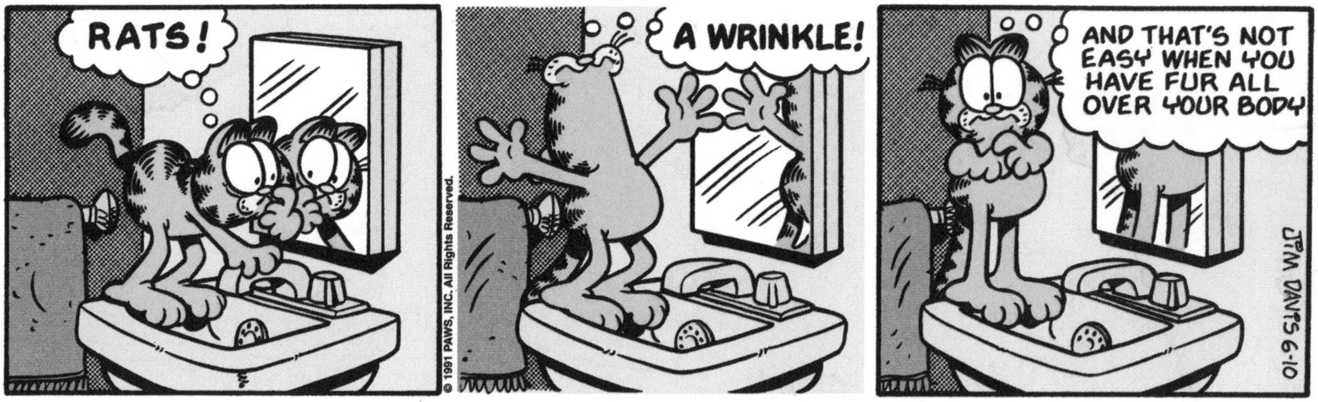
RATS!
A WRINKLE!
AND THAT'S NOT EASY WHEN YOU HAVE FUR ALL OVER YOUR BODY
JIM DAVIS 6-10

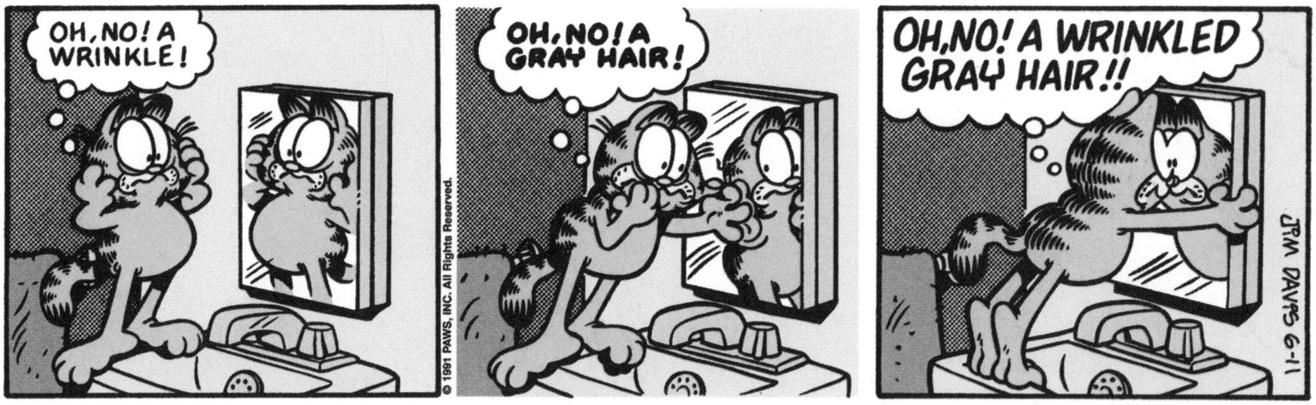
OH, NO! A WRINKLE!
OH, NO! A GRAY HAIR!
OH, NO! A WRINKLED GRAY HAIR!!
JIM DAVIS 6-11

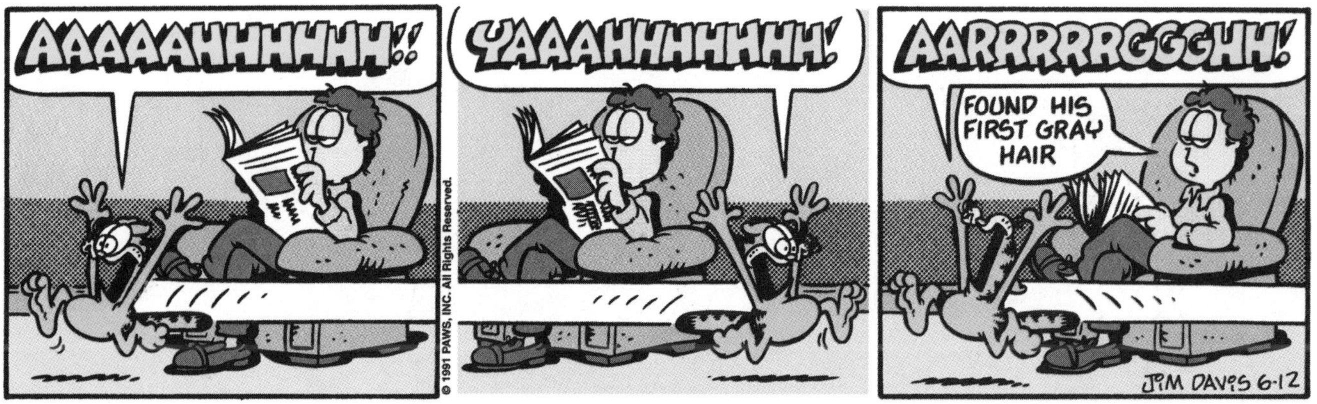
AAAAAHHHHHH!!
YAAAHHHHHHH!
AARRRRRGGGHH!
FOUND HIS FIRST GRAY HAIR
JIM DAVIS 6-12

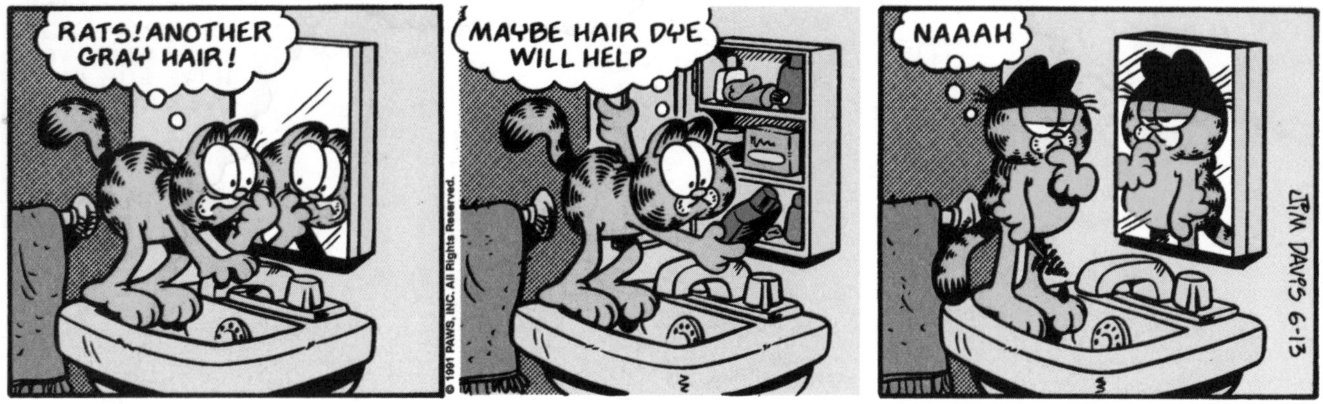
RATS! ANOTHER GRAY HAIR!
MAYBE HAIR DYE WILL HELP
NAAAH
© 1991 PAWS, INC. All Rights Reserved.
JIM DAVIS 6-13

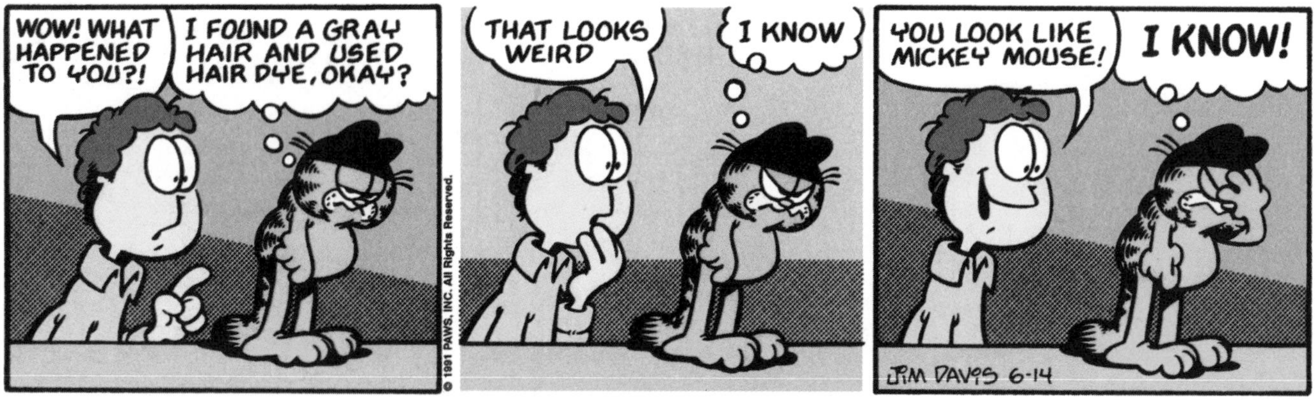
WOW! WHAT HAPPENED TO YOU?!
I FOUND A GRAY HAIR AND USED HAIR DYE, OKAY?
THAT LOOKS WEIRD
I KNOW
YOU LOOK LIKE MICKEY MOUSE!
I KNOW!
© 1991 PAWS, INC. All Rights Reserved.
JIM DAVIS 6-14

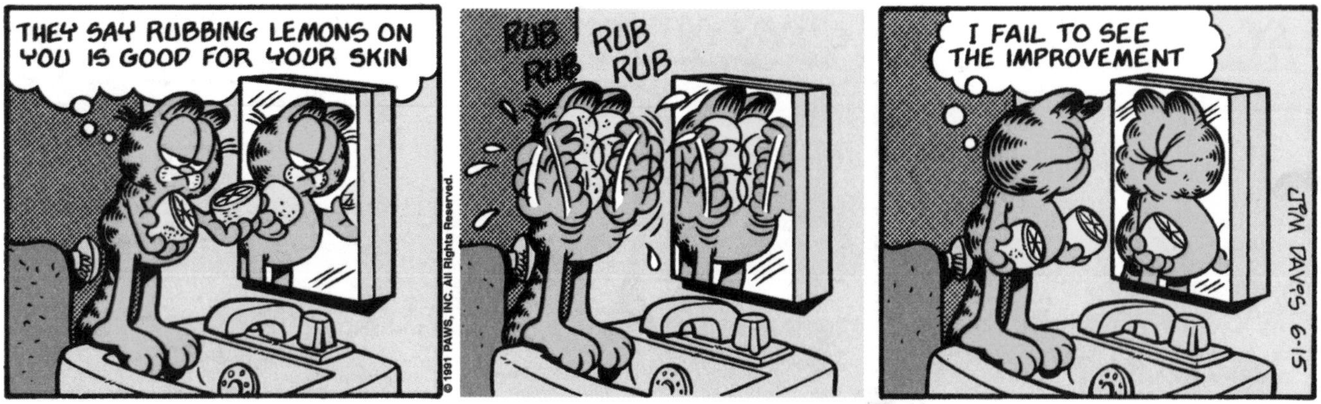
THEY SAY RUBBING LEMONS ON YOU IS GOOD FOR YOUR SKIN
RUB RUB
RUB RUB
I FAIL TO SEE THE IMPROVEMENT
© 1991 PAWS, INC. All Rights Reserved.
JIM DAVIS 6-15

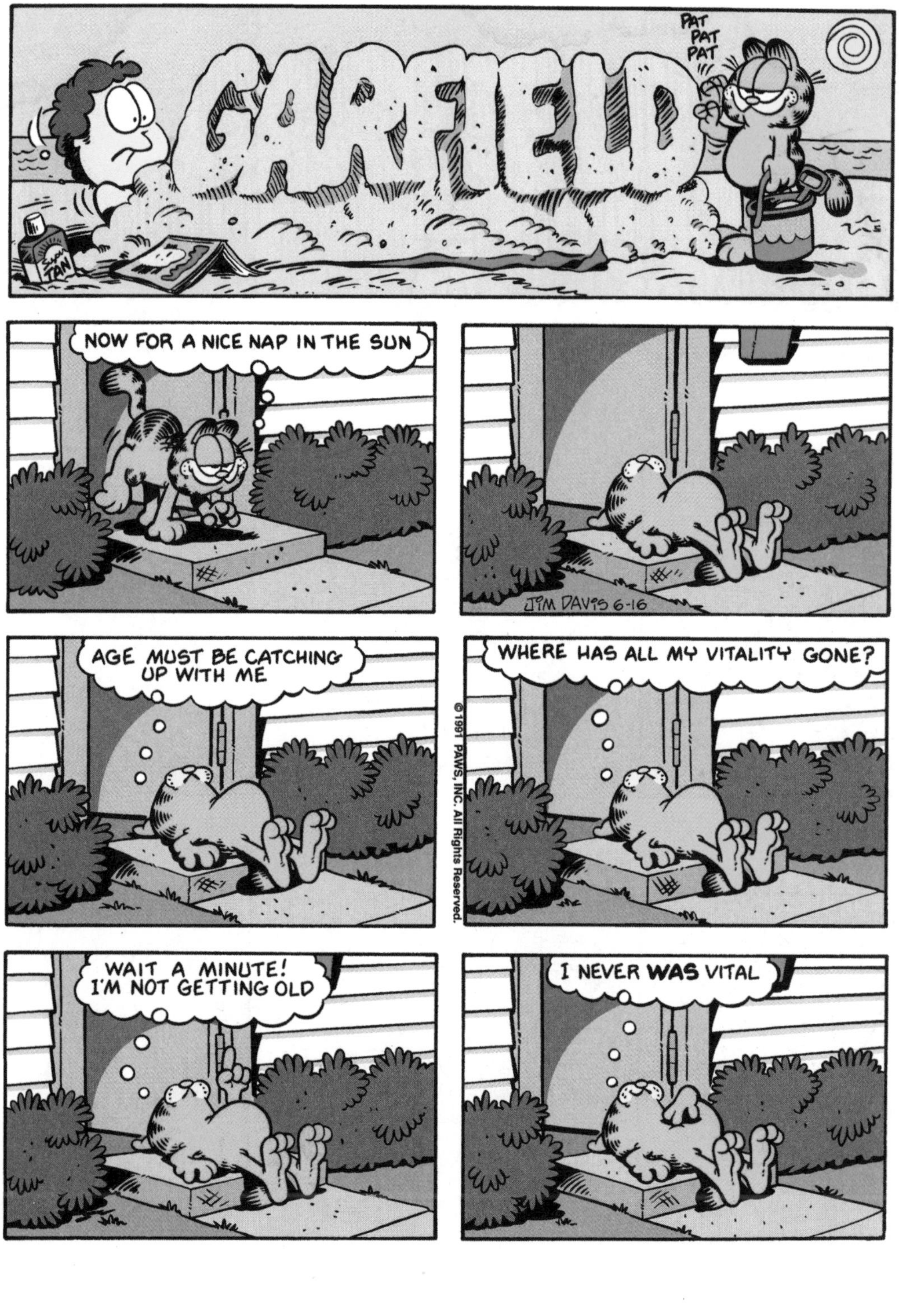
PAT
PAT
PAT
GARFIELD
SUPER TAN
NOW FOR A NICE NAP IN THE SUN
JIM DAVIS 6-16
AGE MUST BE CATCHING UP WITH ME
WHERE HAS ALL MY VITALITY GONE?
WAIT A MINUTE! I'M NOT GETTING OLD
I NEVER **WAS** VITAL

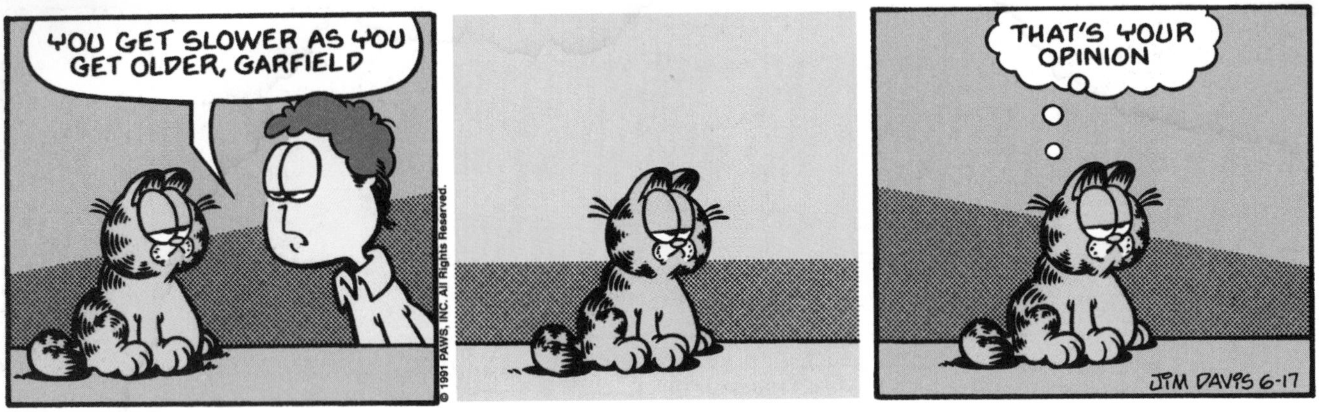
YOU GET SLOWER AS YOU GET OLDER, GARFIELD
© 1991 PAWS, INC. All Rights Reserved.
THAT'S YOUR OPINION
JIM DAVIS 6-17

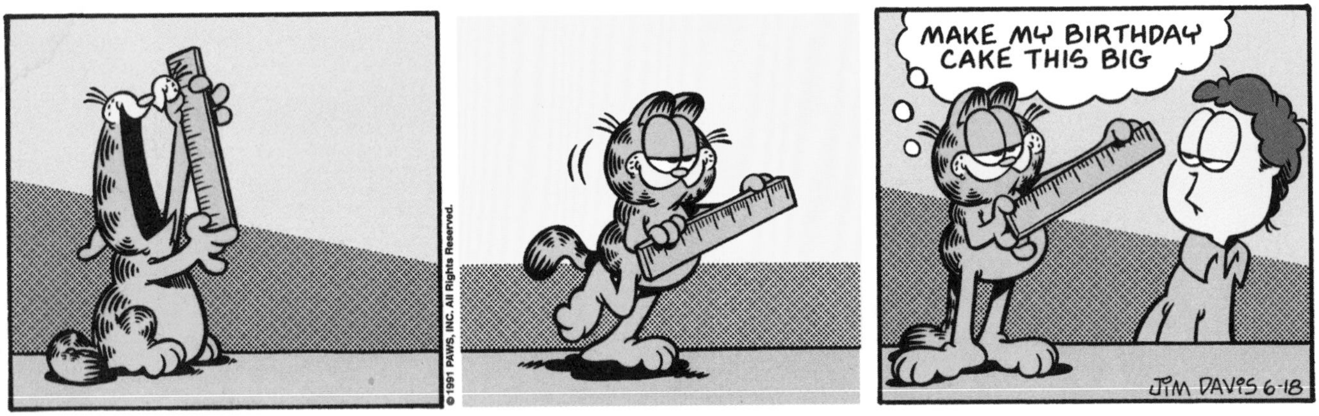
© 1991 PAWS, INC. All Rights Reserved.
MAKE MY BIRTHDAY CAKE THIS BIG
JIM DAVIS 6-18

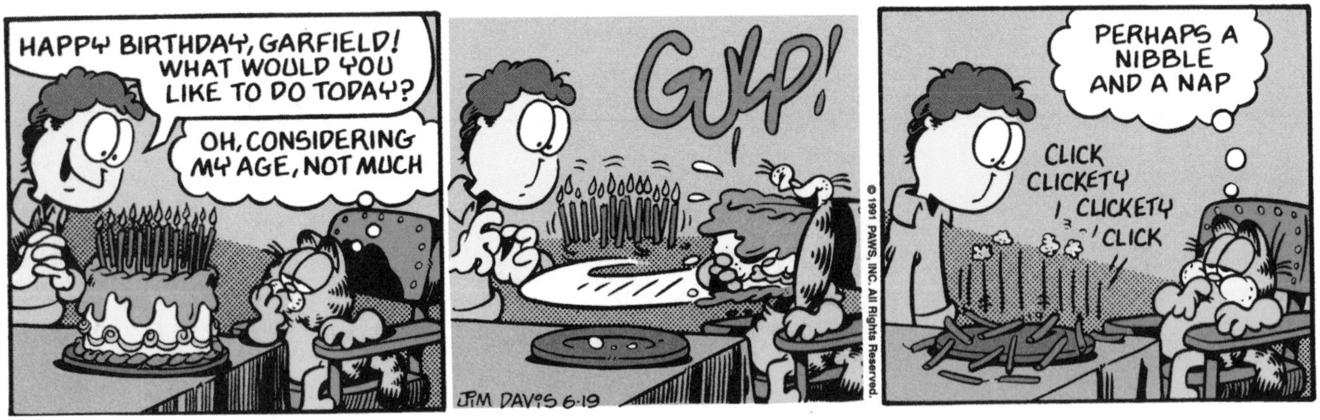
HAPPY BIRTHDAY, GARFIELD! WHAT WOULD YOU LIKE TO DO TODAY?
OH, CONSIDERING MY AGE, NOT MUCH
GULP!
JIM DAVIS 6-19
© 1991 PAWS, INC. All Rights Reserved.
PERHAPS A NIBBLE AND A NAP
CLICK
CLICKETY
CLICKETY
CLICK

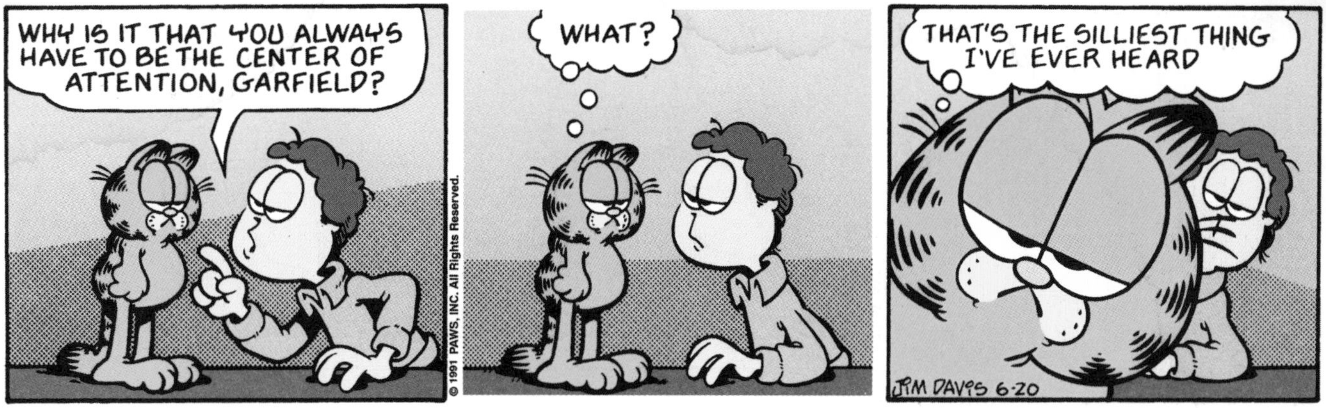
WHY IS IT THAT YOU ALWAYS HAVE TO BE THE CENTER OF ATTENTION, GARFIELD?
WHAT?
THAT'S THE SILLIEST THING I'VE EVER HEARD
© 1991 PAWS, INC. All Rights Reserved.
JIM DAVIS 6-20

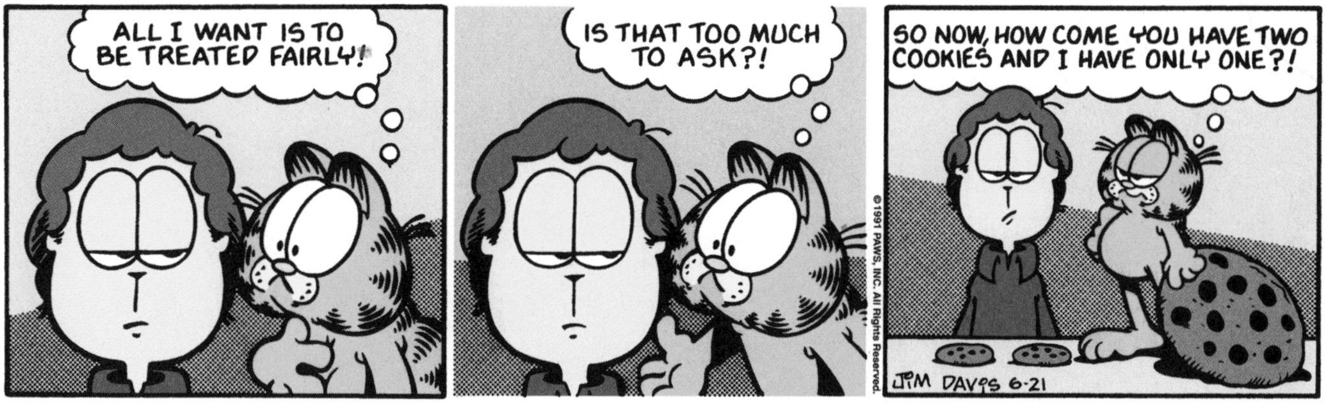
ALL I WANT IS TO BE TREATED FAIRLY!
IS THAT TOO MUCH TO ASK?!
SO NOW, HOW COME YOU HAVE TWO COOKIES AND I HAVE ONLY ONE?!
© 1991 PAWS, INC. All Rights Reserved.
JIM DAVIS 6-21

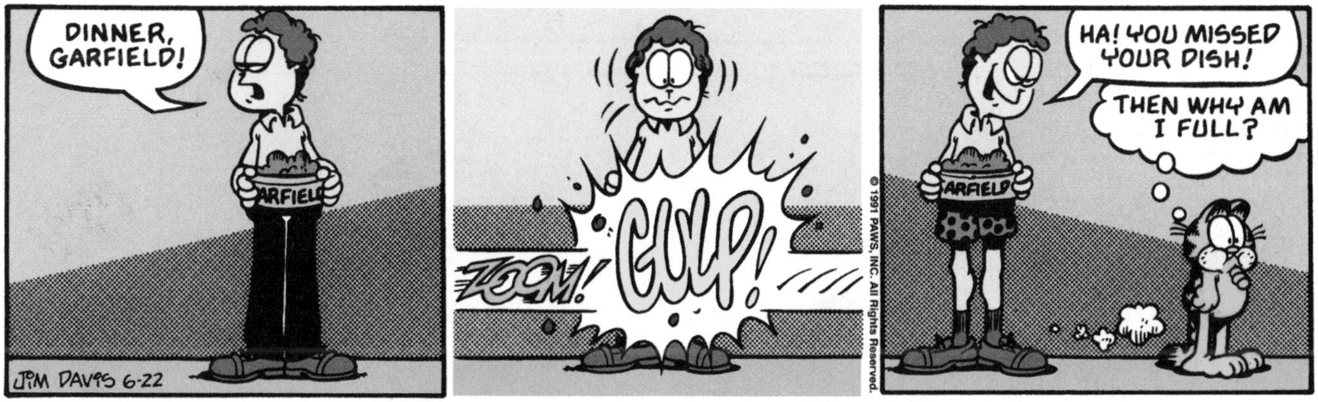
DINNER, GARFIELD!
GARFIELD
ZOOM!
GULP!
HA! YOU MISSED YOUR DISH!
THEN WHY AM I FULL?
© 1991 PAWS, INC. All Rights Reserved.
JIM DAVIS 6-22

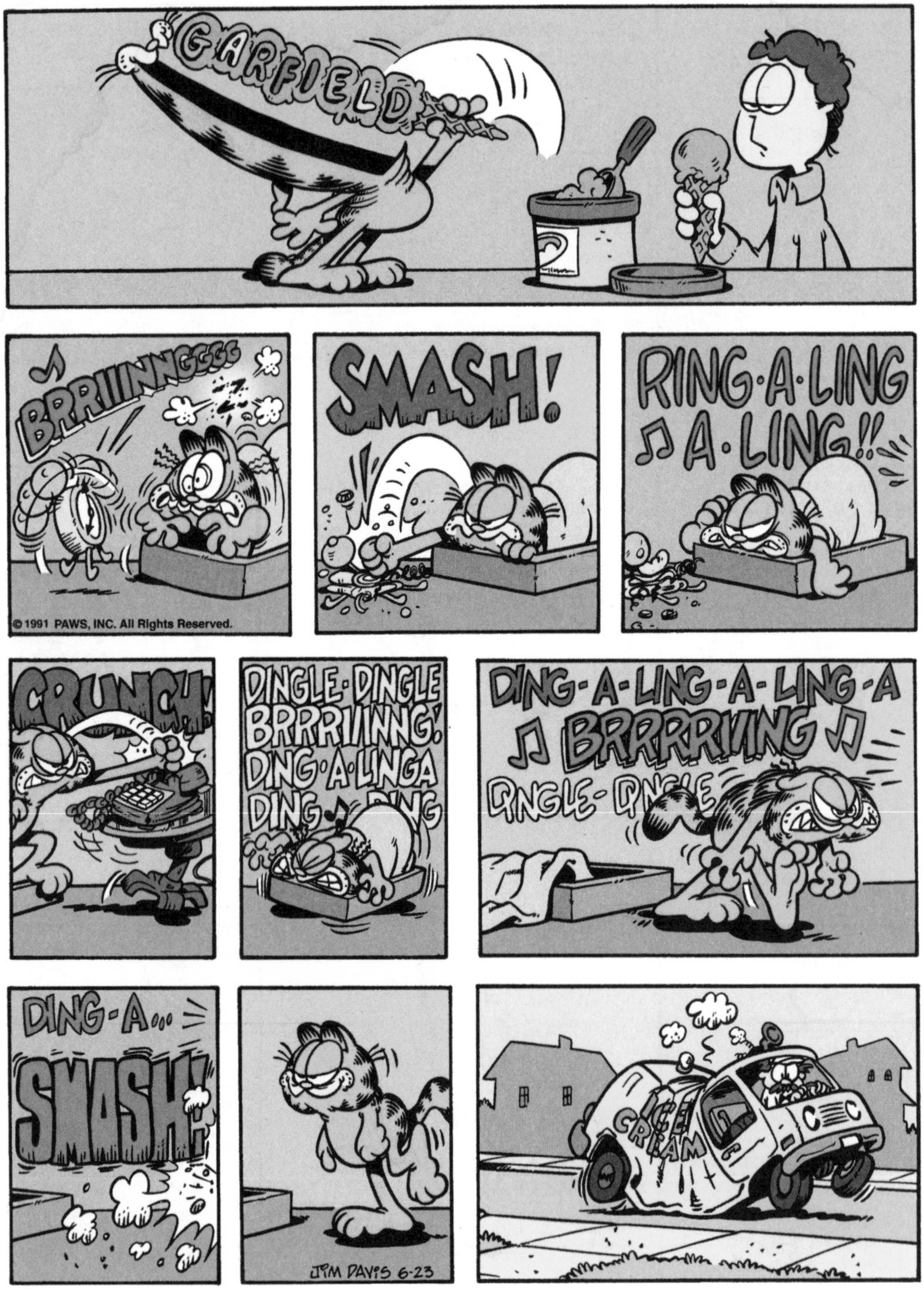
GARFIELD
BRRIIINNGGGG
SMASH!
RING-A-LING A-LING!!
CRUNCH!
DINGLE-DINGLE BRRRIIINNG! DING-A-LINGA DING DING
DING-A-LING-A-LING-A BRRRRIIING
DINGLE-DINGLE
DING-A...
SMASH!
JIM DAVIS 6-23
ICE CREAM

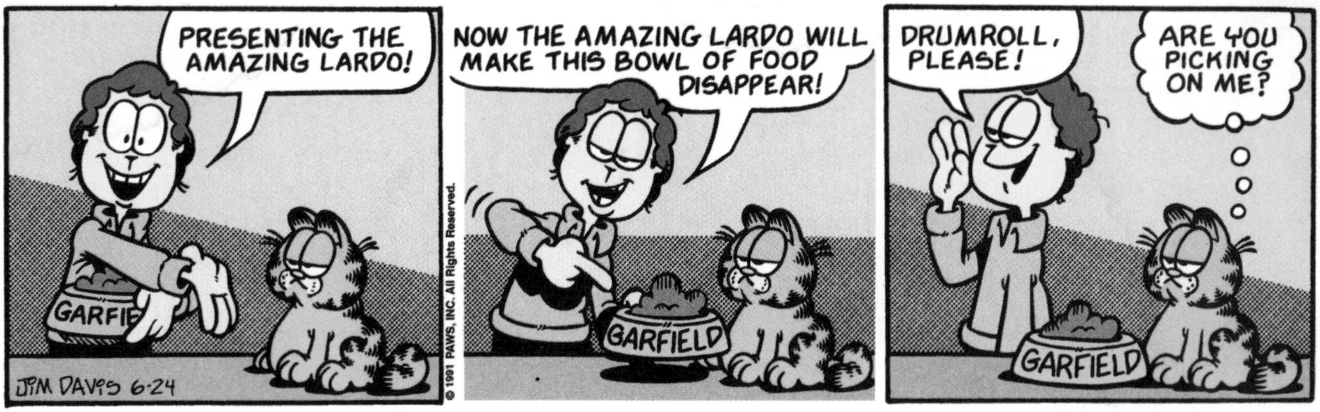
PRESENTING THE AMAZING LARDO!
JIM DAVIS 6-24
© 1991 PAWS, INC. All Rights Reserved.
NOW THE AMAZING LARDO WILL MAKE THIS BOWL OF FOOD DISAPPEAR!
DRUMROLL, PLEASE!
ARE YOU PICKING ON ME?

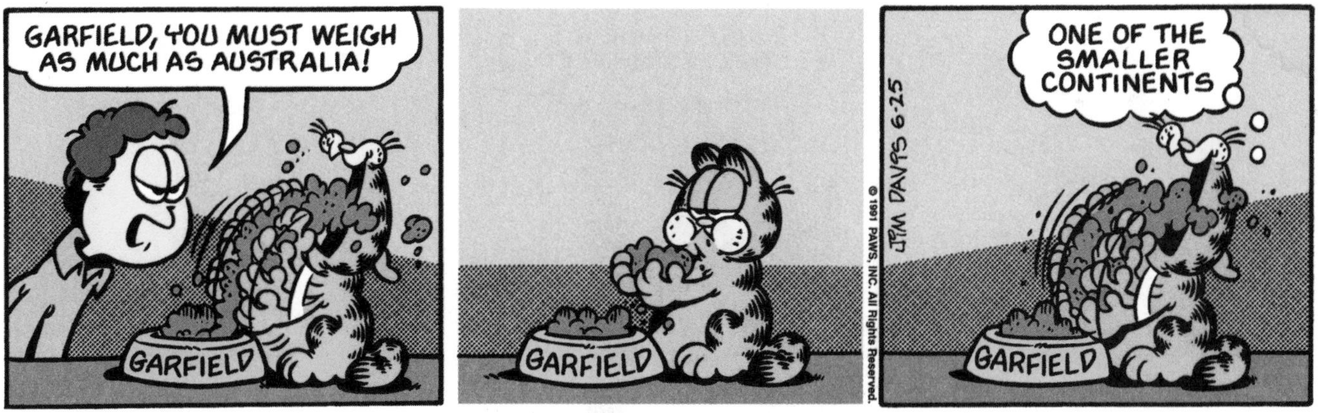
GARFIELD, YOU MUST WEIGH AS MUCH AS AUSTRALIA!
© 1991 PAWS, INC. All Rights Reserved.
JIM DAVIS 6-25
ONE OF THE SMALLER CONTINENTS

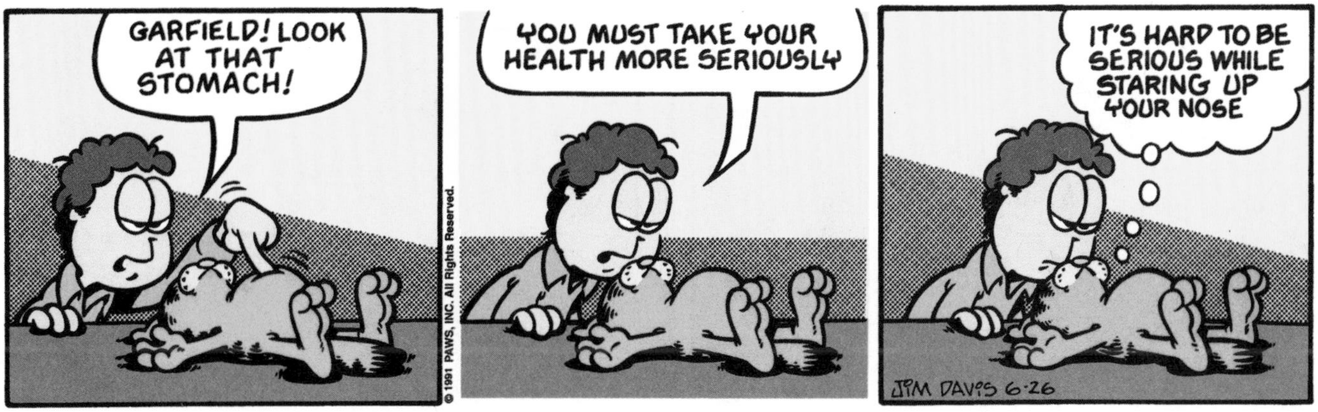
GARFIELD! LOOK AT THAT STOMACH!
© 1991 PAWS, INC. All Rights Reserved.
YOU MUST TAKE YOUR HEALTH MORE SERIOUSLY
IT'S HARD TO BE SERIOUS WHILE STARING UP YOUR NOSE
JIM DAVIS 6-26

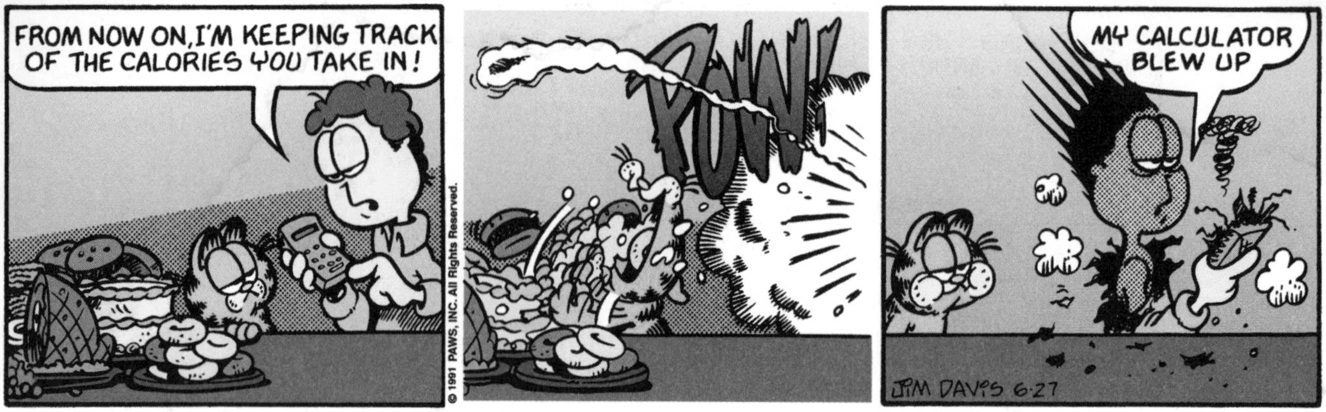
FROM NOW ON, I'M KEEPING TRACK OF THE CALORIES YOU TAKE IN!
POW!
MY CALCULATOR BLEW UP
© 1991 PAWS, INC. All Rights Reserved.
JIM DAVIS 6-27

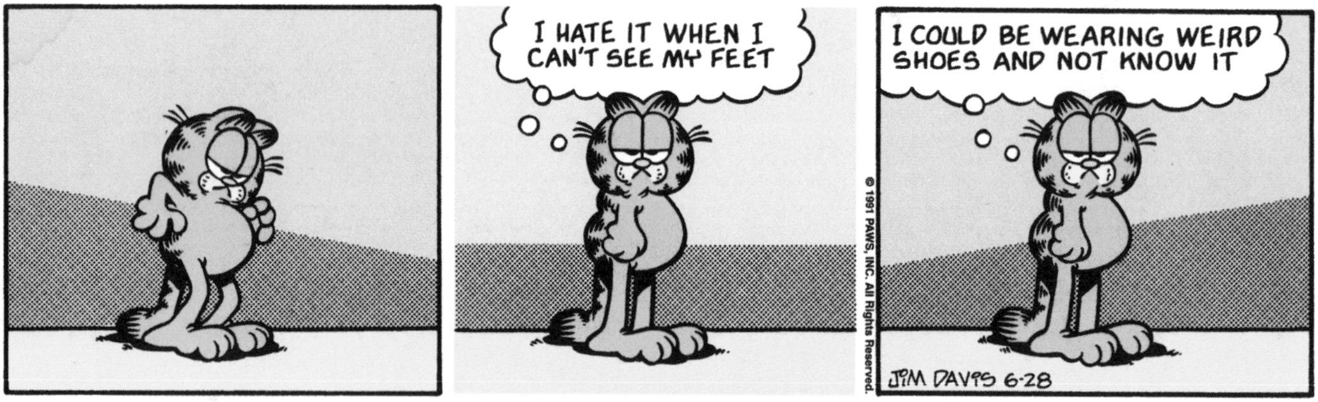
I HATE IT WHEN I CAN'T SEE MY FEET
I COULD BE WEARING WEIRD SHOES AND NOT KNOW IT
© 1991 PAWS, INC. All Rights Reserved.
JIM DAVIS 6-28

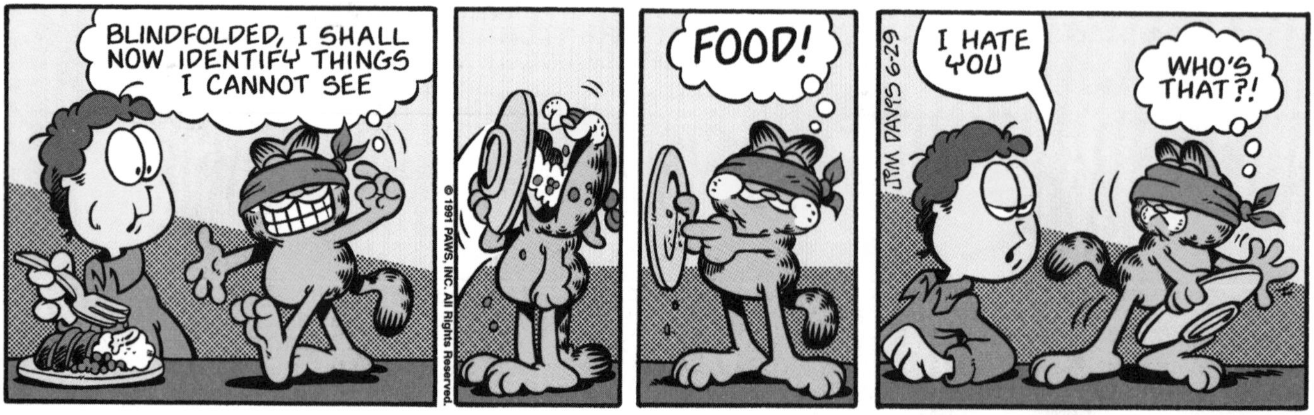
BLINDFOLDED, I SHALL NOW IDENTIFY THINGS I CANNOT SEE
FOOD!
I HATE YOU
WHO'S THAT?!
© 1991 PAWS, INC. All Rights Reserved.
JIM DAVIS 6-29

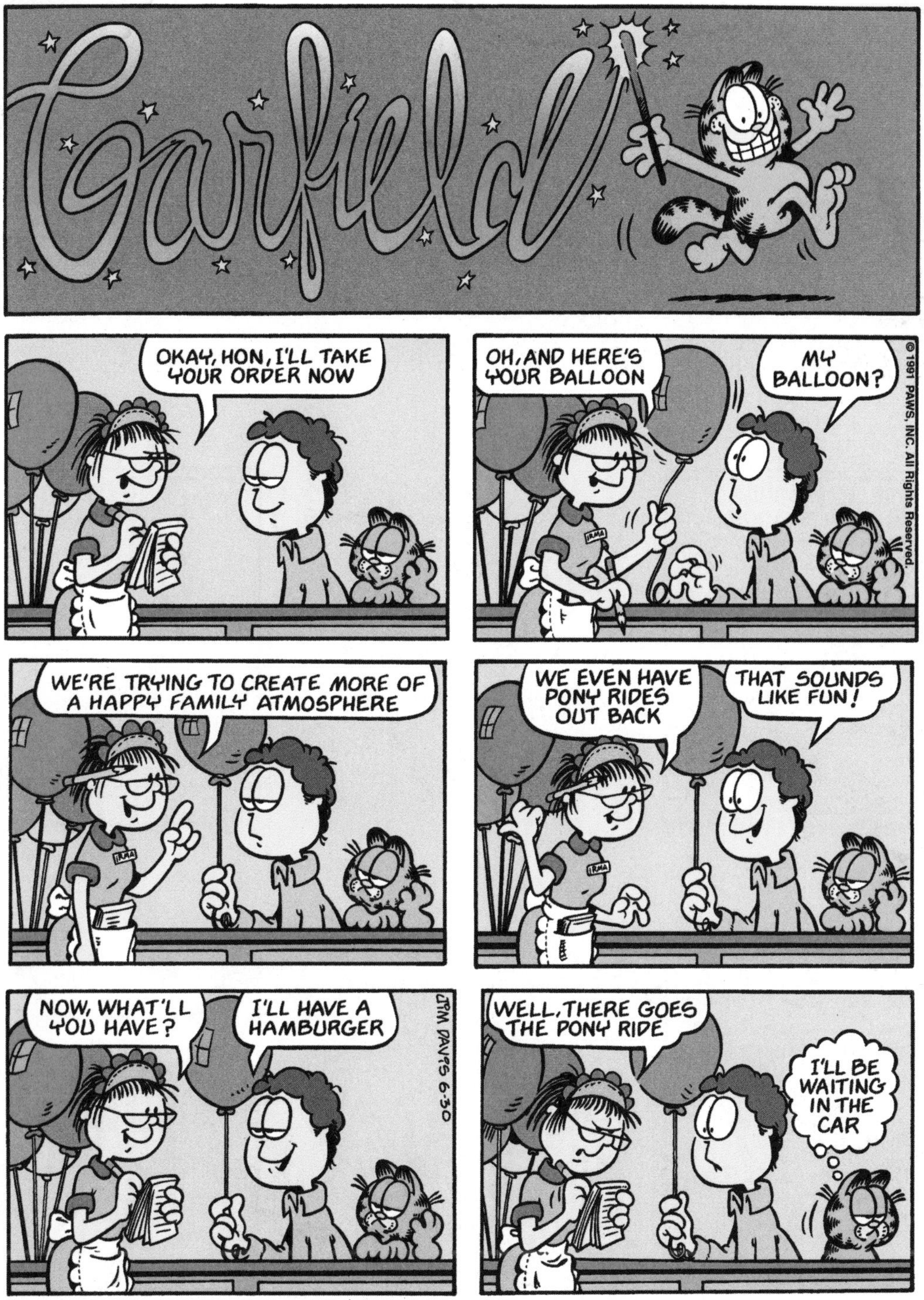
Garfield
OKAY, HON, I'LL TAKE YOUR ORDER NOW
OH, AND HERE'S YOUR BALLOON
MY BALLOON?
© 1991 PAWS, INC. All Rights Reserved.
WE'RE TRYING TO CREATE MORE OF A HAPPY FAMILY ATMOSPHERE
WE EVEN HAVE PONY RIDES OUT BACK
THAT SOUNDS LIKE FUN!
NOW, WHAT'LL YOU HAVE?
I'LL HAVE A HAMBURGER
JPM DAVIS 6-30
WELL, THERE GOES THE PONY RIDE
I'LL BE WAITING IN THE CAR

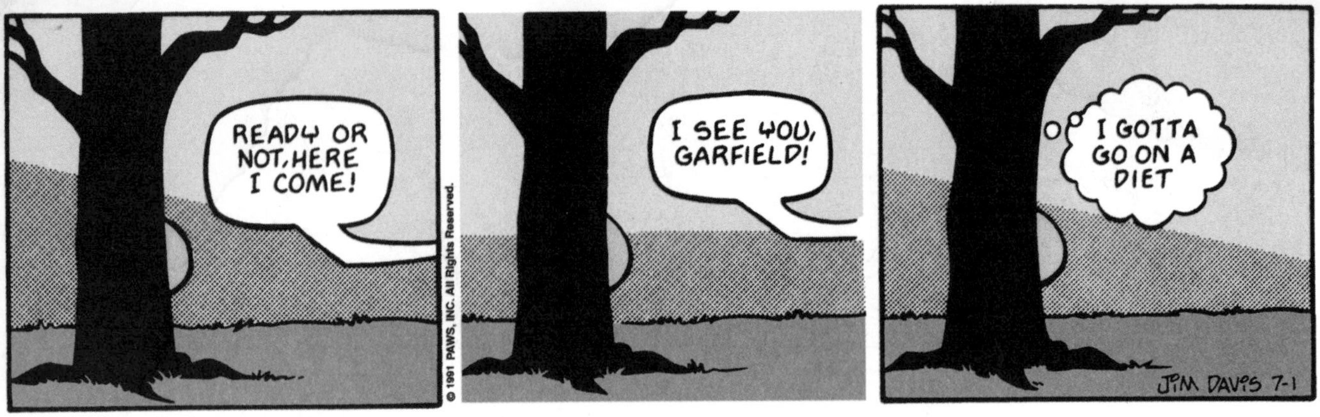
READY OR NOT, HERE I COME!
© 1991 PAWS, INC. All Rights Reserved.
I SEE YOU, GARFIELD!
I GOTTA GO ON A DIET
JIM DAVIS 7-1

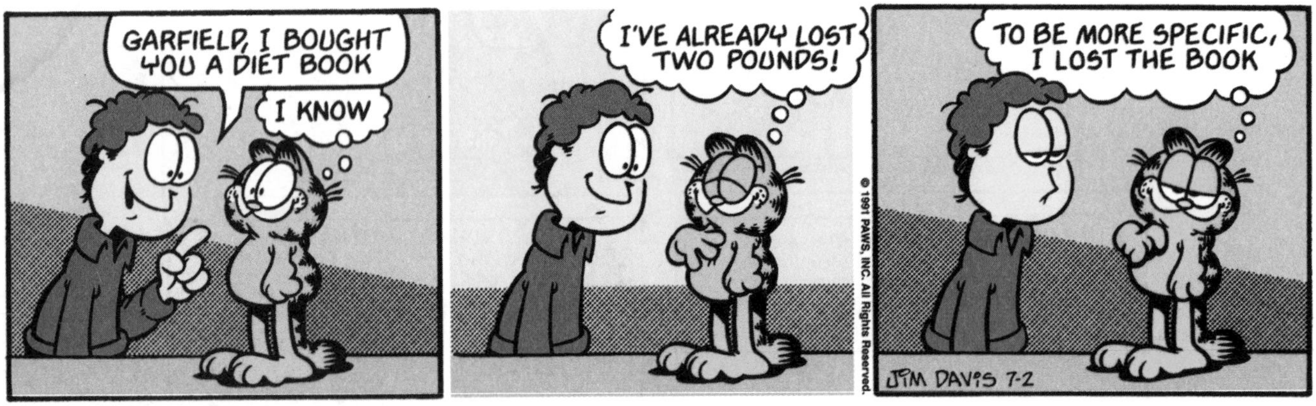
GARFIELD, I BOUGHT YOU A DIET BOOK
I KNOW
I'VE ALREADY LOST TWO POUNDS!
© 1991 PAWS, INC. All Rights Reserved.
TO BE MORE SPECIFIC, I LOST THE BOOK
JIM DAVIS 7-2

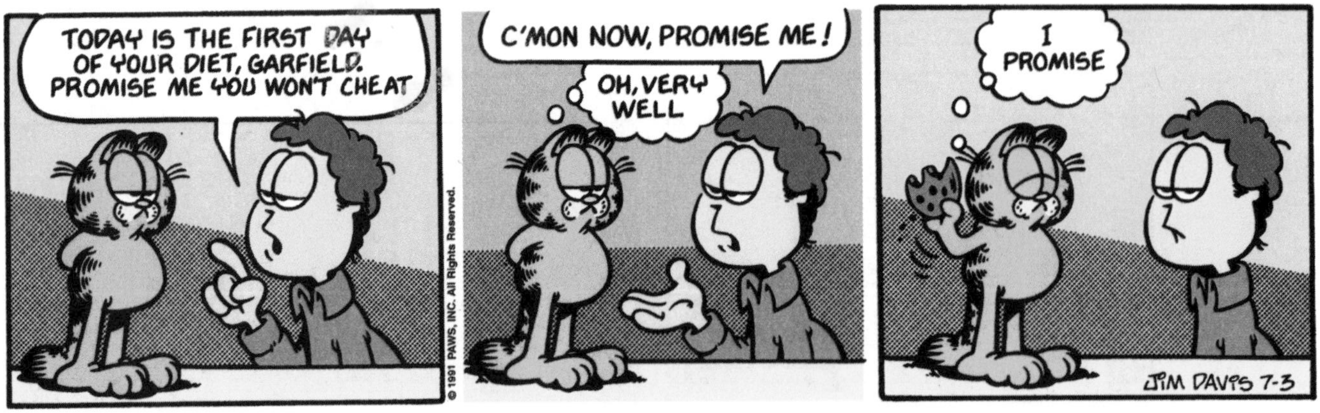
TODAY IS THE FIRST DAY OF YOUR DIET, GARFIELD. PROMISE ME YOU WON'T CHEAT
© 1991 PAWS, INC. All Rights Reserved.
C'MON NOW, PROMISE ME!
OH, VERY WELL
I PROMISE
JIM DAVIS 7-3

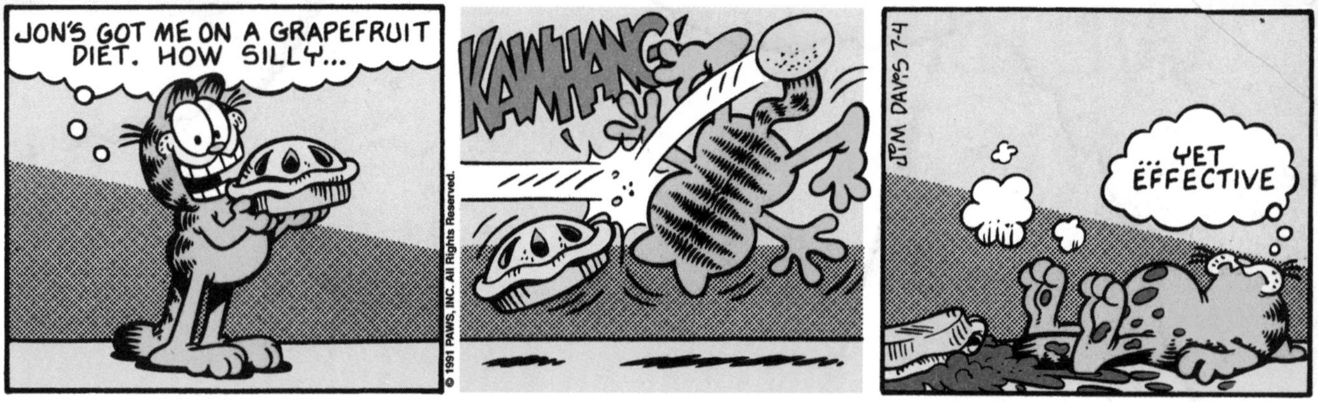
JON'S GOT ME ON A GRAPEFRUIT DIET. HOW SILLY...
KAWHANG!
... YET EFFECTIVE
JIM DAVIS 7-4
© 1991 PAWS, INC. All Rights Reserved.

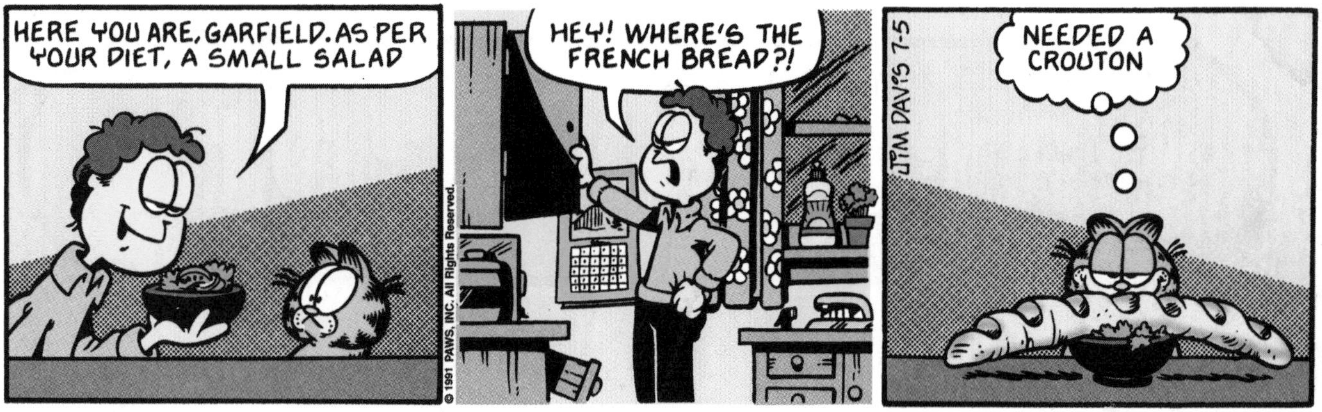
HERE YOU ARE, GARFIELD. AS PER YOUR DIET, A SMALL SALAD
HEY! WHERE'S THE FRENCH BREAD?!
NEEDED A CROUTON
JIM DAVIS 7-5
© 1991 PAWS, INC. All Rights Reserved.

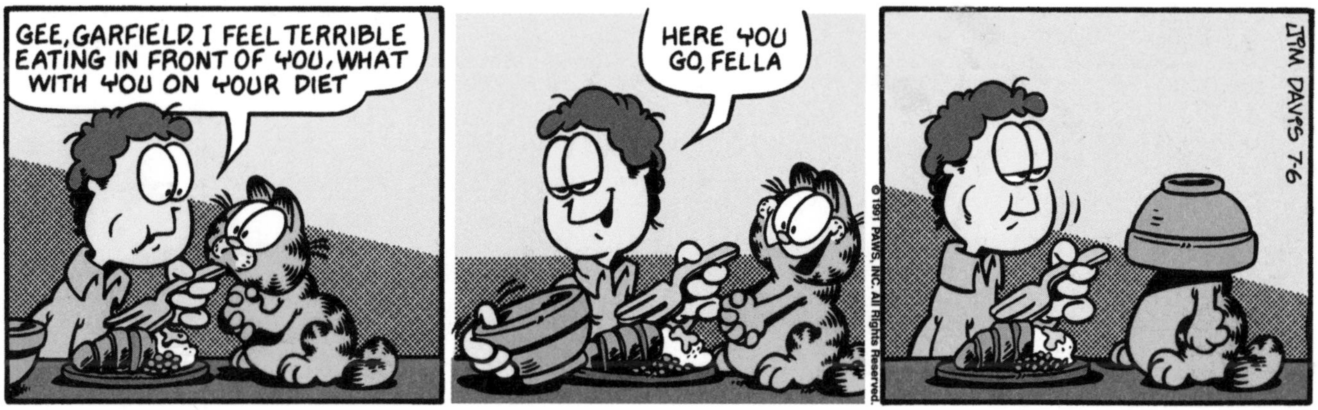
GEE, GARFIELD. I FEEL TERRIBLE EATING IN FRONT OF YOU, WHAT WITH YOU ON YOUR DIET
HERE YOU GO, FELLA
JIM DAVIS 7-6
© 1991 PAWS, INC. All Rights Reserved.